China

THE LAND, THE CITIES, THE PEOPLE, THE CULTURE, THE PRESENT

China

THE LAND, THE CITIES, THE PEOPLE, THE CULTURE, THE PRESENT

Editorial and production co-ordinator: Allan Amsel
Editor: Derek Maitland
Design Concept: Alan Chan
Designers: George Kwan, Annie Choi

Picture credits: All photographs except those credited below have been specially
taken for this book by Nik Wheeler or selected from pictures taken by
Julie Munro over a five year period (1975-1980) working as a photo-journalist in China.

Dean Barrett: 52, 63 (top left and right), 65, 67 (lower), 18 (top middle).

Nancy Nash: 16, 148 (top right).

Published by Lansdowne Press
176 South Creek Road, Dee Why West, NSW, Australia 2099
© RPLA Pty Ltd 1981

This is China was edited, designed
and produced by CFW Publications Limited
130 Connaught Road Central, Hong Kong
Printed in Hong Kong

Contents

The Political Mystery
Richard Bernstein
8

The Cultural Mystery
Nigel Cameron
40

The New Elitism
David Bonavia
70

The Four Modernisations
Richard Breeze
98

The Physical China
Margaret Spackman
146

The Minorities
Dr Hugh Baker
182

The Great Cities
Daniel P. Reid
226

The Tourist Trail
Carol Wright
272

The Sporting Challenge
Bert Okuley
324

The Culinary Mystery
Kenneth Lo
346

Index
378
to
386

Contributors

Richard Bernstein lives in Beijing where he is *Time* magazine's Beijing correspondent.

Born in New York in 1944, Mr. Bernstein graduated magna cum laude from the University of Connecticut, and spent five years at Harvard University studying for a PhD in history and East Asian languages. He worked as a freelance writer in France and Taiwan after he left the academic world for, as he says, "the more fertile fields of journalism."

He started with *Time* magazine in 1973 as a staffwriter, became a correspondent in Hong Kong in 1976, and moved to China in 1980 to open *Time's* Beijing Bureau.

Nigel Cameron lives in Hong Kong where he writes on art-related topics for numerous newspapers and magazines and acts as an advisor to the Hong Kong Museum of Art.

Mr. Cameron was born in Scotland. After obtaining his degree from Edinburgh University, he spent two years travelling through the Middle East, India and the Far East doing research on various aspects of life, art, and history. He is especially interested in the relationship of life to art in China.

He has written seven books on China, including *Peking: A Tale of Three Cities, Hong Kong: The Cultured Pearl*, and *The Face of China 1860-1912.*

David Bonavia is the Far Eastern Economic Review's special correspondent for China and the Beijing Correspondent for the *Times.*

Born in Scotland in 1940, Mr. Bonavia took First Class Honours in Chinese at Corpus Christi College, Cambridge. He worked as a journalist in Central Africa, Hong Kong, Southeast Asia, Moscow and Beijing.

Mr. Bonavia is the author of three books including *Peking* and *The Chinese.*

Richard Breeze is a staff writer for the *Far Eastern Economic Review.*

Born in Great Britain in 1933, he spent 10 years in Africa and 17 years in France. In 1974, when he was working for a Paris-based news agency specialising in French and Black African affairs, he became interested in China. He moved to Hong Kong in 1978 just as China launched its "Four Modernizations."

His articles on Chinese economic affairs, diplomacy, and sports have been published by leading newspapers and magazines around the world.

Margaret Spackman is a journalist in Hong Kong, where she has been studying China, its

people and language for the last 10 years. She is able to speak two Chinese dialects.

An Australian, she first saw China in 1976 from the deck of a heaving sailboat that drifted off course on the way to Vietnam. Since then, she's seen China from many different angles, in many different situations.

"Much has changed in China in recent years," she says, "including the land itself. Enormous development projects have moved mountains, changed the course of rivers and wrenched land from the Gobi Desert wastes."

Dr Hugh Baker is a lecturer in Chinese at the University of London, where he has been since 1967.

He has written numerous articles, broadcasts, and TV programmes about Chinese customs and traditions for the BBC and Radio Television Hong Kong.

Dr. Baker is the author of four books which are based on his observations of Chinese in Hong Kong: *A Chinese Liniage Village: Sheung Shui, Ancestral Images, Chinese Family and Kinship*, and *More Ancestral Images.*

Carol Wright is the travel editor of *House and Gardens* and food writer for the *Daily Mail* in Great Britain.

Richard Bernstein

Margaret Spackman

Richard Breeze

Kenneth Lo

Dr Hugh Baker

Bert Okuley

Her work takes her abroad four to five months each year.

A leading travel and food editor in the U.K., Ms. Wright has authored 23 books on travel and food of various countries around the world.

Bert Okuley began his journalistic career in 1955 as a sports writer with the International New Service, Detroit, Michigan, where he spent the next five years' reporting from Detroit and then Miami, Florida.

After a spell with the U.S. Army Special Services in Washington D.C. Mr Okuley joined UPI as a correspondent in Atlanta Ga., graduated to Foreign News Desk Editor in New York. In 1968 he was transferred to Saigon, becoming UPI manager for Indochina, in 1970. After the fall of Saigon in 1975 Mr Okuley became Deputy News Editor Asia, based in Hong Kong and for the next five years covered events in China and Hong Kong. Burt Okuley presently works as a freelance correspondant writing for various local and international publications.

Kenneth Lo is the foremost expert on Chinese cuisine writing and broadcasting in English.

Born in Fuzhou, China in 1913, he studied physics at Beijing University and later English Literature at Cambridge and London. He has pursued a variety of careers during his time in Britain: as a diplomat, a fine-art publisher, an industrial relations and welfare officer for Chinese seamen, a journalist, a lecturer, and as a professional tennis player. He is best known, however, for his many authoratative books on Chinese cooking and eating.

He has contributed articles and columns to innumerable journals and magazines.

Daniel P. Reid is a freelance writer in the Far East where he continues to pursue his interest in China and the Chinese language.

Born in San Francisco and raised in East Africa, he holds a Master of Arts degree in Chinese language and civilization from the Monterey Institute of International Studies.

Mr. Reid is the author of several books and numerous articles about ancient and contemporary China. He feels that "Chinese culture is a great seductress: She entices you in an infinite variety of subtle ways, but always leaves you with a lingering sense of mystery."

Nick Wheeler is a correspondent for the Black Star Photo Agency in Los Angeles. where He does assignments for *Geo, National Geographic*, and the British Sunday Colour Magazines.

An Englishman, Mr. Wheeler read French and Drama at Bristol University. He started his travels in Greece where he taught English for a year. Following that, he hitch-hiked across North Africa and on to Nepal. He spent three years in Thailand where he illustrated and co-edited a travel magazine and a guide to Bangkok. During the Vietnam war, he was a combat photographer for UPI. He also did assignments for *Times, Newsweek*, and *National Geographic.*

He has published two books, including *Return to the Marshes* in which he describes his life with the Marsh Arabs of Iraq.

Julie W. Munro lives in Hong Kong where she publishes business and other specialized directories to China.

From 1974 to 1977, Ms. Munro worked as a photographer and filmmaker in Beijing. While she was in China, she was very fortunate to travel to many areas which were off-limits to tourists. These areas have only just recently been opened for tourism. Ms. Munro travels to China regularly and continues to photograph and write about China and its people.

Her work has appeared in major newspapers and magazines including *Time, Newsweek, Vogue, Geo*, and the *London Sunday Times Magazine.*

arol Wright

Daniel P. Reid

Nick Wheeler

gel Cameron

David Bonavia

Julie W. Munro

The Political Mystery

Richard Bernstein

If you asked the informed tourist or Western newspaper reader to describe the People's Republic of China today in just a few words, his response would probably be something like this: China is a vast and crowded country that has been through a decade or more of very difficult times, including civil war and serious political chaos. But in the past couple of years it has gone a long way toward putting its problems behind it. China these days is a peaceful, orderly place with a stable, if very authoritarian political leadership that is devoting all its energies to the task of modernising and enriching a backward economy.

There is much that is true in this characterisation. Indeed, the image of the average person interested in China these days, may well correspond to the image most Chinese have of their own vast country. China, the Chinese may well feel, faces the decade of the 1980's with its house in far better political order than it has been in at least 15 years. Its top leadership seems stable and, with a few exceptions, united on sensible policies aimed at achieving what the Chinese call "The Four Modernisations," the economic programme with which it plans to accomplish enormous advances in industry, agriculture, military power and science and technology. At the same time, the Beijing government is making efforts to restore an essential element of government that, during the bad times of the recent past, had all but disappeared from China — namely, a degree of predictability, a confidence that what the leaders say is good today will still be considered good tomorrow. At the same time, after several years of a very cooperative, non-interventionist, outward looking foreign policy, one with a distinctive bias in favour of good relations with the advanced free market world, China has emerged, in the eyes of the West, as a basically benign and friendly force that constitutes a crucial counter-weight to the menace of the Soviet Union.

But while much of this characterisation of China today is certainly true, there is something troubling about its easy simplicity. Indeed, there have been many times in the past, even in certain periods before the Communists took power, when many of the same images of China held sway both in China itself and abroad. And yet, each time, just when it seemed that China was finally about to shed its chronic backwardness and disunity, the country would be plunged into another period of shocking and costly disorder.

Moreover, in the latest phase of Chinese history, the image of China as peaceful and moderate, has implanted itself in the foreign mind so quickly that one almost forgets what China was like only a few short years ago. During much of the late 1960's and early 1970's China was not offering up olive branches to the capitalist West; it was preaching in unequivocal terms the glories of the world revolution, withdrawing all but one of its ambassadors from its foreign missions and even burning down the British Embassy in Beijing. Domestically, the entire nation seemed caught up in one of the century's most sanguinary upheavals, the so-called Great Proletarian Cultural Revolution.

It was then that some of today's top leaders were paraded in disgrace before howling mobs of Red Guards and the Communist Party itself and most of the government ministries were under an assault provoked and encouraged by the late party leader Mao Tse-tung. Even more recently than that, when the Cultural Revolution itself faded away, China remained mired in the midst of a relentless power struggle that saw so many abrupt changes, so many inexplicable twists and turns that analysts in the West could barely keep up with it all. Even today, the Chinese official press admits that the country for several years lived "on the brink of chaos." There is no question that very recently in its history, China was very nearly swept away by disorder and madness.

What is the reason for this near schizophrenic Chinese political personality? And which is the real China — the stable, outward looking moderate entity of today or the place of uncontrollable mobs tearing themselves and their country apart as they scream for the proletarian revolution to engulf the world? In fact, both Chinas are the real China, both political personalities have competed with one another for the last hundred years and more as China, the country that practically invented stable political order, has struggled for a way to cope with and prosper in the modern world.

Indeed, the principal challenge that has faced China over the past century and a bit more is not very different from that facing China today — namely, to reverse a long period of decline and, using modern methods, to rebuild the nation's historic greatness. Similarly, that challenge has produced political turmoil in China not only in recent times but in decades past as well. In the 19th century, for example, there was a sharp division among Chinese leaders between those who wanted to adopt science and technology from the West to help remake the Chinese economy and others, hewing to a very conservative tradition, who wanted to reassert old Chinese values and traditions and saw borrowing from the West as a pernicious threat to China's spiritual superiority. Toward the outside world this overall split between modernisers and conservatives was reflected by two divergent tendencies in dealing with foreigners — one, to mingle with them as equals in an effort to learn from them and two, to rise up against them in a paroxysm of righteous fury and to eliminate their influences from Chinese life. At the same time, lurking in the psychological background, was a shared grief at the indisputable fact that China had lost the preeminent position it once held in the world and had declined to a humiliating second-rate status.

This decline was all the more poignant given the fact that, as any world history test should indicate, China for the better part of two millenia was a stupendously successful political entity. True, it suffered declines and periods of civil war as each of its great dynastic cycles came to an end. True too, China has several times been conquered and ruled by nomadic "barbarians" from the North. But even the foreign-led dynasties became in essence, Chinese. They adopted Chinese ways. And for several separate, long eras, often lasting in excess of 200 years, there is no question that China remained the largest unified country in the world, one of the

great achievements of the human genius, a country that regarded itself as the civilised centre of the world — hence the Chinese name for China, *Zhongguo*, or Middle Kingdom.

This complacent sense of superiority suffered a shock from which it never recovered around 1840 with the unwelcome arrival of European colonialists. The Europeans were, in Chinese eyes, barbarians, and indeed they did resort quickly to violent ways in getting what they wanted from China, including the right to sell large quantities of opium to the Chinese people, thus creating a serious problem of drug addiction which only the Communist government has been able to wipe out. The Europeans were materially superior. They carved China up into spheres of influence. Four times they made war on the unfortunate celestial empire and each time they won. From this rude encounter with the West (and later with Japan) the Chinese developed a keen sense of wounded national pride. And, for decades the Chinese warred with themselves over how to restore their dignity.

Thus, in the late 1960's when China was swept up into a great frenzy of xenophobic hatred of everything that came from abroad, they were expressing again the kind of anti-foreign fury that had engulfed them once before. Indeed, there was, as some scholars have pointed out, an eerie similarity between the rabid Red Guards of the Cultural Revolution, and the superstitious nationalistic mobs of Boxers who, in 1900, rose up to sweep away the hated foreigners, believing, with tragic consequences, that they were impervious to the bullets of the imperialists from across the seas.

When the Communists, after a revolutionary struggle of some 30 years, took total power in China in 1949, they well exemplified this split in the national personality. On the one hand, there is no question that the Communists, like most Chinese, were ardently patriotic. One of their chief goals was to rid their country of the unequal status it suffered with the out-

The People's Republic of China — so much in the news, yet most people know little about it and its people. Despite hundreds of years of trade with the West, from the earliest Arabs who travelled the fabled "Silk Route" to today's businessmen for whom Beijing is just another city on their itineraries, China remains mysterious and seemingly impenetrable to the outsider. China today is struggling with the formidable task of making life comfortable for almost a billion people — a quarter of the world's population.
Opposite: *Nanjing's city square, where portraits of Mao Tse-tung* (left) *and Hua Guofeng* (right) *dominate.*
Above: *Target practice at a primary school.*

side world. On the other hand, the Communists brought with them to their new capital in Beijing a distinctly foreign ideology — Marxism. The Communists established the first true and complete unity that the nation had enjoyed since the Qing (Ch'ing), or Manchu Dynasty began its irreversible decline around the beginning of the 19th century. But though unified and at peace, China under the Communists obviously still carried within itself the divergent and often contradictory responses that the country traditionally had toward the great challenge of dealing with the modern world. Indeed, much of the confusing welter of events in China in the past two decades, much of what has come to be regarded in the West as China's mysterious and often inscrutable political way of doing things, stems from the conflict of earlier traditions.

Before examining the role of these conflicts, it is also necessary first to point out that the Communists made their own unique contributions to China's political behaviour which also contribute to the sense of mystery about China that exists abroad. Indeed, while China in the past two decades has evinced a kind of split personality, there are at the same time certain features of Communist rule that have remained consistent from one period to another.

The most obvious of these characteristics is this: China remains through it all a highly centralised, elaborately bureaucratic state.

True, as we shall see, during the Cultural Revolution, the bureaucracy was shaken to its foundations, so much so that some parts of it ceased to function altogether. But even so, China has always

continued to be run by a secretive, closed political organisation, the Chinese Communist Party. The party maintains branches in every factory, school, commune and military unit. It maintains close control over virtually all forms of information, newpapers, magazines, television, radio, novels, plays, songs, even scholarly and scientific publications. The party — or more properly its 22 top leaders who form the Politburo — formulate policy for the state. Then, they inform the population of this policy through a second major, consistent feature of China's political system.

This second feature is what might be called the mass campaign. Throughout the entire period of Communist rule, no matter what the policy, and no matter how splintered the party organisation, China's leaders have always tried to get things done by mobilising the entire population to accomplish a particular task. The task might be to criticise some fallen party official or to impose new hygienic practices to eliminate a disease like schistosomiasis. But the style of politics is the same. The newspapers and radio stations constantly blare forth a series of catchy slogans. The party committees in each organisation call mass meetings to whip up enthusiasm for the new policy or goal. The party theoretical journal *Red Flag* publishes long articles, with suitable quotes from Marx, Engels and Mao, justifying the new policy. There are demonstrations around the country in support of it, very likely official "emulation campaigns" in which one factory or region or province will compete for better results with another factory or region or province. At the same time, opponents of the new policy will be "exposed and criticised" in the press, on wallposters, or in local meetings held for the purpose. The whole thing takes on the atmosphere of a crusade. In China, everything becomes the moral equivalent of war, whether it is eliminating some "counterrevolutionary traitor" from the party's bosom or working hard in the spring planting so that grain production will rise.

The circumstances of China provide a good reason for this style of political life. Vast, poor and technologically backward, China has one great resource — its enormous population. The country's Communist leadership has differed on many things, but it has always agreed that to accomplish its goals, the basic criteria is to mobilise a huge swell of popular support and activity. The mass campaign is simply the most effective means that the party and government have to encourage China's vast masses to labour harder for a particular goal. In this tightly controlled bureaucratic state, whatever policy is determined at the centre in Beijing must be spread as rapidly and as thoroughly as possible to all 29 provinces and special regions of China.

Logical as it may be however, this mass campaign style has caused a great deal of confusion among observers of China. There are several reasons for this. One of them is the simple fact that policy debates are conducted entirely behind closed doors and the results often only hinted at, rather than openly elaborated, in the propaganda that follows the decision. For example, the newspapers and radio will slowly begin to

The years after the collapse of the Qing dynasty in 1911 were politically vibrant ones. Chou En-lai and other intellectuals went to Europe to study and returned to China filled with ideas and dedicated to rebuilding the nation to its historic greatness.

Mao Tse-tung, a self-styled peasant revolutionary from the backwaters of Hunan province, emerged as the leader of the group that eventually claimed victory over Chiang Kai-shek's Kuomintang forces. On October 1, 1949, Mao stood on the balcony of Tiananmen Gate in Beijing and proclaimed the new People's Republic.

Mao's success gave the world a new political doctrine, a combination of Soviet-style Marxist rule combined with Chinese belief in grassroot organizing of the people.
Opposite: *Soldiers of the People's Liberation Army, which has its roots in the early years of the communist revolution and the "Long March."*
This page: *China's police force, the Public Security Bureau.*

华主席挥手我们胜利前进

奖给 东英施 被评为
三好小朋友毕业留念

announce that people on the agricultural communes who work harder should be allowed to get rich ahead of others — providing that they work harder. What, the China analyst will then begin to ask himself, does this really mean? Is the Communist Party tacitly giving approval in the communes for more private enterprise, to concentrate more, for example, on production on the farmers' private plots for sale on the local free markets? If this is true, then the party has taken a giant step away from Chairman Mao's undying belief that collective agriculture must be stressed and private initiative rigorously discouraged. The Politburo will never admit this latter point, even if it is abundantly clear to every one of the 960 million or more Chinese. But the fact that so much is left unstated introduces, for the outside observer, an important area of mystery.

More important in contributing to the puzzle of Chinese politics, however, is another factor. Frequently, a frenzy of mass mobilisation for one policy will be followed by another equally frenetic burst of activity for a diametrically opposite policy. In other words, the policy may change — or, more likely, there may be a shift in the Communist Party's top leadership. But the propaganda crusade that supported one policy or leadership will suddenly and without much of an explanation support another, competing policy or leadership.

This common, if unfortunate, feature of Chinese politics has left Western analysts more often than not scratching their heads over the devious twists and turns of life at the top in Beijing. The task moreover has not been made any easier by the fact that some of the most portentious changes are preceeded for a long period only by the subtlest hints in the propaganda machinery. Then, even when finally, a full explanation is put out by the Chinese, there always seem to be some elements missing.

Take, for example, one of the strangest political episodes of modern times — the Lin Biao affair. From the mid-1960's until

one fateful day in 1971, Lin Biao, the powerful Minister of Defence was proclaimed with all the considerable bombast that Chinese propaganda can muster, the "closest comrade-in-arms" of Chairman Mao himself. He was the number two man in the all-important Communist Party hierarchy and was designated by nothing less than China's constitution to be the Chairman's successor as party chairman. A cult of personality around Lin Biao almost equalled that which magnified and sanctified Mao himself. Then, in late 1971 something very strange happened. Lin Biao simply disappeared. He vanished from his usual place beside Chairman Mao at all important state and party functions. His photographs, of which there were literally tens of millions, were suddenly not around any more. Equally mysterious, there was not a word of explanation for the once mighty Lin's abrupt entry into the status of non-personhood. Months went by, and the Chinese press said nothing. Foreign visitors, who at that time included U.S. President Richard Nixon, were advised not to ask about the disappearance of Lin Biao.

After more than a year of official silence, suddenly the authorities in China put out an official explanation of Lin Biao's disappearance. It turns out, or so went the official account, that Lin and a small group of co-conspirators, had tried to assassinate Chairman Mao and seize power in a coup d'état. When they failed, Lin and his immediate family attempted to escape to the Soviet Union in a Trident jet, but their departure was so hasty that they were unable to completely refuel the airplane. Their sad end: a crash in the Gobi desert of the Mongolian People's Republic (dominated by the Soviet Union) in which Lin and all the other passengers on the plane were killed.

That explanation was then followed by one of China's mass campaigns, and a campaign that, after some fits and starts and changes, still continues today. With characteristic moral fervour, the Chinese propaganda machinery pounded away at

In 1979, the country celebrated 30 years of Maoist rule. In all that time, there had only been two leaders, Mao and Hua Guofeng (who was appointed leader shortly after Mao's death on September 9, 1976).
Opposite: *A model worker's home in Shanghai in 1980, with typical decor: pictures of Mao Tse-tung and Hua Guofeng (that's Hua with his arm outstretched), family photographs and certificates of achievement on the wall, the ubiquitous vacuum flask filled with hot boiled water and, a sign of the times, a portable radio.*
Above: *P.L.A. soldiers in Beijing.*

the villain Lin Biao, using him as a negative political example of the dread consequences of straying from the correct political path. The problem with Lin Biao was not only that he was a "scab" and a "traitor." His ultimate goal was to turn back the tides of revolution in China and to reestablish capitalism.

Thus, in the space of a few months, a figure who was adored by the entire Chinese nation was transformed into one equally detested. All the elements of China's political mystery were present: an abrupt and complete change, secretiveness, the mass campaign.

The history of Lin Biao was completely rewritten, with the ironic result that his counter-revolutionary behaviour turns out to have been the dominant feature of his character even in the days when he was Mao's revered closest comrade-in-arms. And while Lin Biao may be the most obvious example of the hero inexplicably turned traitor, and a negative model for the entire nation, he is by no means the only

one. On the top level of the Politburo, the same thing happened to Lin's predecessor as Defence Minister, a man named Peng Dehuai. On the lower level, that fate also befell literally tens of thousands of cadres who had attached themselves to one or another of the fallen leaders. In the latest such episode, the fall of the so-called "Gang of Four", it was not only the top leaders who were cashiered and disgraced; followers of the "Gang" all over the country were less publicly axed.

After Lin Biao, the most celebrated victim of China's capricious politics is the man now regarded as the effective guiding hand of China's march toward modernisation, Vice-Premier Deng Xiaoping, except that, if anything, Deng's case is even more complicated than the unfortunate Lin's. Indeed, the rollercoasting career of Deng Xiaoping is an almost perfect reflection of the larger torment of the Chinese nation as well as of the mysteries of its politics.

While the history of the Chinese Com-

In China, where all publications are controlled by the government and official permission is necessary to purchase newsprint, printing equipment and supplies, the leadership is able to control the kind of information that reaches the people and when. When the time is right, all the media carry the same pronouncements with little variation in style or content. Details of the "news" appear on large wall posters, or dazibao, *pasted on hoardings, walls of buildings and inside classrooms, offices and factories.*
Opposite: *A driver stands by his military jeep in Guangzhou.*
This page: *Wall posters on a Beijing street.*

munist movement is one of extraordinary triumph, it is also one of almost continuous internal conflict. Founded by a small band of just 12 men in Shanghai in 1921, the Chinese Communist Party in the space of little more than 40 years grew to a membership of several million and, more important, succeeded in seizing power in the world's most populous nation. But the historical wake of the party is littered with the corpses of those revolutionary leaders who fell, not at the hands of the Kuomintang enemy but as purge victims of their fellow revolutionaries. In the very early years of the revolution, the 1920's, the leadership of the then fledgling movement changed at least three times. By the early 1930's, the movement was split into two major groups. One consisted of those who believed that the revolution would, as Marx claimed, have to be based in the industrial areas among urban workers. The other, centred around a youthful visionary named Mao Tse-tung, believed that the revolution could rely in rather unclassical Marxist fashion on the country's rural masses. By the mid-1930's, while the Communists were on their epic Long March to escape encirclement by the Kuomintang,

Mao's forces definitively triumphed. And, from then until his death in 1976, nobody ever openly challenged the supreme leadership of Mao as party chairman. But though Mao's position remained supreme, there were numerous debates and quarrels within the top party leadership, both before and after the Communist victory of 1949. Before the "liberation" the most serious challenge to Mao came from a Russian-trained intellectual named Wang Ming who, to this day, remains in the Soviet Union at the head of a tiny splinter group called the Chinese Communist Party.

The first several years after the takeover in 1949 were, in terms of inner party conflict, rather uneventful — at least on the surface. Allied closely to the Soviet Union, China followed a Russian model of development. Gradually, a corps of Soviet-like bureaucrats emerged to run the ever-growing machinery of the state. Heavy industry was emphasised. Until 1957, China made an impressive economic recovery from the years of war that had preceeded the Communist victory.

What few outside of China predicted, however, was what might now be called

the Maoist factor in Chinese politics. Mao, who possessed powerful poetic and romantic impulses, was impatient at a number of things, including domination by the Soviet Union and, perhaps more importantly, the tendency, as he saw it, of the Chinese Communist movement to spawn a large, conservative privileged bureaucracy that did not share Mao's own romantic identification with the impoverished masses. Beginning around 1956, Mao began to experiment with the revolution, to yank it down previously untravelled paths, to shake the bureaucracy out of its complacency. It was his experiments and his campaigns which led directly to the bitter and even bloody political struggles of the last decade and a half, to the strange up-again-down-again fortunes of Vice-Premier Deng Xiaoping.

Mao's first great experiment was the so-called "Hundred Flowers" campaign in 1956, a brief period of official tolerance of criticism. When the criticism threatened to get out of hand, the Communist leadership clamped the lid down on the Hundred Flowers and transformed that movement into a wide-ranging campaign against rightist tendencies in the country. Then, in 1958 came what historians will probably regard as Mao's first colossal mistake, the Great Leap Forward. Mao was impatient with the rate of economic development in China. More important, with his almost mystical belief in the creative power of the masses, he felt that the Soviet Union's rather conventional approach to economic change was failing to use China's greatest resource — its vast population. Defying all the rules of conventional economics, Mao wanted to break through in one glorious stroke to a new economic era by unleashing the power of the masses. The result was the Great Leap Forward.

Hundreds of millions of farmers were herded onto rapidly created agricultural communes. Inefficient backyard blast furnaces sprang up all over the country. Statistics came to have no meaning as over-enthusiastic factory managers outbid one another in claims of production quotas

overfulfilled. The result, not surprisingly, was a disaster. Combined with bad weather it produced what the Chinese still call the "three hard years" from 1958 to 1961, during which millions came close to starvation.

But the Great Leap was more than an economic disaster. It also produced a deep cleavage within the Communist Party leadership that endured for the better part of the next two decades and caused much of the seemingly inexplicable political instability, the purges and counter-purges and hysterical campaigns that became characteristic of the Chinese political scene. In essence, the Chinese Communist Party began around the time of the Great Leap Forward to crystallise into two main factions. This was by no means clear at the time, perhaps not even to some of China's leaders. But it was to become clear to almost everyone later. On the one side, there was Mao and those closest to him. This group represented a more radical approach to China's revolution. It believed that the key ingredient to China's transformation was the correct revolutionary spirit, the right "proletarian" ideology. Mao and the radicals were very fearful that China would produce a privileged class of technical experts such as existed in the Soviet Union and that such a development would ruin their vision of a truly democratic, classless society. That meant, in turn, that most policies had to hew to what the Maoists called the "mass line." In education, for example, the best opportunities had to be given not necessarily to the best qualified academically but to those with the best political attitude, preferably from a genuine worker or poor peasant family background. At the same time, Mao, who had had almost no experience abroad, exhibited a powerful xenophobic streak, a profound distrust of foreigners. He broke with the Soviet Union at around the time of the Great Leap Forward and began to formulate a concept of extreme self-reliance. China, he determined, would do everything on its own. It would not depend on foreigners for technology or

capital or aid. All China needed to solve its problems was the energy of its masses, properly directed by truly selfless, revolutionary cadres.

Some of these views, particularly the dislike of the Soviet Union, were shared by others in the leadership. The lines that divided the Maoists from others in China were never crystal clear. Yet, as a result of the disasters of the Great Leap Forward there is no doubt that large numbers of people within the Chinese bureaucracy began to distrust and passively oppose Maoist policies — though, of course, never the sacrosanct Mao himself. Many of the members of this faction represented precisely those people who were threatened by Mao's sometimes extreme populism and disdain of a technological elite. They were the thousands of party and government bureaucrats who emerged into positions of leadership and responsibility during the early 1950's. They were often the very people with well-developed administrative and technical skills. Among them, for example, was China's head of State Liu Shaoqi. Another key figure in this more pragmatic, cautious group was Deng Xiaoping.

In 1959 the Maoists scored one great internal victory in the slowly developing power struggle. They successfully purged and disgraced the then Minister of Defence, a revolutionary hero named Peng Dehuai. Peng had personally attacked Mao at an important party meeting at Lushan, in Jiangxi Province, for ignoring the laws of economics and causing untold suffering among the Chinese masses. But even though Peng was dismissed — to be replaced by the then ardently Maoist Lin Biao — in the years that followed, real power gradually seeped away from Mao and into the hands of Liu Shaoqi and the more moderate bureaucrats. By the mid 1960's, Mao was hinting that he had been put on the shelf like an old statue. He told visiting French writer Andre Malraux in 1965 that he was "alone with the masses, waiting."

What Mao was waiting for, it turned

Much of the world was shaken by events during the hey-day of the "Great Proletarian Cultural Revolution." Photographs of rabid Red Guards waving their "little red books" of quotations by Chairman Mao and shouting revolutionary slogans appeared in the major newspapers in the West. Mao's call to "bombard the party headquarters" was heard throughout the land.
To this day, monuments to this period, such as this one in Nanjing, (opposite) remain.

out, was the momentous cataclysm of the Great Proletarian Cultural Revolution, which was designed once and for all to eliminate the conservative elite from the country and to enshrine forever Mao's cherished mass line.

Essentially, what Mao did was turn to those groups in Chinese society who had some feelings of alienation or discontent with the veteran bureaucrats, led by Liu Shaoqi, who were in power. Among these, for example, were tens of thousands of idealistic youths, particularly those youths who did not come from cadre families and were thus resentful of the privileges enjoyed by the children of the bureaucrats. These provided the basis for the swarms of so-called Red Guards who, for the better part of a year in 1966 and 1967, carried out Mao's reckless order to "bombard the party headquarters." Often aligning with other groups such as low-paid workers, the Red Guards raided party and government offices around the country, paraded thousands of bureaucrats through the streets with dunce caps on their heads, then began to fight, often with knives, battering rams, and even guns, with other groups of Red Guards, or more conservative workers, or local military commanders, who rose up to oppose them. The Red Guards and their allies accomplished a basic task for Mao. They helped him eliminate his most powerful enemies in the party leadership — including Liu Shaoqi, who has since died, and Deng Xiaoping. At the same time, Mao himself rose to the top again surrounded by a personality cult that exceeded even that of Joseph Stalin during an earlier period in the Soviet Union. But eventually, faced with increasing chaos among the unruly and violent Red Guards, Mao called in the military, led by his close ally Lin Biao, to restore order. The Red Guards, having served their purpose, were disbanded.

During this entire period, Mao also had to seek support from leadership groups, generally outside of Beijing, who had axes to grind against the veteran bureaucrats. Among the most important leaders he

turned to was the one-time B-grade actress from Shanghai, Jiang Qing, who was in fact his fourth wife. He also approached a group of zealous ideologues from Shanghai who both shared his near-religious faith in the masses and who longed, like him, for supreme power. This group, along with Jiang Qing, became the now-despised "Gang of Four."

Indeed, the process of the Cultural Revolution transformed what might have been a genuine ideological conflict into a naked struggle for power which, in many ways, still dominates Chinese politics. For in trying to create a new leadership group, Mao gave birth to another leadership elite, one that replaced the thousands of veterans who had been cashiered and disgraced during the Cultural Revolution itself. Many of these new leaders, who began to fill in important positions throughout all of China's provinces, were far more youthful than the veterans they replaced and often far less experienced in running the affairs of state. Later many of them were given the contemptuous

sobriquet "helicopter cadres," meaning that they shot from the bottom to the top very quickly because of the vacuum created by the decimation of the old leadership.

In the years that followed the end of the violence of the Cultural Revolution, from 1968, until the death of Mao in September 1976, the main feature of Chinese politics, the principal cause of near-constant instability at the top, was the rivalry between this young, new bureaucracy that owed its position to the Cultural Revolution and the old veteran bureaucracy that had been in power before that tumultuous event.

A key figure in this turmoil was China's brilliant and crafty survivor, Prime Minister Chou En-lai. Chou, who enjoyed a prestige almost as powerful as that of Mao himself, had tried to remain above the immediate political fray. Still, in ideology, Chou was clearly not a Maoist. He believed in the necessity of a skilled, professional bureaucracy that could work without the constant disruptions of Maoist campaigns for ideological purity. But pragmatic to the core, Chou also knew that some kind of order in Chinese society would require a great deal of compromise between the two main political factions.

So, Chou struggled for order and compromise. In the years immediately after the Cultural Revolution, he skillfully played his self-effacing charade of remaining always behind others in the party hierarchy. He stayed, for example, in the shadow both of Mao and of Mao's designated successor, Defence Minister Lin Biao. But when Lin fell in his alleged coup attempt against Mao in 1971, Chou stepped in to pick up the pieces of a newly devastated party, becoming not exactly an ally of Mao himself, but nonetheless a man whom Mao couldn't do without.

In the months and years that followed the Lin Biao episode, Chou played his skillful balancing act. He never excluded the Shanghai radicals, always including them in the major affairs of the Party and the state, such as the 1972 visit to China of President Richard Nixon. But even so, the radicals correctly identified Chou as an obstacle to their ambition of seizing complete power in all of China, or, at least, of being in a position to rule the country when the aging Mao finally passed away. Chou's principal flaw, from the radicals' standpoint, was that he worked slowly but unmistakably to restore many of the key victims of the Cultural Revolution, the old veteran bureaucracy, to their former positions of power and influence. Most horrifying to the Shanghai group around Mao's wife Jiang Qing was Chou's rehabilitation of none other than Deng Xiaoping, the second most important villain of the Cultural Revolution and an inveterate enemy of the radicals. During much of 1974 and 1975, Chou worked to enshrine the pragmatic Deng as his own successor as prime minister. At the same time, the radicals, definitely on the defensive now, used their control of China's propaganda machinery to launch oblique, indirect attacks on Chou himself.

The final stage of China's political

drama was set when Chou died early in 1976. With Mao's apparent blessing, Deng Xiaoping was passed over as prime minister in favour of a dark horse compromise candidate, Minister of Public Security Hua Guofeng. In striking this compromise, the party leaders clearly did not accept Chou's own favoured candidate, Deng. But the compromise was by no means a victory for the radicals either. They wanted one of their own number to become prime minister — very likely the First Party Secretary of the Shanghai region Zhang Chunqiao. Equally important, they wanted to be in a position to name a member of their faction, most likely Jiang Qing, to become party chairman after the death of the fast fading Mao. And so, the radicals went on the offensive.

First, they continued their indirect but unmistakable efforts to tarnish the posthumous reputation of Chou En-lai, largely by blocking any efforts at a nationwide memorialisation. In April, 1976, on the Ching Ming festival during which the Chinese have traditionally commemorated the dead, a huge and violent riot broke out in Beijing's vast Tiananmen Square. The riot was evidently caused when local militiamen, following the orders of the radicals, removed thousands of memorial wreaths that the people had put up in honor of Chou. But the radicals seized on the pretext of the Tiananmen incident to launch a new struggle for power. Most important, they got enough support in the Politburo behind them to send Deng Xiaoping into disgrace and purge still another time. And they launched a nationwide propaganda campaign to criticise the "counter-revolutionary" Deng and, again by association, Deng's late benefactor Chou En-lai.

Then, on September 9, 1976, five months after the Tiananmen incident and the purge of Deng, the portentious event for which the Chinese nation had been bracing itself for years occurred — Mao Tse-tung died at the age of 83.

Mao's death brought about a climax of

The Cultural Revolution turned into a no-holds-barred struggle for power that ended with the arrest of the so-called "Gang of Four" in October 1976, less than a month after Mao had died. The most celebrated victim of this power struggle was Deng Xiaoping, a pragmatic communist who had the backing of China's most respected politician, Chou En-lai.

Deng has been purged from senior government and party ranks three times; the last time was in the spring after Chou's death on January 8, 1976. Workers were called into the streets to demonstrate in support of the purge (opposite).

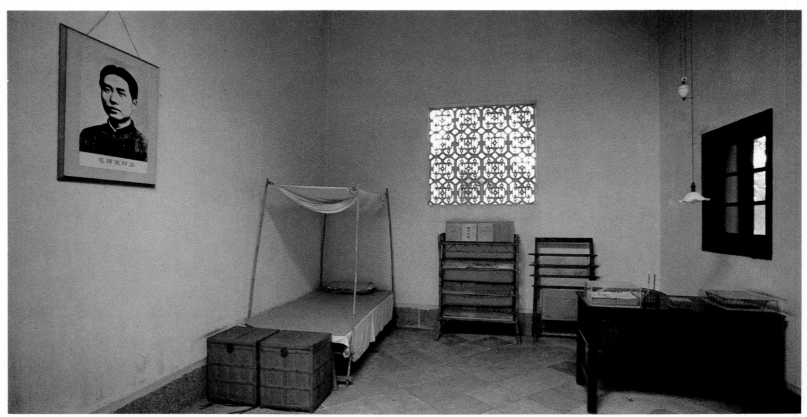

sorts in the political confrontation that had been building since the Cultural Revolution — indeed, since the great party divisions that had emerged during the Great Leap Forward. With Mao removed from the scene, the Chinese nation was bereft of the imposing figure that had served as a kind of focal point for national identity, as well as symbol of the legitimacy of the Communist revolution itself. Moreover, in the months that had led up to the death of the Great Helmsman, there had been scattered but unmistakable signs of a loss of discipline among the population at large, of a strong degree of cynicism and malaise at the spectacle of constant back-biting and jockeying for power among the top leaders. The Chinese people, while not as confused about developments in the Politburo as many Western observers, were probably tired of the erratic swings from one side to another, the sudden transformation of heroes into villains that had been caused by the radical-moderate schism. There were strikes and demonstrations in various Chinese urban areas. Thousands

of youths who had been sent to work in the countryside had returned illegally to the cities where they lived clandestine, underground lives. There were even signs of unofficial organisations of youths, with roots going back to the Cultural Revolution, which threatened the party's monopoly of power.

At the same time, not only was Mao dead, but so too was the country's near-indispensable moderator and conciliator, Chou En-lai, while in his place was a relatively unknown and untested newcomer to the leadership scene, Hua Guofeng.

It seems clear in retrospect then that it was crucial for the Communist Party to resolve its debilitating internal differences; and, after a month of preparation, it did so in spectacular fashion. On the night of October 5, the detachment of the People's Liberation Army responsible for protecting the top leaders, arrested the four main radical leaders — Mao's wife Jiang Qing, Shanghai first Party Secretary Zhang Chunqiao, and Politburo Mem-

bers Wang Hongwen and Yao Wenyuan. With a dramatic stroke that would have been impossible while Mao was still alive, the moderates made an all-out effort to resolve the power struggle by striking at the centre of power of one of the major factions. To do so, they had to win the allegiance of certain key power brokers. One, obviously, was Hua Guofeng himself who became not only Prime Minister but Party chairman as well, a position of formal power that not even Mao himself had ever attained. Others that needed to be brought along on the anti-radical stroke were a majority of the country's powerful regional military commanders and the head of the Beijing palace guard, an old Mao loyalist named Wang Dongxing. The bold stroke at the radicals also assumed that China's restive masses would approve of the elimination of what soon came to be called the "Gang of Four". In this, the leadership seems to have been right. It appears very likely that the radical faction in the party, which was widely viewed as responsible for China's constant, intrusive political campaigns was widely disliked and resented by large segments of China's population. Their arrest seems to have been greeted with a great collective sigh of relief.

The question is: Did the elimination of the "Gang of Four" provide conditions for long-term political stability in China? If one remembers the complex nature of the power struggle, it becomes obvious that the simple arrest of four individuals and a few of their close allies could not immediately quell the turbulence of Chinese politics. The radicals, or the Cultural Revolutionary faction, while disliked by many in China, did at the same time have a strong constituency. Also, during the years that they had been in power, they had succeeded in placing thousands of young officials into positions of authority throughout China's provinces. To truly unify China's leadership, it became necessary after the fall of the "Gang of Four" to purge the legions of officials who had, since the Cultural Revolution, thrown in their lot with the radicals and their programme. This alone was bound to cause nationwide friction. At the same time, at the top levels of the Party Politburo, there remained a group of powerful figures who clearly owed their own rise to the Cultural Revolution, and who visibly supported the final campaign of the radicals — the nation-wide assault on Deng Xiaoping that followed the riots at Tiananmen Square. Given that the main factional lines coincided with those in power before the Cultural Revolution and those who came to power as a result of it, the Chinese political scene remained fraught with tension and potential conflict.

Not suprisingly, that conflict has surfaced on a number of occasions, though always in the muted, indirect way common to Chinese politics. One way the conflict has shown itself is in repeated calls in the propaganda machinery, fully three years after the fall of the "Gang of Four", to "criticise and expose" those many officials around the country who have tried to cover up their mistakes and who refuse to repent the errors of their ways. This alone is a strong hint that factions continue to exist, if not remain strong, in various places. At the same time, certain top level leaders have periodically been criticised in wallposters — very likely supported by other top level leaders — for their roles in the anti-Deng movement in suppressing the Tiananmen incident, and there have even been calls for their dismissal.

Dispite these signs of continued tension, there is no question that the moderates have been able to dominate the political scene, and that the key element enabling them to do so was the surgical removal of the four main radicals. Several months after the anti-gang attack, for example, Teng Hsiao-p'ing was restored to the several key positions he had held before his purge, including vice-chairman of the party and vice-premier.

Despite the fact that Hua Guofeng was his formal superior in the hierarchy, most outside analysts believed that it was Deng, as the leader of the old veteran bureaucrats, who wielded effective day-to-day control over the affairs of China. Certainly, the moderate, pragmatic programme that he promoted has become the official policy of the state. This includes such decidedly non-Maoist aspects as significant purchases of foreign technology, the restoration of purely academic, rather than political, standards in the universities, a greater degree of free market activity by China's collectivised farmers, and a tolerance of traditional, non-proletarian plays, novels, and movies.

Probably, the long-term political stability of China depends on Deng's success in coming up with clear results with his programme of pragmatism. If he can succeed in raising living standards and perceptibly improving China's long-stagnant economy, then the chances are that his scheme, and the backers of it, will entrench themselves in China's driving seat for some time to come. In the long run, political stability in China will depend on a belief among the majority of China's people that the government in power is

On April 5, 1976, an event occurred which shook the Beijing leadership to the core. Thousands of people gathered on the steps of the Great Hall of the People, demanding to speak with the country's leaders. When they were frustrated in this attempt, a huge and violent riot broke out in Tiananmen Square. Deng and his supporters were blamed and the "Gang of Four" sent Deng into disgrace. That was their last hurrah.

Opposite: *Mao Tse-tung once slept here, in Guangzhou.*

producing benefits for them.

If, on the other hand, Deng and the current leadership fail to restore a measure of success, then the heritage of Maoism and recent power struggles could well introduce another era of chaos. In a sense, the last 20 years of Chinese history — the events since the ill-fated Great Leap Forward — have introduced into the country a political tradition which the present leadership is obviously edging away from. That tradition, among other things, consists in an extreme egalitarianism, the belief that might be summed up in Mao's notion of the continuing revolution. During the Cultural Revolution, millions of youths — who are now in their late 20's and early 30's — experienced the heady, if short-lived satisfaction of attacking their elders and insisting on a kind of extreme equality. "To rebel is justified," Mao proclaimed. If youth becomes dissatisfied again, that rallying cry could acquire new meaning.

In fact, it is not hard to imagine that opportunistic leadership groups could try to exploit popular grievances to dislodge the moderate group from power. If any kind of political practice had remained constant in China it is the habit of each successive victor in the power struggle to use the vanquished as a scapegoat for all that is wrong in the land. The "Gang of Four" did that to Deng; Deng and his allies are now blaming the "Gang of Four" for all of China's failures of the past decade, and more, using all of the hyperbole that is contained in the considerable verbal arsenal of China's propaganda machinery. Deng, at 74, has probably not very many years of productive labour ahead of him. If he should die or if the current leadership should fail, it is not inconceivable that China could enter a new period of instability.

The current leadership, at least, seems well aware of that danger. On the one hand, it seems anxious to allow the people to let off some steam. In late 1978 and early 1979, a considerable degree of criticism of the leadership was tolerated in the form of wallposters put up on Beijing's so-called "Democracy Wall." But the regime has also strictly regulated the extent of the criticism and even arrested a number of dissidents who went beyond permissible boundaries. What may be particularly frightening to the Politburo is precisely the prospect that dissatisfactions among China's teeming youth, many of whom have been required to spend years labouring on rural communes, could reach some kind of political smouldering point.

Whatever may be the future, however, it is clear that for now at least, one of the inclinations of recent Chinese history has triumphed over the other. The pragmatic component of the Chinese response to the 20th century challenge prevails over the radical, xenophobic element. In a still broader sense, China, ever since the Opium Wars of the last century, has been searching for a successful approach to a new era in Chinese history. The country has experienced the self-strengtheners of the 19th century as well as the Boxers. It has leaned toward the Soviets and branched out on its own path of extreme self-reliance. It has been through numerous, often violent, struggles for power which, on each occasion, have diverted the nation from its attempt to reestablish its historical greatness.

The latest stage in this long search is summed up by the Chinese themselves as the Four Modernisations. It is represented by the image of a peaceful, orderly, united, pragmatic China that prevails in the West now. But whether China has finally found its formula, whether this is the China of the future or just another stage in China's long search, that only the next several years will tell.

In 1956, Chairman Mao declared the "Hundred Flowers" period as a time for disgruntled people to voice their complaints about the government and its policies. When criticism became too strong, and challenged basic tenets of Maoism, Mao declared that the criticism must stop. Hundreds of intellectuals and former businessmen were removed from their homes and sent to the countryside. Some, like the outspoken woman writer Ding Ling, were rehabilitated (restored to their former positions) only in the past two or three years.

Under Deng's leadership, criticism was tolerated again. Although it too was brought to a halt by government edict when communist ideology was questioned, only a few dozen of the "Democracy Movement" dissidents seem to have been arrested.

Opposite: A statue of Mao Tse-tung in Chengdu.

LAO SHE

"Thou shouldst be living at this hour" is the most fitting epitaph for Lao She (real name: Shu Sheyu), China's greatest post-revolutionary writer, who died in 1966 as a result of Red Guard persecution. He is officially said to have drowned himself, but a big question-mark hangs over his demise, as it does over the fate of thousands of other intellectuals of the old school.

For pathos and compassion, Lao She's writing is matched only by that of the 1930s author, Lu Xun. His satirical tale "City of Cats" is similar in spirit to Lu Xun's more brilliant "Story of Ah Q." But unlike Lu, who died in 1936, Lao She witnessed the first seventeen years of socialism in China, and was publishing until shortly before his death.

Lao She was one of the dwindling Manchu race whose ancestors conquered China in the 17th Century and presided over the last imperial Dynasty overthrown in 1911. Born in 1898, he spent his youth as a teacher of Chinese in England, later at Nankai University in Tianjin (Tientsin).

He visited the United States in 1946 after his novel "Camel Xiangzi" became a hit there in translation as "Rickshaw Boy."

Lao She, already a famous writer, returned to China immediately after the proclamation of the People's Republic in 1949, and was active in international movements to sponsor peace and friendship with the East European socialist block and the Third World. He lent his name to ban-the-bomb movements, reform of the Chinese written language, revival of the Beijing Opera, commemoration of Lu Xun, and friendship with the Soviet Union, North Korea and North Vietnam, while continuing to write plays and poems.

Lao She's friend Cao Yu, also a victim of Red Guard persecution and a well-known writer, wrote of his warm and generous character: "He would feast, visiting friends from afar on money he had obtained by pawning or selling his own clothes. He liked to drink wine, though he could not take much. After a few cups, he would start singing, his resonant voice shaking the four walls of his tiny room."

Cao claims that he persuaded Lao She

to return to China at the instigation of the late Premier Chou En-Lai. Lao She has become a culture hero of post-Mao China, and a symbol of the mass martyrdom of the Chinese intelligentsia in 1966-67.

Lao She's critique of Chinese society was fundamental and unsparing, and much of it is valid still today. In "City of Cats" he wrote of a decaying social order in which nobody cared for anything but a mysterious substance called "poppi" (drugs? money? corruption? national deceit? — apparently a symbolic amalgam of them all).

Had he lived, Lao She would have witnessed the demoralisation and disorder which descended on China as a result of the Cultural Revolution, though this showed signs of being put straight after the 1976 purge of Mao's former supporters, the "Gang of Four", and the institution of rational policies at the apex of the Communist Party. His suicide is made doubly unlikely by the sentiments he attributed to his rickshaw-puller, Camel Xiangzi: "Had he been a spirit in hell, he would probably have made the best of his surroundings."

Opposite: *The house in which the Chinese Communist Party was formed, on July 1, 1921 in Shanghai. Chou En-lai's picture hangs on the wall.*
This page: *During the Cultural Revolution, dances of minority nationalities lent a little colour and gaiety to otherwise dull performances. The rifle is a Cultural Revolution addition to bring political content to the dance.*

Opposite, top left: *At the height of the 1970's power struggle, Deng Xiaoping stands in front of Hua Guofeng* (left) *and Yao Wenyuan, a member of the "Gang of Four."*

Opposite, top centre: *Soldiers in front of a portrait of Mao.*

Opposite, top right: *A P.L.A. motor cycle patrol in Hangzhou.*

Opposite, bottom: *Mao's portrait is carried through the Beijing streets in a celebration in the summer of 1977.*

This page: *A big-character-poster is written on a wall.*

Above: *Despite official protestations against personality cults, these portraits of Mao and Hua hung in every public place.*

Right: *A billboard in Guangzhou celebrating 30 years of the People's Republic.*

Opposite: *A 1958 quotation from Mao: "Go all out, aim high and achieve greater, faster, better and more economical results in building socialism".*

鼓足干劲，力争上游，多快好省地建设社会主义。

毛泽东：《在中央会议上的讲话》

一九五八年三月二十日

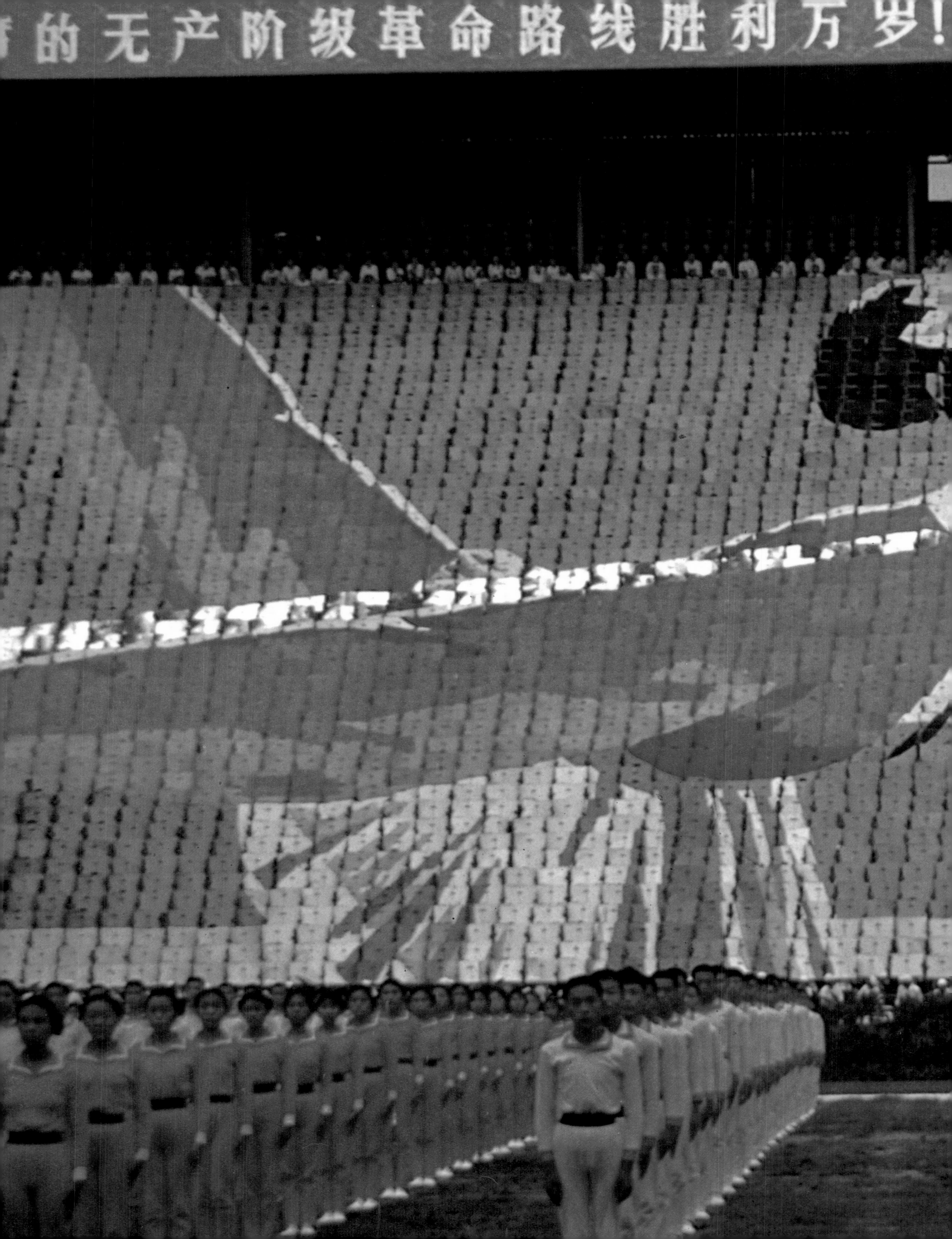
的无产阶级革命路线胜利万岁!

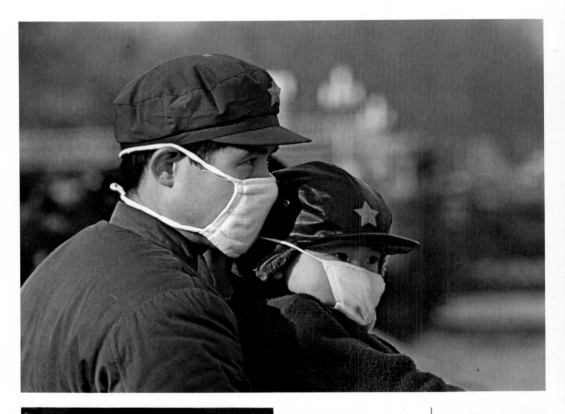

Preceding pages, opposite: *A display of flash cards in Beijing.*

This page, top: *A soldier dresses his son in matching clothes.*

This page, bottom left: *A young woman mourns the death of Chou En-lai.*

This page, bottom right: *In front of the Sichuan Exhibition Hall, Chengdu.*

Opposite: *Putting up a new message in Shanghai.*
    This page: *A youngster at the Kunming Zoo.*
    Following pages: *A painting stressing the importance for good physical fitness.*

The Cultural Mystery

Nigel Cameron

The two most vital dates in all 4,000 years of Chinese history are undoubtedly 221 BC and 1949 AD. With the first came the initial unification of the Chinese heartland under Qinshihuangdi. With the second came triumph of the Communist Revolution. And with both, China entered on an entirely new epoch of its history. With both, China was apparently totally altered, root and branch. Moreover, a colossal attempt was made in both cases to completely extirpate the past and all that pertained to it. And each effort was remarkably, but not completely, successful.

The full impact of what has taken place in China as a result of the revolution of 1949 can hardly be fully comprehended without some general knowledge of what happened 2,300 years before, at the time of the first unification of territorial China under the Qin ruler Qinshihuangdi who seized power in 221 BC. And we are much too close to the events of the Communist Revolution as yet to form more than tentative conclusions. But any assistance that can be had from the bottomless archives of written Chinese history, especially those with some analogous bearing, must be worth careful study. The events which occurred on the two widely separated dates, although very dissimilar in many respects, still have some fundamental likeness to each other.

From a congeries of feuding states the ruler of one, the Qin, welded together by force of arms a unitary state composed of all the others under his autocratic rule. The customs and usages of other states were cancelled and the new unified state was governed by Qin laws. The majority of the ruling and noble families of these other states were either put to the sword or brought to reside in the Qin capital, and thereby politically and militarily neutralised. Vast resources were speedily mobilised and employed with almost incredible efficiency. The fragments of walls that had been put up by previous rulers in part protection against the onslaughts of the "barbarians" outside, always envious of rich Chinese lands, were rapidly joined up by forced labour; and the perhaps one million who died in the process passed into Chinese folk memory — like those who participated in the Long March to Yenan over 2,000 years later. Poetically, but with a degree of realism, the builders of the wall who secured the first Chinese state, and the participants in the Long March who, in a very important way contributed to the triumph of the Communist Revolution of 1949, may be equated as the two most important functional elements in changing the pattern of Chinese life.

The Qin emperor ordered the burning of all books not of purely practical use in husbandary and the like. Especially sought out were the histories of other dynasties in China before him, and the records of the philosophical movements to which he was opposed — among them the material dealing with the socio-political thoughts of Confucius who had lived and travelled among the palaces of the states Qinshihuangdi had destroyed. Those who harboured such books were sent to forced labour building the Great Wall.

Inherent in this whole process was the embryonic development of a Chinese national consciousness. Then and tentatively later, people began to think of themselves as belonging to the single state that was now China — and as members, therefore, of the same race (however untrue the "race" idea was even then, for the inhabitants of the Qin state were racially mixed). The effect of the formidable barrier of the Great .Wall was not only physical in excluding the nomadic peoples outside its confines, but quite as importantly it was a spiritual and potentially nationalist divide, separating in the minds of the Chinese inside it their cultural achievements from those of the nomads, which were demonstrably of a lower level. In a sense the effect was rather like that of the sea barrier isolating the British from the European continent. The resulting spiritual isolation was in many ways productive of a special culture with all that that implies.

Another fundamental alteration in Chinese society at this time brought about unification in the manner of writing, on which so much later was to depend. For, from this time, the Chinese language could be fairly easily read by all literate persons within the state. Since the revolution of 1949 there's been another major overhaul of the language in an effort to simplify the complexity of strokes in the most common and most difficult written characters; and this will doubtless in due time lead to some sort of Romanisation of the language at the expense of the ancient written ideograms. The Qin were also responsible for what at first sight seems a trivial step — the standardisation of the axle length in all wheeled vehicles. In a land of mostly unpaved roads (such as existed in Europe until the 19th century, with no such measure ever taken) this meant that all vehicles could use the same ruts and thus in weather, fair or foul, communications were relatively efficient. Weights and measures, too, were made uniform throughout the state — another stablising factor. Yet the Qin state that was to have lasted for ever, by the very fundamentalism of the acts that created and supported it, aroused such a turbulence and resentment that a matter of four years after the death of its creator it was toppled by a man of the common people — the first emperor of the Han dynasty. Two things are noteworthy in this. The first is that the new dynasty came of common stock and not from some noble or formerly aristocratic or ruling family; and second, that the Han did not cancel most of the Qin achievements but on the contrary used them to maintain unity under their rule.

What little use the new rulers had for philosophy and religion was at first channelled through the old semi-magical formulation of spiritual heritage called Taoism. But gradually the Confucian doctrines which had been suppressed came back with new vigour, the books irretrievably lost rewritten from the memories of former scholars and savants. From some point in the second century BC, the philosophies of Confucius began to dominate imperial and bureaucratic thought and acts. Thus Confucianism, a system designed long before for use in the very courts that Qinshihuangdi had destroyed, a system designed to bring back the alleged glories of a mythical "Golden Age" to courts and states whose feudal society was in ruins, now took the reins and, with a tenacity that perhaps meant it was ideally suited to Chinese

temperament and social basics, held them with a sureness all but unparalleled in a non-religious, non-mystical philosophy for the ensuing 2,000 years.

Putting it in a few words, the traditional Confucian concept of the State from emperor through the ranks of the official bureaucracy and dowh to the peasant and even the mendicant, may be characterised as that of one huge, ramifying, but still closely-knit family. The family obligations worked basically from the bottom upward, while the family power descended from the emperor downward.

Confucian formulations of the mythical "Golden Age" of ancient and perfect rulers as the keystone to the health and prosperity of the nation, was complemented by another doctrine — Filial Piety. This was doubtless a codification of ancient ancestor-worship of former times, and enjoined on all the ritual ceremonies of respect and honour to be paid to ancestors. Thus the current emperor, regarded as the holder of that Mandate of Heaven descending to him from the perfect rulers of the "Golden Age" — when all was for the best in the best of all possible Chinese worlds — revered and honoured his own ancestors and ritually communicated the state of the realm and kow-towed to Heaven (a somewhat vague entity). His subjects were expected to revere their ancestors also, and in terms of filial piety children unquestioningly respected their parents, sisters their brothers, wives their husbands, and everyone his or her superior in the social hierarchy. Since the emperor was often one who had succeeded his dead father, he had, apart from Heaven, only his mother to defer to — hence the vast power of some dowager empresses in Chinese dynastic history.

It was this strange set-up, whose central concept was the fundamental stabilising process of reverence for ancestors (quite as stabilising as the Western submission to the rule of God or worship of Him), which early Jesuit intellectual missionaries at the Chinese court in the 16th and later centuries struggled to understand. Some of them did understand, but failed to convince their masters in Rome; and Rome at one point sent a Papal Legate who, in Chinese eyes, had the temerity to argue the point with an emperor. The downfall of Jesuit efforts stemmed from the Western conception that the Chinese *worshipped* their ancestors, when in fact this was hardly the case — as the emperor told the Legate before sending him packing from China.

It was this system of morality which sanctioned the structure and work of the government of China, and proved in this respect to be the longest-lived energiser of any socio-political system ever devised by mankind. Taken together with the fact that the Chinese, in their compact but very large territories, were probably always the most numerous homogenous group on the face of the earth, this continuity in basic principle needs to be firmly grasped in order to understand just how deeply China and the Chinese are in a category all of their own. With a non-religious concept as ruling principle, China was never torn apart by religious wars. The nearest to a holy upheaval was perhaps the Taiping Rebellion of the 19th century, which in fact took to itself many of the outward forms of the Confucian bureaucracy although it was inspired by a muddled Chinese version of Protestant Christianity.

A strong case could be made for the idea that Confucian tenets, while imposing strict lines of moral and social conduct, of guiding the ruling hands, of forming the sturdy framework of conduct or law by which the country was ruled in every aspect, nonetheless allowed the citizenry to continue observing all those comforting beliefs and superstitions and magical practices which man in his earliest times had begun to elaborate in the face of unendurable nature and calamitous personal life. The strength of Chinese traditional rule lay partly in its general permissiveness in the area of beliefs and local customs; and this tolerance was greater than that of most state systems. For the ordinary person, as for the holder of high state office,

Mythology and religion have always played an important role in the people's daily lives and in the affairs of state. The moral code of modern China has its roots in Confucianism.

In violent reaction against the pervasive hold of religion bands of young people in the late 1960s sought out symbols of the spirit world and destroyed what they could find (above, heads of Buddhas shattered in this stone cave, Hangzhou).

When the official taboos against religion eased, one of the first signs was the burning of incense in front of these luohans in the Temple of the Azure Clouds outside Beijing (opposite).

the essential and seemingly timeless guidelines were there. Within them, in matters other than official, and in matters personal, a whole firmament of beliefs and spiritual observances could, and did, exist.

In China both before and after the Qin state, and right up to and after the 1949 revolution, it was not religion but magic that was called upon in daily assuaging of cares and troubles — ritual observances that had little or nothing to do with the Confucian grand design. Even now in China, in isolated little places, occasional sticks of incense are to be seen burning at the foot of a tree in what was once the village's sacred grove, the copse that protected it from the evils of northern influences (and at the same time, on a pragmatic level, supplied many herbal materials, colourants, materials for medicines, fruits and nuts, canes and bamboos for handicrafts, and the like). And in the country areas of Hong Kong, that remnant of pre-revolutionary China, these and a host of other traditional observances are still readily seen. Animism mingles with geomantics in the common use of a *fung shui* (auspices) expert before a house is built, and alteration made, even a bed placed, and then the incense burned, or the paper replica ceremonially burned on the pavement-side on a given day. There is nothing particularly different at least in the intent in such observances, between those of China and those practised in the countryside of pre-industrial England. China did not encounter industrialisation on any major scale until the 1950's and in the Chinese countryside even now — in commune life, with its sweeping away of the gruelling miseries and starvation of what was a dying social system — there remain many remnants of homely superstition.

Religion in China, as in many huge areas of the Eurasian continent, was not a homegrown matter, any more than it was in England. The great world religions, and also many of the minor ones which came to China, such as Mazdaism and Zoroastrianism, all originated within a comparatively small geographical area bet-

A curious aspect of Chinese religious activity was the growth of popular folk religions, which combine elements of Buddhism and Taoism with local legends and myths to create hundreds of gods and demons to fit virtually every physical or spiritual need one might possibly have.

Fierce-looking guardians at temple gates scare off any uninvited demons (here, in a Taoist temple in Kunming). *Newcomers to Chinese culture may be excused if they see some similarities between traditional Chinese religious spirits and the highly stylized masks of traditional opera characters* (opposite).

ween the shores of the Eastern Mediterranean and the Arabian sands, and the northern part of India and southern Central Asia. Buddhism arrived in China in the first century AD, gradually gathering a corpus of adherents. Not surprisingly, the school of the faith that came was the Mahayana with its ready-made pantheon of gods and godlings, its plethora of good and evil spirits — all of which, together with the Buddha himself (quite contrary to his apparent intentions), were the subject of worship and veneration and supplication. Buddhism of this type would seem a religion ready-made for China. But in fact the pragmatic Chinese soon interfused it with many of the subtleties of their much older Taoism, which was a systematisation of a multiplicity of very ancient and popular magical and other beliefs and cults. It was perhaps Taoism itself which came nearest to being a religion for Chinese. By the mid-course of the Tang dynasty in the 9th century AD, the fusion of the two systems was such that it is hard to sort out what came from which.

But during that dynasty, the Chinese perhaps came closest than at any time before or since to espousing religion in the manner of other nations. By the mid-point of the dynasty, which ruled from the early 7th to the early 10th century, religions other than Buddhism had penetrated the country in varying degrees, largely by infiltration along the Silk Routes across the wilderness of desert and mountain and steppe lands of Asia. From the Western fingers of those routes came Mazdaism, Manichaeism, and the heretical Nestorian form of Christianity — all of them spurred on in some degree by the expansion of Islamic militants after the death of Mohammed. Such was the press of Westerners in the Tang capital of Changan (modern Xi'an) that, apart from being the most populous city of the world at that time, and the most sophisticated by far, it was also the most cosmopolitan. And such was the attraction of various exotic religions for the Chinese — temporarily somewhat blinded by the glamour of all these foreigners and their customs — that for a time they relaxed their normal self-containment in relation to the outer world. It seems too that the traditional Chinese assumption of their own absolute superiority over the peoples of the rest of the world began to crack around this time.

This outlook, and others related to foreigners, their strange religions, and the altering quality of Chinese life, was eventually to come under official disapproval.

Official orthodoxy, when it acted, was sharp and characteristic of what was to take place on many an occasion in the future when similar events occurred. It is worth taking note of the statements made at the time and the action taken to suppress the organisations concerned; for these are the first statements of such ponderous gravity concerning the absolute rule of Confucian philosophy as a state system, and the attitudes expressed at this time of the Tang held good for the remainder of dynastic history, right into the 20th century.

The emperor, at a moment when it was felt that the stability of his dynasty was threatened, blamed much of the disarray into which China had fallen on the incursions of the foreigners and their religions. In an edict of 845 AD, severe and straightforward in wording, he declared: "Under our three famous dynasties no one ever heard of Fo (Buddha). It is since the Han and Wei (from the time of Christ onward) that the sect began to spread in China. Since then foreign elements have established themselves without our people being sufficiently on their guard . . . and the State suffers in consequence . . . In all the cities, in the mountains, there are nothing but priests of both sexes. The number of monasteries grows daily . . . A great deal of gold is wasted on embellishing them. People forget their traditional rulers in order to serve under a master priest . . . Could anything more pernicious be imagined? Today an infinite number of priests . . . live upon . . . the sweat of others, expend the time of an infinite number of workmen in building . . . at great expense their magnificent edifices. Need we seek further for the cause of exhaustion of the empire?"

The emperor goes on to castigate his immediate predecessors for permitting this state of affairs to arise — however tendentiously argued were his supposed reasons for it. And he thunders his determination "to dry up this vile source of errors which flood the empire." More than 4,600 monasteries were destroyed, 260,000 men and women were to return from them to the temporal world and to pay their proper taxes. Monastery lands were to be confiscated and the 150,000 slaves working them to be returned to the bosom of the Chinese people. All this, he added with emphasis, "so that in the customs of our empire there shall be no mixture."

The key words are "no mixture." The idea was to be repeated again and again as the Chinese strove at all levels of what they conceived as the correct paths of life to protect what they saw as their unique culture and their unique social attainments. Thus Buddhism, Nestorian Christianity, the temples and congregations of Zoroaster, and the Manichaeists too, along with all the other foreign and organised religions and their adherents, were dissolved, reduced, harried, or otherwise frowned upon in various ways from time to time over the centuries in favour of the omnipotence of orthodox Confucian state principles. The Confucian Han monolith, with its heavyweight and irresistable philosophical and socio-political message, rolled on. Even poets were delighted at the downfull of religion. The great Bo Zhuyi, who died the year following the edict, had lamented:

"No more do I hear the sound of music-making, but only bells and chimes:
On the gates of temples in golden words the Imperial Patent shines.
For nunneries and wide Buddhist courts plenty of room is found;
Here moss under the brilliant moon, acres of vacant ground;
But in the crowded homes of ordinary folk there's hardly space to live."

Such sentiments in essence echo the orthodox view, a view accepted by most Chinese — anti-clerical and suspicious of religions as basically foreign things. The antagonism did not stop at religions. At various times in the Tang dynasty and right through to the Cultural Revolution of the 1970's it appeared in more or less violent forms affecting foreign people and their actions and organisations within China. Yet the Moslem minority peoples within the borders of China, principally in the northwest, were not frowned upon — perhaps because they had for long been familiar. Neither was there any disapproval of the large Moslem Arab settlements in certain southeastern coastal areas

Temple walls and gates were an important repository of the arts. Stone carving, such as on this panel found in a Moslem mosque in Xi'an, enables modern scholars to study centuries-old artistic styles.
One of the most significant archaeological finds in modern China is the tomb of Chinese emperor Quinshihuangdi (221-210 BC). In the spring of 1974, thousands of life-size terra cotta warriors and horses (opposite) were apparently discovered by local peasants digging a ditch. These figures were buried in the tomb, as was customary at that time, to indicate the wealth and importance of the monarch. The site is said to cover more than 36,000 square kilometres.

in former times when the seaborne trade of China was largely carried in Arab boats. Recent archaeological work has conclusively proved this. The Moslems, of course, were not fanatic about converting unbelievers to their creed.

Running through this pan-Confucian climate of living, with its insistence on the chain of filial piety linking the social pyramid, there ran another concept, ancient in its origins, sanctified by long acceptance, and related to the "grand concept." This was the idea commonly called *yin-yang*. *Yin* is the female and *yang* the male principle in this duality. The idea of the essentially complementary male-female relationship is extended to form a bi-polar system applicable to all aspects of nature and human life. *Yin* is cool, *yang* is warm; hence, the north-facing side of a hill is *yin* and the southern *yang*. Hollows are *yin*, and complemented by rises or upstanding things which are *yang*. The sun is *yang*, the moon *yin*. This concept of complementary opposites extended to everything. The many systems of Chinese physical exercise are not thought of in the Western fashion as being just good for the health; the seemingly limitless items in the Chinese pharmacopoeia, the clearly defined lines of acupuncture points and their use in treatment, are not simplistically considered as modes of direct influence on disease of abnormalities in this or that condition: all are considered and formulated in the light of adjusting an ill-adjusted *yin-yang* balance that is in itself essential to health.

This emphasis on balance, on the equable ordering of opposites in a nonviolent manner, underlined the spirit of compromise that prevailed not only in ordinary Chinese life but in intellectual discussion and the formulation of right policies too, and in the settlement of disputes among people by peaceful means. Studying the writings of Mao Tse-tung, in which he analyses social problems and divides them into antagonistic and nonantagonistic contradictions, one discovers that the former must be corrected by force, but the much more common non-

antagonistic ones are to be solved by persuasion. This thesis has the same roots as traditional Confucian thought on the subject. Confucianism put its emphasis on virtue as a sort of balancing act that goes on through life, in which impulse is tempered by cooler thought, anger by contemplation of the subject in terms of responsibility, punishment in terms not only of the actual wrongdoer but also of his family or associates. The doctrine of group responsibility stems from the idea that had the family or clan or associates of the wrongdoer regulated its members and its affairs correctly the crime would not have been committed; therefore all are in some degree responsible. A famous example of this occurred during the first Opium War when a party of drunken British sailors were on Chinese soil. In a brawl, one Chinese was murdered. The Chinese demanded that the murderer be handed over to them for punishment. The British replied that they could not establish which sailor was actually the murderer and therefore they could not hand one over. The Chinese said this was a frivolous reply as, clearly, the group murdered the man and *any one of them* would do as culprit. The British were outraged, unaware that in the Chinese mind this request was perfectly normal.

In such matters and in many other similar ways, the Chinese in times of peace and strong rule were to a very great extent a self-regulating society. There was no formulated written code of criminal law. Guilt was evident in terms of transgression of the binding Confucian ethic or code of normal conduct. The balance of provocation and group, as well as individual, responsibility entered into the making of a judgement. Popular opinion was based not on religious principles, as in the Christian West or in the Islamic or Hindu worlds, but on a complexity of Confucian standards whose sanction was that they had proved themselves by having worked well for a very great number of years before. In a sense, it could be said that this was a more rational basis for legality and right

conduct than religious belief, which is in essence arbitrary.

The point concerning the secular basis of morality is fundamentally important. However superstitious the Chinese were, Chinese life was regulated by a purely secular system. When we come to examine the Communist Revolution we therefore encounter two principal ingredients in the national consciousness (or the knowledge of being Chinese). First, an innate discipline. However broken down the system was in the last century before the revolution (a fact attributable largely to Western interference in China) discipline was an inherent part of Chinese society right down to village and family levels. Second, the religious-cum-spiritual aspect of Chinese life included a wide spectrum of beliefs more or less equally valid in Chinese eyes. Chinese-style Buddhism, Taoism, shamanist cults, simpler cults of virtually Neolithic antiquity, vied for prominence with the customary observances linked to the incidents of the agricultural year — the regulation of which was decided by government boards and issued as an annual calendar by Imperial Edict. There was no body of powerful vociferous religious adherents automatically ranged against the secular Socialist-Communist theory and practice that revolution brought.

Merely to contrast events in Christian Russia at the point of its revolution and after, is to establish that in China the picture was totally different. The bi-polarity of the secular system and a massive spectrum of superstitions mingled with some (generally heretical in purist terms) belief in organised religions, was the norm of human life in China. The tiny educated class were of course much less addicted to placating malevolent and encouraging benevolent spirits than were the multitude of the ordinary peasants and the uneducated. The educated man paid homage to and revered his emperor to intercede with Heaven on behalf of himself and the Chinese people — in ceremonies of extreme antiquity and formality. And from time to time at tur-

Excavations around Foshan in Guangdong province have unearthed 600-year-old pottery kilns and workshops. The pottery made in Foshan today (above) *copies the style of traditional Han dynasty figurines and Shiwan artistic pottery.*
Opposite: *The pottery army near Xi'an.*

ning points in his personal and family life — births, death, betrothal, marriage — he might turn not only to Confucius in a temple dedicated to the man who was in a way an archetype of all ancestors, but also to Buddhism, or Taoism, or indeed to a bit of all. Such was the interpenetration of the various religious and Confucian systems coexisting in China, that at time of stress all were called upon in the hope that in one major secular and many spiritual insurance policies some sort of safety or other solace might result.

Few Chinese, apart from the actual priests and adherents of religious sects, were wholehearted believers, and not even all of those — for there was many a "rice-Christian," and in times of famine the priesthood of other sects swelled noticeably. Adding up the total of adherents of all the sects in China in 1949, it is hard to arrive at a figure greater than eight to nine million. The population at that time was in the region of 400-500 million. A mere decade after the revolution, the rapidity of the change in this picture of what Westerners sentimentally called "enduring China" (if enduring is taken to mean suffering rather than long-lasting, the phrase is nearer to truth), could readily be seen in every aspect of life. A very popular song of that period was sung with great pride and deep satisfaction by people who, all over China, felt that their eyes had been opened by facts and their minds were now free to apply themselves to solving actual problems rather than to placating spirits, and it is fairly typical of the national mood.

> "There's no Jade Emperor in heaven,
> No Dragon King on earth.
> I am the Jade Emperor,
> I am the Dragon King.
> I order the three mountains and five peaks:
> 'Make way! Here I come!'"

The song sounds much more rousing in Chinese. But within its new expression of personal freedom, we still have recourse to an ancient phrase about ordering "the

three mountains and five peaks" to encompass the idea of great power. A new language to express new ideas is long in forming. However naïve the sentiments may be, the song tells much of the conquest of former superstition, as of the abolishment of the Confucian system. Under both, no such verse would have been made or sung. Just as the deep-rooted superstitions of the English peasantry evaporated in the steam of the Industrial Revolution, so the multiplicity of Chinese superstitions were vulnerable to a new secularism. In China there was no widely held religious belief proper, so what there was, was equally vulnerable to the revolutionary doctrine. We may contrast this with the still deeply-held Christian and Jewish faith in Russia after more than half a century of revolutionary theory and practice. In China a new secular philosophy replaced a traditional one, and with it swept away the greater part of beliefs of a non-rational nature. The demonstrable benefits of the new over the disordered remnants of the old in China were apparent to all Chinese — and non-Chinese visitors. But the coming of a Socialist principle to government in China presents a unique case in that it did not have to overcome deeply rooted religious life. For this reason the possibilities of rapid change in China were greater than elsewhere.

Examining China today, it is impossible to escape the fact that the Chinese, within the new fabric of their revolutionary society, have managed to infuse many aspects of the old one. Just as they did with organised religions in the past, they have treated Marxism with a cavalier high-handedness and made it Chinese.

Maoism as a social doctrine was quite far removed from Marxism, for the basic and very good reason that the Chinese economy was massively agricultural and only infinitesimally industrial. Peasants, not urban proletariat, made the revolution. Marxism was tailored by Mao to fit the facts of China. Once the first fruits of the revolution had ripened, there came a

There is no lack of imagination in the kinds of characters that abound in Chinese mythology, whether they are folk heroes of village legends, powerful gods of local mythology or evil demons of a favourite Beijing opera (opposite).
Despite the country's emphasis on industrialization and modernization, artisans, like this potter (above) in Foshan, are still trained in the age-old crafts.

53

period of great turbulence. Its precursors, even in the initial period of ripening, included the "Hundred Flowers" period in which the idea was to let all schools of thought air their views and all flowers bloom together. Such a diversity of schools and blossoms sprang up immediately that it was apparent China had not properly digested the revolutionary Socialist doctrine. But in the process of this much-maligned episode, what emerged was a furthering of the national consciousness (among intellectuals at least, and among others in part) in relation to a new order in life. It was obvious that huge chunks of antique thinking survived in China. It was equally obvious that they were completely out of step with the times. Their time is coming now, 20 years later, in the aftermath of a necessary social consolidation and an immense social and political experience that the Chinese have shared.

One more example of pragmatism within the Maoist context was the Great Leap Forward. As an example of Chinese humour touching right on the spot, an interpreter of minority peoples' languages in the deep southwest of China, on being asked how long he had been married, replied, "Six years." And how many children did he have? "Seven." After a moment he added with a cheerful smile: "The Great Leap Forward!"

But what the Great Leap Forward was really all about was making iron and steel in the communes so that the peasants would understand something of industrial processes. In fact, the products of this activity, which convulsed the nation and was highly detrimental to the agricultural economy, were very low-quality pig iron, for the most part, which commune members beat out into equally poor quality tools. But the *real* product was something quite different. In a country and at a time when, even then, the majority of people had never seen a light bulb and regarded industrial products as the work of absolutely superior beings, the Great Leap Forward taught Chinese in a year or so that technology was like the agriculture

they understood — an ordinary activity performed by ordinary people, and not in any way the magical thing it seemed to most of them. The Great Leap Forward was an economic disaster but an educational success.

One further result of the ripening of revolutionary fruit was the Cultural Revolution in which ultra-left separatist groups attempted to force a return to what they saw as the original Maoist purity of doctrine. Irresistibly, we are reminded of that Tang emperor's decree on the upstart religions which he wiped out in order that "in the customs of our empire there shall be no mixture." Faced with the realities of both the Chinese and the Chinese-in-the-world picture, the Cultural Revolution faded away — but again, not without the tremendous educational lesson of involvement in a mass movement and what it actually means in terms of human reality.

Two other aspects of post-revolutionary China should be given their place. Although the Cultural Revolution probably put paid to the last remnants of filial piety, the Chinese family emerged with remarkably few scars. Vast numbers of youths were deployed far from home in the deep country to work on the land. The attempt was to encourage knowledge of China's main base, agriculture, and simultaneously to prevent the growth of cities and towns as consumer aggregations. With the ending of the Cultural Revolution and the conquest of the Gang of Four, there has been some filtering back of this youthful workforce — and some accompanying violence in cities. But the impression gained in visits to many parts of China, both countryside and cities, and from conversations with many different people in various stations in life, is of the continuity of the family as a living and worthwhile institution. Certainly, it is hard for older people to accommodate to the absence of the automatic respect of the type they could command under the old scheme of things. But it should be considered that everyone in China who was aged about 20 in 1949 is bound to be 50

Hefei, the capital of Anhui province, was just a small market town until the communist revolution. It became a centre for iron and steel, and started to develop handicrafts, including embroidery (above) *and electric wire painting* (opposite).

now, and their children most probably aged from 30 downward. Many are indeed grandparents by now. Thus, the composition of the total population of China is quite largely composed of people who never knew the old system, or knew it only in their youth.

The ties of family are still extremely strong. One example may perhaps be allowed to stand for many. During the Cultural Revolution a man and his wife were separately interned for alleged need of re-education in political thinking. The father was first to be released, and on the release of his wife she arrived home to their flat to find that the authorities had arranged for their children, who had been working in distant parts of China, to be home to greet her. The salaries of both man and wife were not withheld and were presented in a lump sum to them on

release, thus further strengthening the parental core of the family.

The continuance of old institutions such as the "street committees" has been construed by the outside world as some sort of official spying on the people. It could be used as such, perhaps, but in fact represents the present continuation of a grass roots element of the old self-regulating population in today's new world.

One other aspect of continuity of tradition, among many others, is worth a mention — the cult of heroes. Chinese mythology was always filled with the tales of heroic figures. On example was the Great Yu, who was said to have been Minister for War in the reigns of the Emperors Yao and Shun in the faraway "Golden Age." In a time of great floods he was appointed to drain the land, a task which he accomplished, regardless of his personal circumstances, in nine years. The famous tale has him passing by the gate of his own home, where his wife and children could be heard lamenting his long absence, but without paying any heed. Time made the Great Yu into one of the Three Transcendant Powers, with Yao and Shun, whom he is said to have succeeded, and also made him the inventor of irrigation and water conservancy in general.

This placing of the shining mantle of pre-eminence in one or other field of endeavour is a highly popular national characteristic today when "model peasants" and "model workers" are heroes of the whole country, their stories told on radio and their faces familiar on the commune TV. Model production brigades and model factory teams are also brought to light in great emulation campaigns which are merely an up-to-date rendering of the popular tales of the heroes of old. Apart from emulation and its pay-off in increased production, the increase in popular solidarity is an important result.

For the time being under the vice-premiership of Deng Xiaoping, China is entering one of the infrequent periods of opening out to the world. But this phenomenon is probably the result of the

need to repair quickly the lost impetus and semi-chaos which occurred under the extreme leftist policies of the Cultural Revolution and the Gang of Four — when the "no mixture" purification of the Socialist base and the connected xenophobia left China more or less static for a decade. The present pragmatism, whatever the purely material need for it, is a sign of the flexibility of Socialism — and this in many ways, too, reflects the flexibility of the traditional state doctrine when it was in sure power.

But for imperfect humanity (perhaps imperfectible humanity would be correct) there is always the need for whatever comforting daily observances can be found. New Chinese legends, many that spring from actual events during the period when the revolutionary forces were still struggling to defeat both Japanese and Kuomintang forces in simultaneous warfare, are already well entrenched in the popular mind. The way they are told echoes the manner of telling of the old legends to a surprising degree. And although New Year is no longer at the Spring Festival as of old, but on January 1, the real festival of the popular year is still the Old Spring Festival as the world of winter succumbs to softer airs and life in response surges back from the dormant earth. It will probably take a very long time before the Chinese feel that the year starts in January. And perhaps it would be best, not only for them but for other people, to stick closely to the seasonal year — for *homo sapiens*, alone among the earth's flora and fauna (and rather recently, too) has altered the natural rhythm of terrestrial life.

In China, and considering the closeness of former Chinese life to that natural rhythm, one has often been struck by the propriety of conforming to it. The secular "Grand Concept" of rule and society did not, and should not now, exclude the innate response of human beings to natural phenomena.

Tianjin, an industrial centre and major seaport east of Beijing, had a national reputation for producing hand-painted "New Year's pictures" and museum-quality terra cotta figurines (right). Quality suffered seriously in the late sixties when Cultural Revolution's leaders insisted on political content in all art works, from theatre and drama to painting.

The street was once a hub of neighbourhood activity, especially on festival days. Some of this activity is returning — vendors sell sweets or noodles from carts in some cities, and dragon dances (opposite) are held on special occasions. Other traditional art forms, especially in music, remain popular. Highly talented youngsters can look forward to government-sponsored scholarships to national or provincial academies of music, art or drama.

MA YINCHU

The severe ideological and political problems associated with China's economic growth and massive surge of population increase form the framework of the career of the near-centenarian economist Ma Yinchu.

Born in the rich coastal province of Zhejiang in 1882, he was educated by missionaries in Shanghai, later attending Yale University where he took his bachelor's degree in 1910, following up with a Ph.D. in applied economics at Columbia. During a spell as Professor of Economics at Beijing University in 1915-27 he advised the Bank of China on currency problems, founded the Shanghai College of Commerce and the China Economics Society and published anti-Marxist works on economic theory.

In 1927 Ma returned to his native province as a Professor at Zhejiang University, and in 1928 was elected a member of the Kuomintang-dominated parliament. During the war against Japan, he taught economics at Chongqing (Chungking), and turned his critical pen against the Kuomin-

tang government — for which he was held under house arrest for two years.

After the war, Ma became a still more committed political activist, participating in demonstrations at Shanghai and Hangzhou and eventually fleeing to Hongkong. When the Communists were victorious in 1949, he returned to the mainland and held numerous posts teaching and advising the new government on economic policy.

But even in his seventies he was not to retire from the arena of political controversy. Ma made himself increasingly unpopular with the Communist Party by publicly proclaiming his belief in the Malthusian concept of disastrous population increase — whereas the Marxists of the day held that "people are the most precious capital."

After publishing an article defending his ideas in 1959, he was dismissed from the presidency of Beijing University, but continued to serve on titular bodies until the Cultural Revolution, when he was denounced by Red Guards and disappeared from view for over a decade.

In 1979 Ma was rehabilitated and his

ideas vindicated in a series of important articles in the Party-controlled press. He was portrayed as having fallen a victim to the "Gang of Four" and his theories on population control were acclaimed as vital to the solution of China's birth-rate problems.

Had Ma been heeded earlier, the Chinese authorities might not have found it necessary to take the measures applied from 1979 onwards — severe social and economic penalties for any family which bore more than two children, and strong persuasion of parents to let themselves be sterilised after they had borne one child.

The present rate of growth of China's population — probably around 12 million new mouths every year — has become the most important single factor holding back a rise in living standards. But this will hardly give satisfaction to Ma who predicted it, for his career has been one of bold and devoted service to his native country, finally recognised and duly praised.

Opposite, top right: *In Hangzhou, a 380-metre-high temple guard carved from a solid piece of camphorwood.*

Opposite, top centre and left: Luohans *in the Hall of 500* Luohans *in the Temple of the Azure Clouds in Beijing.*

Opposite: *The Western Garden Temple in Suzhou, a Buddhist temple built in 1635, destroyed during the Taiping Rebellion, completely rebuilt at the turn of the century.*

Above: *The entrance to Shanghai's Jade Buddha Temple.*

Opposite: *The Lingyin Si (Temple of the Souls'
Retreat), Hangzhou. The original temple was
apparently built at the beginning of the fourth
century, destroyed and rebuilt 200 years later,
abandoned in the mid-ninth century during a
period of religious persecution. Destroyed again
in the mid-1800s, it was rebuilt and is now a
monastery.*

This page, top left: *Monastery of the Souls'
Retreat.*

This page, top right: *The Jade Buddha
Temple, Shanghai.*

This page, bottom: *One of many stone
sculptures in Hangzhou caves.*

From ancient times, palaces, temples and private homes of officials and scholars have been decorated with the finest examples of statuary, friezes and wall paintings, only some of which has been carefully preserved or reproduced.

63

Chinese opera is an art form in its own right, not a musical version of a literary work (as is usually the case in the West). Some famous traditional operas date back as far as the Yuan dynasty — 700 years ago. The best-known style is the Beijing Opera, but regional operas with their own distinct provincial characteristics are also very popular, though seldom found outside their own regions. Musical variety shows, with acts featuring solo performances of traditional musical instruments, comedy routines, acrobatics and ethnic dancing (this page, top), are traditional.

Chinese operas make heavy demands on backstage support staff, requiring elaborate costumes, scenery and decorations (this page, centre and bottom right).

The skill of the craftsman and artist can be found in the making of an ordinary umbrella, porcelain figures and vases. Hand-carved wooden door panels and hand-painted glass insets were important decorations in the finest homes and gardens.

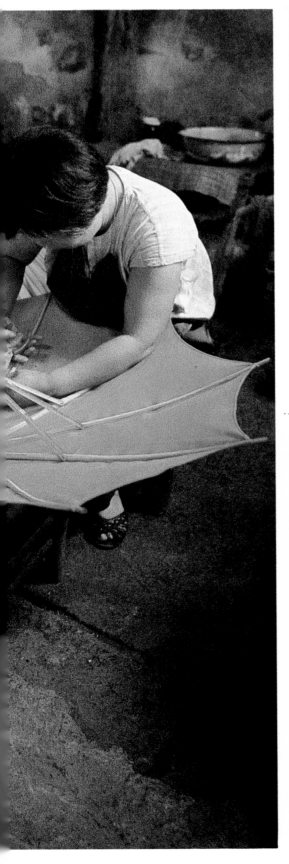

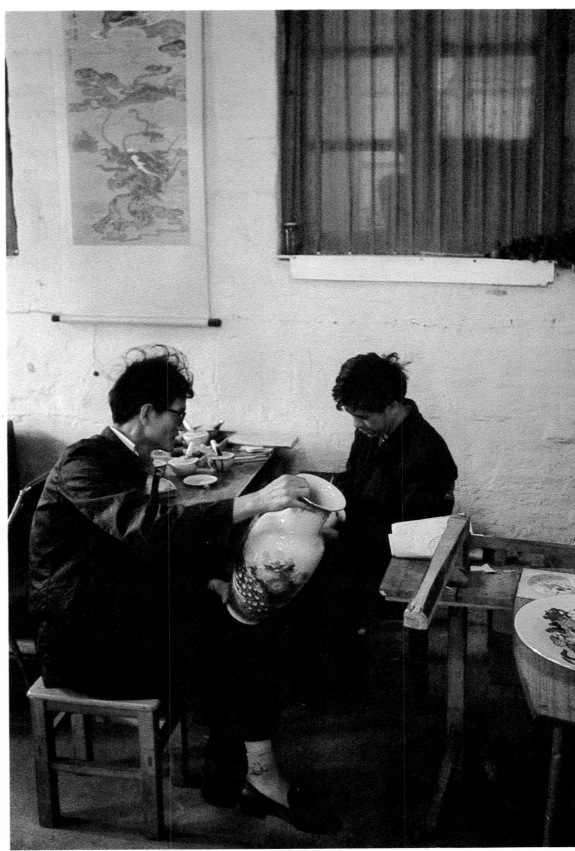

Formal art education is reserved for a relative handful of young people, some of whom are selected for study in the main institutions of culture in Beijing and Shanghai.

Some students at the Temple of Heaven try their hand at an unfamiliar art medium, painting in oils (this page, top) while others practice the accordian (this page, bottom), an instrument which is probably more popular now in China than in the west.

Weiqi, a type of Chinese chess game similar to the Japanese game, Go, is often played in parks during holidays, and draw large crowds of spectators.

The New Elitism

David Bonavia

In the spring of 1979, the huge city of Shanghai was buzzing with rumours about a spectacular heist which had just been perpetrated there by a young man called Zhang Longguan.

Zhang, a high-school graduate, wanted a ticket for the first Shakespeare production to be put on publicly in China since the early 1960's. It was "Much Ado About Nothing", and its staging marked the end of the long freeze which Madam Mao (Jiang-Qing) had imposed on the Chinese theatre before her overthrow in 1976.

For the theatre-goers of Shanghai, it was a stunning novelty to see Chinese actors and actresses dressed up in European Renaissance costumes, courting each other in flowery language. There was a terrific demand for tickets, and no one could get one easily without special connections. Zhang had the bright idea of simply ringing up the theatre, impersonating the chief of the municipal propaganda department, and asking for a ticket for "the son of a senior leader" who would be coming to Shanghai from Beijing and who wanted to see the play. The theatre company, unable to find a single free seat in the auditorium, placed a special chair in the aisle for the "important" young guest, and later transferred him to a choice seat in the stalls which was willingly surrendered for him by some senior local official.

Having apparently enjoyed his VIP treatment, Zhang rang the theatre company again and persuaded a woman opera singer to let him have another pair of tickets. When she offered to deliver them in person, he told her: "No, don't do that. I'm staying at the East Lake guesthouse and you might have difficulty getting in. I'll pick them up myself." This convinced the singer that Zhang must be the son of a very important person, and she subsequently invited him to her home and laid on an elegant meal to entertain him. Zhang, who had been giving himself the alias of Li Xiaohong, allowed her to jump to the conclusion that he was the son of General Li Da, an important staff officer. And he consented to her eager offer to help find him a girl friend in Shanghai. With her help, he picked out a girl who was the daughter of a former Shanghai capitalist. Like many of his type, the old man had lived comfortably enough on a state allowance until everything was confiscated by the Red Guards in 1966. Now, in accordance with the post-Mao leadership's policy of making restitution of funds seized from such people, he had overnight become a rich man again. He was interested, too, in acquiring family connections with the son of an important official, to avoid repeating his unpleasant experiences of the Red Guard period, should such a thing ever recur. He invited Zhang to move into the family's plush apartment, and his wife actually made him a gift of her own wristwatch, in a move clearly intended to hint at eventual marriage with the daughter of the house.

Through his other connections, Zhang made friends with a senior official in the Culture and Propaganda Department, who was so pleased to be acquainted with the "young master" that he gave him free use of his own car — a luxury enjoyed by only the most important people. The mere fact of having access to a car meant that Zhang and his girl friend could go wherever they wanted — they were simply assumed to be important. So they spent their time driving around and making excursions to the picturesque city of Suzhou, China's "Venice."

But the working people who lived near the home of Zhang's prospective father-in-law became suspicious about the credentials of this young man who never went to work and spent all day amusing himself. They took the matter up with the authorities, and finally someone checked with the General Staff in Beijing. There was no such person as Li Xiaohong — it transpired — and Zhang was duly arrested. Cross-examined by the police, he denied that he had impersonated a general's son. "That's just something you all assumed," he said. And when asked whether he admitted his guilt, he came back with the unanswerable retort: "Supposing I had been a general's son? Would what I did have been a crime then?" Zhang's insinuation that what he did was criminal only because he was *not* the offspring of a senior official touched on some very deep-seated nerves of socialism in China. Especially since the downfall of Madam Mao and her political clique in 1976, there have been numerous exposés of fraud and abuse of office by Chinese officialdom, and the Beijing press has inveighed against the assumption held by many of them that their rank alone puts them above the law.

The tendency for high officials and their families to regard themselves as elites is common to all Communist countries, and China is probably the one in which the most determined efforts have been made to combat the rise of what Yugoslav dissident author Miroslav Djilas called "the new class." The Cultural Revolution — for all its wild excesses — was aimed at least partly at the abolition of class privileges which the Communist Party, the army and the government had been accumulating for themselves. However, élitism is not simply a matter of officials creaming some "perks" off their countries' social and economic systems. Extreme disparities of income, privilege and opportunity still exist in China — between the urban and rural populations, the intellectuals and the workers, soldiers and civilians, Chinese citizens and foreigners. If they do not immediately strike Westerners visiting China — who tend, on the contrary, to gain an impression of uniformity and egalitarianism — that is because they are more carefully disguised, and take different forms from the élitism and privilege accepted as normal in Western countries. And the general standard of living in China is so low that particular disparities are harder for Western eyes to spot in what at first looks like a featureless mass of people.

It is important to remember that four-fifths of China's one billion population live on the land and make their livelihood from farming and related activities. Most of them are very poor by the standards of the developed world, receiving each year just enough food to stave off malnutrition, a few yards of cotton cloth, a very little cash — and having access to only quite rudimentary medical services, for which, contrary to what is often believed, they pay themselves through co-operative welfare schemes. They have little or no chance of

migrating from their native villages to the cities, or sending more than a tiny number of their children to study at universities. A young persons's best hope of advancement in the rural areas is to become a tractor driver, or — dream of dreams — to be one of the few selected for service in the armed forces.

By comparison with the peasants, the working class in the urban areas is a relatively privileged group. Millions of peasants would like to migrate to the cities, if they were allowed to, and in fact there was just such a mass movement of population in the late 1950's, when Mao launched his "Great Leap Forward" to revolutionise the Chinese economy. The "Leap," however, was an economic and organisational disaster. The country was brought to the brink of starvation, and when Mao finally backed down in 1961, millions of peasants who had flocked into industrial jobs were packed off home to their communes because agriculture was again seen as the main priority for national salvation, and because the cities just could not support them all.

To ease the strain of the rapidly increasing urban populations in the 1960's and 1970's, Mao's ruling group sent millions of young high-school graduates off to the farms and remote border regions, where they were supposed to settle down for life. Nothing could have more cogently brought home to the young town-dwellers how great were the disparities between their living conditions back home and those they had to share with the peasants on the communes. Country life is no idyll in China. It means back-breaking work, sometimes for more than 16 hours a day in busy farming seasons, being outdoors in all kinds of weather, enduring meagre food rations, rudimentary sanitation, mud, dust, bad smells, coarse manners, ignorance, and everything else one associates with a poor peasant society. So most of the "rusticated youths," as they were dubbed, heartily disliked their life on the land, and frequently failed to hit it off with the peasants — who for their part tended to

regard the soft young city kids as a burden on their own over-stretched means of subsistence. Far from inspiring the peasants with the feeling that the government and the urban dwellers really cared about them and wanted to ease their burdens, the seemingly effete ways of the youths from the cities often served to rub in how great was the disparity between town and country. Mao himself recognised this as one of the great contradictions in China's society, and one which he earnestly attempted to solve through a process of social levelling.

Mao's successors, however, are conscious of the unpopularity of the "rustication" programme, and have begun winding it down. Where there were previously no jobs in the cities for school-leavers, jobs are now being created through the setting up of co-operative ventures to do everything from hairdressing to furniture making. Few young people are now being assigned to the countryside — at least not for long or indefinite spells, as before — so that even the slight mutual acquaintance which grew up between town and country dwellers over the past decade or two will eventually fade from peoples' memories.

The industrial workers are considered a privileged class in China, because however crude their living conditions, and however dreary their jobs, they have the basic comforts of city life which people in rich countries take so much for granted. These include enough fuel to keep reasonably warm in winter; stone or brick houses; freedom from the effects of flood, gales, hailstorms and droughts; relatively good schooling facilities within easy reach of a child's home, and access to university for the brighter ones; fixed working hours and no child labour (which also means freedom for the children to do more homework and thus improve their chances on the educational ladder); better access to consumer goods; public transport; closer proximity of hospitals and clinics, access to a wider range of medicines, and highly-subsidised medical care; and in some cases the chance to pass one's job on to one's offspring upon retirement.

Of the many tragedies that occurred because of the Cultural Revolution, one of the most deeply felt today is the loss of an entire generation of young people who were unable or unwilling to get even a minimum level of schooling during that tumultuous time. Universities were closed for two or more years; teachers were sent for "re-education"; courses of study were disrupted by routine periods of manual labour in the fields (following pages) and in the factories for both the students and the teachers; discipline broke down almost completely in the elementary and high schools. People complain that today's youth (opposite) playing cards in Xi'an has no appreciation for hard work and struggle.

Despite the outcry against elitism in the late sixties and early seventies, sons and daughters of officials (above), *military officers and politician could still enter colleges and institutes through "the back door," using family influence. Some, who had earlier planned teaching careers, changed their minds after observing the lack of discipline and of formal schooling* (opposite) *in the classroom during their practice teaching sessions.*

These are some of the reasons why hardly any Chinese worker in industry would change his job for a place on a commune. The young people in Western "communes," who drop out of society to set up their own subsistence economies, would seem little short of ludicrous to people in China, who know the real meaning of hardship and the real benefits of organised urban society.

At the heart of the ongoing controversy about élites and privileges in China stand the intellectuals or *zhishifenzi* — a rather loose word in Chinese, meaning more or less anyone who has graduated from high school and works with the brain rather than the body. It can, of course, also indicate a person of high intelligence and fine academic qualifications. Mao, himself a largely self-taught intellectual, had a deep-seated disdain for the products of formal education. Under his rule they were sometimes abused as the "stinking ninth category" (in addition to the so-called eight categories of political undesirables). Chinese intellectuals underwent their most severe persecution for over 2,000 years during the Cultural Revolution — many of them having unwittingly set themselves up as targets when they accepted the Party's invitation to voice frank criticisms of the way the country was being governed and were denounced as "rightists" as long ago as 1957. Mao's anti-intellectual stand — itself a major revolution in Chinese terms — brought educated people under terrible pressures at the onset of the Cultural Revolution in 1966-67. Professors, doctors, engineers, writers, artists, schoolteachers, diplomats, actors, musicians and even athletes were exposed to maltreatment — beating and arm-twisting, exhausting and humiliating "struggle and criticism" sessions. Those who did not die of injuries or stress-conditions such as ulcer and heart attack, or commit suicide, or go mad, were subjected to various degrees of detention or supervision with menial labour for several years thereafter. Some were treated as social outcasts for more than 20 years following the 1957 campaign.

Between 1972 and 1975, Premier Chou En-lai and the rehabilitated Vice-Premier Deng Xiaoping did their best to reinstate intellectuals ousted from their jobs, if only because the country's education system, science, technology and military research would undoubtedly decline if those with specialised knowledge were not allowed to use it. But it was not until 1977, after the downfall of the Gang of Four, that a policy of thorough mass rehabilitation was applied. Intellectuals returning from the countryside, or emerging from retirement or obscure labouring jobs, were given back their full status and prestige, and told to think of themselves as a new vanguard in China's drive for modernisation.

The intellectual aristocracy was thereby reinstated. Of course, some of the privileges of an intellectual élite are part and parcel of the job. It is simply not economic for teachers or scientists to do their work in conditions of extreme heat or cold, or to exhaust themselves with physical labour to the detriment of their mental toil. The chances are that an intellectual will live in a city, in conditions at least as good as those of industrial workers, and probably better. High salaries can be earned for mental labour which would never be paid for manual work. And intellectual work often entails a strong element of creativity, one of the deepest satisfactions known to mankind.

Before the Cultural Revolution, a senior professor or surgeon could earn well over 300 Yuan monthly (about US$190 at 1980 rates of exchange) — five or six times the average wage for a worker, and many, many times more than that of a peasant. These high wages, which were generally docked or "voluntarily" surrendered in the Cultural Revolution, are now being reinstated. Universities and research institutes, in addition, provide quite comfortable housing for their senior staff, though there may be waiting lists. Medical care, welfare, pensions and ration cards are supplied by the place of work, and the social atmosphere is helpful to children's schooling. Intellectuals are in the front

ranks of those Chinese citizens who are permitted to travel abroad — a great privilege for people who may not hope to exercise it more than once or twice in a lifetime, if at all.

Unfortunately, it seems that some of the lessons of the Cultural Revolution are being forgotten only too quickly. Reinstated to their former rank and prestige, the intellectuals are already acquiring a reputation for arousing resentment among others who are less well-qualified, but who managed somehow to ride out the storms of the Red Guard rampage and subsequent upheavals, even at the cost of their intellectual integrity and professional standards. It is rather as though a nation's war-dead had returned to life and claimed for themselves the status of "brightest and best" on account of their martyrdom — thus pushing out the less heroic types who had stayed alive and made a life for themselves in the ruins.

Intellectual snobbery and pedantry are only too obvious temptations for the scholars, teachers and scientists of a nation which has meticulously preserved a 2,500-year-old respect for knowledge and educational refinement. Underlying the Cultural Revolution's assault on intellectuals was the idea that they were not living up to the trust which society resided in them — to use their knowledge and talents for the good of all, and not just for their own material benefit or self-glorification. The tremendous gap between urban and rural life, which we discussed above, is also in the Chinese cultural tradition, which saw the peasantry as an ocean of necessary but ignorant and uncultivated helots lapping around the islands of civilisation which were the cities and the estates of the gentry.

The Chinese intellectual in the modern era has an additional and difficult role to perform — that of mediating between Chinese and foreign culture and knowledge. Needed — vitally needed — on account of his or her knowledge of foreign languages or foreign-originated technologies, the intellectual runs the risk of being considered disloyal to Chinese values through becoming too deeply immersed in the values of the West. Thus, in 1974, when Madam Mao was launching her last great onslaught against the intellectuals, she concentrated her fire on their role as purveyors of Western culture and Western knowledge — even going so far as to deny the aesthetic quality of Western music and question the need to purchase Western industrial technology which, so her followers proclaimed, Chinese workers could just as well originate themselves.

Now, however, everything is going the intellectuals' way. Scientific and cultural knowledge are being lauded above political rectitude. It is suddenly better to stray to

the "right" than to the "left." The country recognises its need for foreign research and foreign products, and for Chinese exports to adapt them to revive the flagging technology of a country once famed for its inventiveness. Everything is being done to make the intellectuals confident and happy, to save distracting them from their work, and to bring on new generations of young educated members of the elite. It is observable in many countries that intellectuals are to some extent a hereditary class. Traditions of scholarship in a family, a quiet place to a study, and a good private library, are among the best forms of stimulus for children and adolescents to become scholars like their parents. The working-class or farming family may oppose bookishness among its children — either because their labour is needed or because the parents do not understand academic subjects and are suspicious of them or hostile toward them. The influence of a child's circle of friends also tends to propagate the desire for study in some peer-groups, while mocking or suppressing it in others.

Another important elite in China is made up of the armed forces. There is no universal conscription, and the chance to serve as a soldier, sailor or airman is viewed as a great privilege. Military service enables young people to do exciting and prestigious things like firing guns and flying aeroplanes, which they could never hope to do in civilian life (except perhaps popping off a few rounds of ammunition once a year in militia practice). It provides the opportunity for travel, for deeds of valour recognised and rewarded by the state, and for access to some of the most advanced areas of technological knowledge. The main career disadvantage facing Chinese servicemen is the difficulty of finding equally rewarding or interesting work when their term of service comes to an end. In theory, veterans receive preferential treatment, but in practice they may find they have missed the boat for a comfortable factory job and may have to become plain farmers — something which

they generally resent, even if they came from communes in the first place. Big cities in China over recent years have repeatedly been swept by murmurs of discontent from unemployed veterans — sometimes public demonstrations and wall-posters voicing protests.

While in the armed forces, a Chinese serviceman can feel justly proud of belonging to the country's main élite group, whose role as founder and guardian of the Revolution is constantly trumpeted. Senior officers travel "soft class" on trains — even when it means letting them mingle with "dangerous" foreigners — and they make up a high proportion of those permitted to travel on the domestic civil air network. Their clothing, quarters and food are provided free. From the rank of battallion commander upwards, they are allowed married quarters. In the cities, they seem to commandeer the largest fleets of vehicles, both private cars and jeeps. They have special hospitals, and special schools for the children of senior officers. And the close links maintained between regional and local military commanders on the one hand, and the civilian party administration on the other, mean that many areas of covert privilege — called "going through the back door" — are open to them. On top of all this, the army provides a possible route to entry into the national leadership.

In the early years of the Communist victory in China, the army was the main administrative body because of its monopoly of communications and coercive power. But its role was soon subordinated to that of the Party, and prominent army commanders who dared to challenge Mao's authority were dealt with promptly and severely. In 1967, however, the army again had to be entrusted with huge areas of civilian administration because of the breakdown of law and order brought about by the Cultural Revolution. China came close to being a military dictatorship until 1971, when the Defence Minister and named successor to Mao, Marshal Lin Biao, was officially claimed to have died in

Most people consider themselves fortunate to own their own bicycles (opposite, top in Shanghai). *The State continues to allocate the annual production of new bicycles so that anyone wishing to buy one must first obtain permission from his organisation.*

In schooling as well, it often helps for a high-ranking official to use his contacts to obtain admission for a family member to one of the handful of prestigious nursery schools (opposite, bottom).

Until recently, beauty parlours (above) *and western-styled clothing were available exclusively to the elite.*

People living in the cities are by and large far better off than peasants and have more time for personal activities and relaxation (above). *Unemployed teenagers playing cards on city streets* (opposite) *rather than taking jobs in the countryside have been publicly criticized for their attitude.*

an air crash in Mongolia while trying to flee the country after an unsuccessful coup attempt. From then on, the presence of military officers in civilian organs of power declined, as Madam Mao and her group of civilian propagandists and theorists made their last bid for power in the period 1974-76. With the overwhelming support of the Chinese army commanders, the other top leaders locked her and the rest of the "Gang" up in October, 1976, less than a month after Mao's death. Military influence in policy formulation again became strong, as the twice-rehabilitated Deng Xiaoping rewarded his military supporters with jobs on the Politburo. During his two spells of political disgrace, Deng had depended heavily on his friends among the army commanders, particularly in South China, for his safety and eventual political comeback. They were a powerful force working in favour of his anti-leftist policies in the series of personality and power struggles which divided the leadership between 1976 and 1979. This restored level of military influence in the government of China naturally led to fresh prestige and power for army officers at the local levels — and it is perhaps significant that our Shanghai con-man, Zhang Longguan, let himself be assumed to be the son of a general.

But having reviewed the privileges enjoyed by industrial workers, intellectuals and soldiers in China, it remains to discuss the most privileged élite of all — the party and government hierarchy, which meets at its apex in the persons of the Chairman of the Party (concurrently Premier at time of writing) and several Vice-Chairmen (mostly Vice-Premiers as well). Exercise of power is the biggest privilege of all, and in China that means power over almost one billion people. But the bearing of office extends its privileges right down to the level of the rural production brigade (a group of farming villages within the framework of a commune). Officials on the communes are to a considerable extent exempted from manual labour — the more senior they are, the fewer labour days they are expec-

ted to put in. And it devolves on them to translate into action the policies laid down at congresses of the Party and meetings of the Politburo and Central Committee. Many members of this army of bureaucrats are conscientious and well-intentioned people, frugal in their life-style and anxious to do the right thing and fulfil their duties to the leaders and the people. But in a country where, by historical tradition, officials were expected to pay their own salaries out of exactions from the common people, the temptation to abuse one's position is still strong and violations of "socialist morality" are frequently reported.

Since the fall of the "Gang", the press has been giving more and more details about the excesses committed by individual cadres and their relatives. These range all the way from intolerance of criticism from below, to sexual coercion, abuse of funds, large-scale embezzlement, black-marketeering, wrongful detention and even judicial murder. In part of the continuing campaign to control and eradicate such abuses, the Party press has extolled the virtues of a long-gone emperor, who is commemorated for having actually offered rewards to officials brave enough to criticise his actions — the biggest reward being for criticism made to the Emperor's face, the next for submitting criticism in writing, and the third for voicing objections to the emperor's style of government in some public forum from which the criticism would eventually come to the august personage's ear. By doing so, he sought not only to learn about his own shortcomings, but also to encourage officials to drop their habitual intolerance of criticism from below. If the emperor could accept criticism, why not the mandarinate?

Admirable though the idea behind this royal prescript may have been, it made little impact in the long run on the perfectly human dislike of criticism from one's subordinates. Visitors to China, who have responded openly to the often-voiced invitation to offer "criticisms or sugges-

tions," usually find that this casts a pall over their relations with the Chinese hosts. The invitation to criticise is mainly a form of politeness, to which the visitor is actually expected to reply with the equivalent politeness of finding nothing at all to carp at.

Unfortunately, Mao himself did not set a good example, despite his approval in theory of criticism from below. Mao once said: "Whoever criticises us (i.e. the Communist Party) in good faith is not blameworthy. However sharp his criticism or severe his censure, he is not to be blamed or punished or given tight shoes to wear" (a Chinese metaphor for victimisation). But Mao himself was demonstrably intolerant of criticism, and many who let themselves be cajoled into speaking out against the Party in the 1950's and 1960's paid for their naïveté with demotion, ostracism, imprisonment or death. The dividing line between "comradely criticism" and "counter-revolutionary propaganda" is exceedingly fine.

Present-day officials have been blamed by the Party leadership for using their position to promote their private interests. "They concentrate on stirring things up," wrote a commentator in a major provincial newspaper, "and start rumours, confound black and white, distort facts, make sneak attacks on one another and always want to use schemes and intrigues to disrupt the situation and overthrow some comrades who adhere to the Party spirit." In addition, these officials are blamed for "eating three square meals a day and not working, establishing luxurious and sluggish habits, and paying no attention to the well-being of the masses." The life-style practised by such officials might not seem very luxurious to people in rich, advanced countries. But in the context of the national austerity and strict rationing of food, clothing and consumer goods in present-day China, it sticks out like a sore thumb. The following description of overbearing behaviour on the part of office-bearers might seem in the West to be little more than a description of the way a successful

businessman would have things organised: "They go in for extravagant eating and drinking, give dinners or send gifts in order to curry favour, and spend without restraint. When some get to the top, all their friends and relations get there with them."

One of the problems impeding the abolition of such élitist practices in China is the lack of a set of coherent rules and regulations laying down the exact privileges of rank and the life-style to which officials should accustom themselves. When the reform of China's legal system was under discussion in 1978, a senior judge actually had to remind magistrates that they must not accept gifts from either party to a dispute!

The English-language weekly *Beijing Review* (formerly *Peking Review*), which sets out to propagandise the best aspects of modern Chinese society for the benefit of foreigners, published in 1979 an account of a house-building spree which took place on a commune in the northwest province of Shaanxi. Local people had nicknamed the rows of neat new villas "authority street" because of the number of heads of department, committee chairmen, bureau directors and factory managers who were taking up residence there. The case was exposed when a worker in a local factory wrote to the national press complaining about the waste of funds and resources: Apparently nearly all the trucks in that county had been commandeered for the building work, and tractors were also requisitioned while they should have been used for ploughing. Local peasants had been co-opted into working on the new houses, affecting farm production.

A few years ago, such revelations would not have found their way into even the Chinese-language press, for fear that foreigners would seize on them to denigrate the entire socialist system. Nowadays, however, it is considered virtuous to disclose the existence of abuses, in order to bring home to the people how determined the leadership is to put a stop

to them. This made it all the more serious when someone as august as a Party Vice-Chairman and former security aide to Mao, Gen. Wang Dongxing, was accused in wall-posters in 1979 of having squandered public funds on a big new house for himself and his family, right under the noses of the other leaders, in the Zhongnanhai office and residential complex in the very heart of Beijing. This extravagance was probably one of the pretexts used by Deng Xiaoping, Wang's long-term rival, to cut off Wang's powers and render him a political non-entity.

Influence peddling is common right down to the man-in-the-street level, where it is called "going through the back door." Shop assistants are among the main culprits, for in a scarcity-ridden economy like China's they are in a position to do others favours in distribution of goods. A cartoon in the Chinese press shows an old man going to his local fish-shop, accompanied by his cat. The shop-assistant tells him: "We're all sold out." As he goes dejectedly home, his cat rushes round the sales counter and grabs a fish which was hidden there — chased by the indignant

Virtually no individual owns an automobile, but many bureaucrats take advantage of their positions to take wives shopping or families on Sunday outings in the "company" car.
This bundled-up toddler will probably never get the chance of riding in a Shanghai model car (opposite).

shop-assistant, shouting: "That's mine!" Hardly rapier-like wit, but it makes its point.

Every totalitarian socialist system the world has known has been plagued by black marketeering and diversion of scarce goods — the Soviet Union being a prime example. In China, the authorities have sought to eradicate it by police work, propaganda and reliance on informers. Now, the leaders are evidently resigned to letting the world at large see these warts on China's socialist face, if it is thought that satire and public ridicule can help root out such behaviour.

Another form of privileged élite is composed of the wives and families of men in influential positions. Some of the most acute power struggles in revolutionary China have centred on the jealousies among such senior public figures as the widow of the disgraced former head of state, Liu Shaoqi, and Mao's wife, Jiang Qing. Madam Liu was held up to scorn and mockery in 1966-67 for having worn attractive *cheongsams* while on foreign visits. Merciless cartoons showed her as a decadent, Westernised countesan. Ironically enough, similar charges were flung at Madam Mao when she fell from power, and Madam Liu has now been released from the maximum-security prison where she spent over 12 years. The *People's Daily* has this to say about wives of influential men: "If the husband is a leading cadre, she will also enjoy treatment she is not entitled to, and may even consider herself to be a cut above others and ride roughshod over people."

Yet another élite group is formed by the relatives of Chinese living abroad who send money to them, and by returned Overseas Chinese — for instance, those whom persecution drove back to China by the shipload from Indonesia in the 1950's and 1960's. Beijing's policy towards these people was to give them preferential treatment in housing, food supplies and access to consumer goods, partly because they were already used to a higher standard of living than that enjoyed by ordinary people

In a so-called egalitarian society, some jobs are better than others. Richshaw- and trishaw-pulling are two of the least attractive work assignments (opposite, in Guangzhou); *whereas joining the Public Security Bureau as a traffic policeman* (above) *may be even better than working in a factory.*
Pages 86, 87: Visible signs of increasing wealth in the cities: owning a pet; getting married with a handsome dowry or a bountiful wedding feast; a regular appointment at a hair salon.

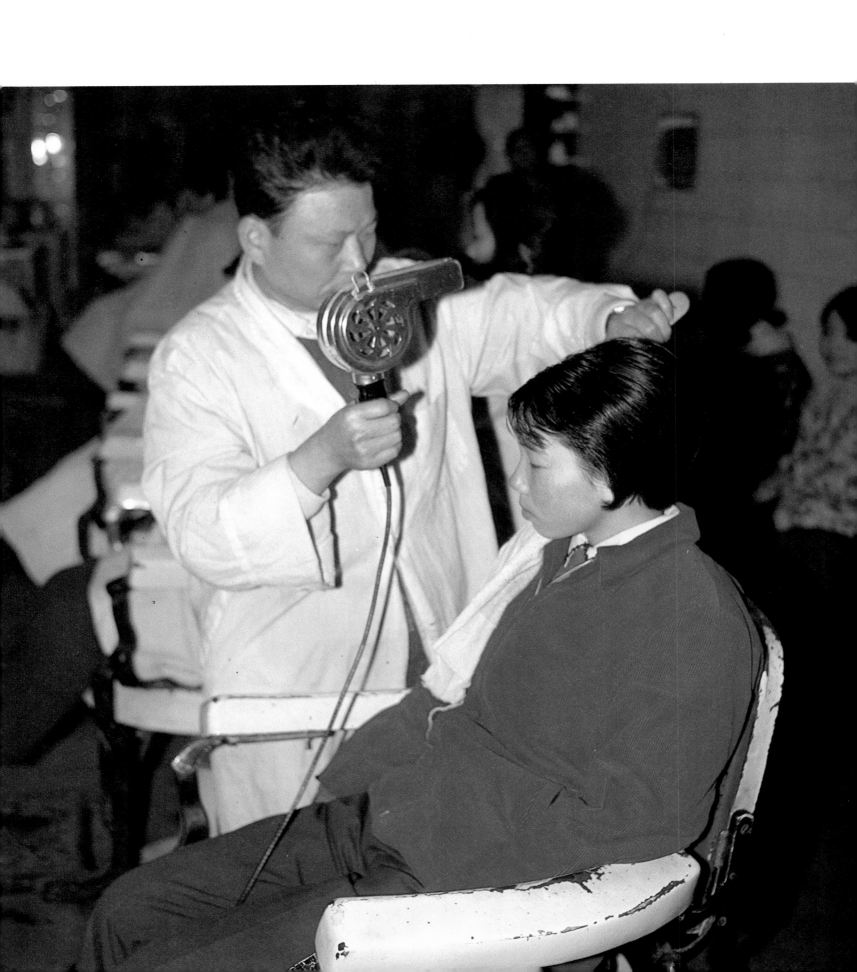

in China, and partly to encourage them to spend their hard currency and get more sent in from other relatives still abroad. They had special villages, special shops, and extra ration coupons. Not surprisingly, this caused much resentment in parts of China where the Overseas Chinese or their relatives were settled — most in the south and southeast. In the egalitarian fury of the Cultural Revolution, they were stripped of their material privileges and placed under suspicion of being spies and subversives. One of the most damaging things that could be said about a person in those days was that he or she had "overseas connections."

After Mao's death, the new leadership reversed this state of affairs, restored the material privileges of the Overseas Chinese, and even tried to attract more to come back to work and invest in the motherland. Particularly welcome were people with capital, business training or technical expertise. High salaries were offered to Overseas Chinese specialists just to come back and lecture for a year or two. Special export processing zones were set up primarily to attract investment from the Overseas Chinese and the business communities of Hong Kong and Macau. It seems inevitable that this new round of privileges for the Overseas Chinese will resurrect the old resentments against the but the leadership apparently considers this is less important than exploiting the Overseas Chinese in the interests of China's scientific and economic modernisation.

People with relatives in Hong Kong are also in a fortunate position, since they may recently, duties have been waived on consumer durables brought in as gifts for big difference to the family budget of a peasant in the mainland. And more recently, duties have been waived on consumer durables brought in as gifts for friends and relatives — the favourite items being colour TV sets and cassette recorders. Expensive watches and audio systems are also keenly sought after — so that in parts of southern China one may

witness the ludicrous sight of a peasant family with a colour TV and a Rolex watch, but with barely enough rice to go round!

The entire trend of Chinese social policy under the post-Mao leadership is towards the re-establishment of élite groups as the only way of providing incentives to people to work hard and creatively out of enlightened self-interest. This policy is a gamble, because it may well lead to increasing stratification of society, and a bigger gap between town and countryside, which will be damaging to social and political stability. The greatest attempt at egalitarianism ever made in the history of mankind is being wound up with few regrets, except over the time wasted in trying to make it work.

More than 100 institutions of higher education receive central government funding as "key schools". With the recent reinstatement of annual examinations, children of non-intellectuals, such as this street sweeper (above, in Guangzhou), *have little hope of entering one of the top elementary schools, and graduating into a white collar job. The new system favours children such as those opposite.*

Plastic toys such as this blow-up doll (above) in Shanghai and foreign-made goods, such as these Hitachi consumer and industrial products displayed in a Beijing store window (opposite), are stuff of today's dreams.

Popular entertainment ranges from simple toys such as this whistle (right) *to first-run domestic movies* (opposite).

THE PANCHEN LAMA

The Chinese Government's treatment of and attitude towards its ethnic minorities is symbolised especially by the case of the Panchen Lama of Tibet, more accurately known as Panchen Erdeni Chuji-Deltseng.

Born in 1937 in China's western province of Qinghai (Ch'ing Hai) adjoining Tibet, the Panchen was "recognised" in 1943 as the reincarnation of a 15th century Panchen, and installed in a monastery as the spiritual brother of the Dalai Lama in Lhasa. While still a teenage boy, he was used by the Chinese authorities as the symbol of Tibet's historic acceptance of Chinese suzerainty — a tradition which had been disturbed by the British incursions into Tibet in the 19th and early 20th Centuries.

While acquiring his religious education, the Panchen spent much time touring China and appearing at functions, both political and religious. He and the Dalai Lama travelled in 1956 to India to attend the 2500th anniversary of the Buddha.

The Dalai Lama fled to India in 1959, following the outbreak of the anti-Chinese rebellion in Tibet, and the Panchen Lama was installed in Lhasa as acting chairman of the Tibetan regional government under Chinese supervision. To celebrate his installation, foreign correspondents were invited to Lhasa to witness the religious rites. The Panchen was then brought to Beijing, where he attended numerous ceremonies for Buddhists from Tibet and other parts of China.

Interviewed by American writer Anna Louise Strong, the Panchen said: "The Buddhist classics are extensive; their study takes many years. I have in them two tutors. Since liberation I also study politics, especially the works of Mao Tse-tung and other Government leaders. These works also are extensive and take time."

After three years in Beijing, the Panchen returned to Tibet, where Chinese rule had been irrevocably established with the suppression of the rebellion. He was given a symbolic position in the regional government, but was under the direct control of Gen. Zhang Guohua, the Chinese commander for the region.

In 1964, irked by the slow pace of reform and the recalcitrance of the Tibetans, Gen. Zhang accused the Panchen of being a "reactionary" and supporter of the exiled Dalai Lama. He was dismissed from his titular offices, though he retained membership of the key government committees. Apart from this, no formal punishment was decreed for him at the time, despite a 17-day trial in which he was accused of attempting to restore serfdom, murdering a worker, planning to launch a guerilla war, illicitly co-habiting with women, opposing China, supporting the Dalai Lama and plundering religious buildings of precious objects.

Discredited and shorn of his influence, the Panchen came under heavy attack in the Cultural Revolution and was deported to Beijing where he is believed to have been imprisoned. But after the death of Mao, when the new Chinese leadership was trying to repair the damage done to relations with ethnic minorities, he reappeared in a leading position at the National People's Congress session in 1979, and was expected to return to Tibet at least from time to time.

The second generation of children born under communist rule is already in school and will soon be taking on adult responsibilities. The quality of life for this generation will be affected by today's policies toward population control, public health and the importation of foreign products, technology and culture.

This page, top: *On a Beijing street.*

This page, bottom: *A Uygur couple strolls in a Xi'an park.*

Opposite: *A movie billboard in Nanjing.*

Pages 96, 97: *In the Beijing Workers Stadium, a flashcard display of a "barefoot doctor" illustrating acupuncture points of the ear.*

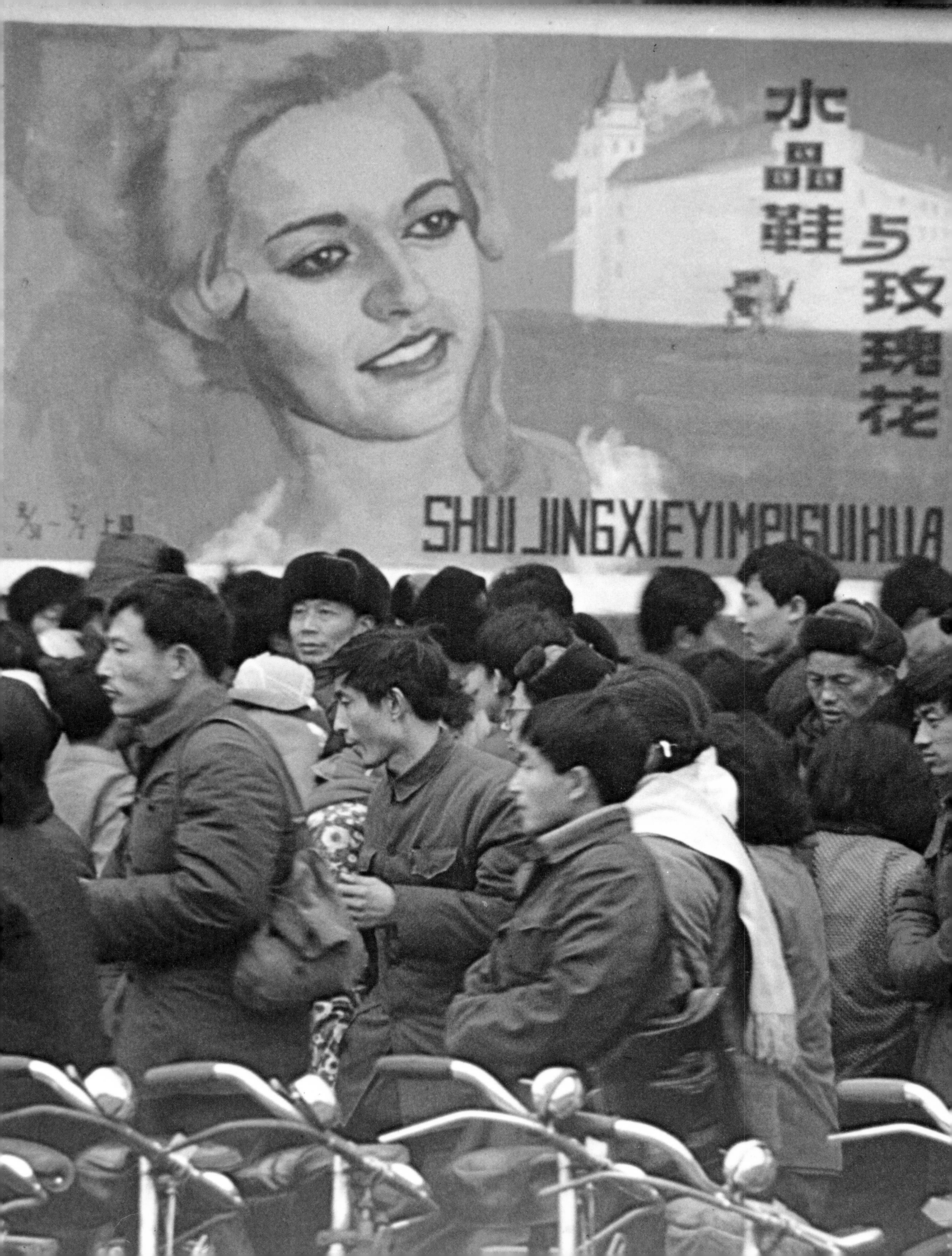
水晶鞋与玫瑰花
SHUIJINGXIEYIMEIGUIHUA

The Four Modernisations

Richard Breeze

At a remote desert base in central China, senior officers and scientists watched, taut with tension, as the towering, three-stage rocket belched its first flames. Their tension was transformed into elation as the missile lifted off alongside its gantry and rose with a deafening, triumphant roar to arc away to the south with its wake of flame. It was May 12, 1979 and China had joined the élite thermonuclear club with an Intercontinental Ballistic Missile (ICBM) which could carry a holocaust to Moscow, Europe or the continental United States.

Napoleon once remarked: "When China wakes, the world will tremble." This ICBM test, which was successfully concluded when the missile flew 5,000 miles to the Pacific, was perhaps one of the most spectacular public achievements of this long waking process — the modernisation which China seeks to achieve by at least the end of the century.

In its flight the rocket crossed a land which provides some of the most startling contrasts in the modern world. China is the world's youngest nation with 60 per cent of its population under 30 while many of its leaders are over 80. The Chinese represent a quarter of the world's population and many of them are impoverished farmers continually fighting to make a living from a hostile land mass which is mainly desert and mountain. China is a country with too many people and not enough food, where in some towns beggars burst into restaurants and snatch the scraps from tourists' tables. Yet it is a nuclear power, one of the Big Five in the United Nations Security Council and a country which has put satellites aloft. It is the first country to have produced a detailed medical map showing the incidence of cancer among the population. Its doctors have developed a highly efficient birth control pill and carried out a heart transplant. In fields such as lasers and high-energy physics, China is among the leaders. But across the country people still work like draught animals.

China has failed to realise its overall potential draught as it has been torn over the last 30 years between the right and left factions of its ruling Communist Party. Twice the country has been thrown to the left as Maoist doctrines gained the ascendancy — in the Great Leap Forward of the late 1950s and then the Cultural Revolution a decade later. And twice the country was brought to its knees.

After the death of Chairman Mao Tse-tung in 1976, the pragmatic or right-wing faction headed by Deng Xiaoping Zhao Ziyang, came to the fore. It was Deng and his associates who had pushed the modernisation of China which had been first outlined in January, 1975. Speaking before the Fourth National People's Congress, then Premier Chou En-lai defined China's task for the 1980s and beyond as "to accomplish comprehensive modernisation of agriculture, industry, national defence and science and technology so that our national economy will be marching in the front ranks of the world."

The Four Modernisations, as the plan has come to be known, requires massive investment in 120 large scale projects. This investment was aimed at increasing industrial production by more than 10 per cent each year from 1978 while the rate of annual growth of agriculture was set at more than four per cent.

By 1978 it was already clear that China's planners had been too euphoric and had ignored harsh economic realities. In 1979 plans were scaled down, often dramatically, and at least three if not five years will be needed before the country's economy is sufficently readjusted and restructured so that it can be placed on a correct modernisation path.

The Dengian faction of course blames the poor overall state of the economy on damage caused by the Cultural Revolution and the ensuing period of radical rule under the influence of the Mao's widow, Jiang Qing, and the much maligned Gang of Four. But a word of caution: It has long been the tradition for Chinese dynasties to write the history of the preceding dynasty. And to prove the successors' legitimacy, it was customary for these histories to be as black as possible. Thus could it be demonstrated that the preceding emperor had deservedly forfeited the mandate of heaven and that the people had been justified in rising up to overthrow him. This tradition has been continued by the communists in Beijing and the country remains one where facts are carefully concealed in Orwellian Newspeak. Given the vital role of defence this essay on modernisation could conveniently commence with an examination of the military establishment, whose three services are known jointly as the People's Liberation Army (PLA). For Mao, the PLA was the instrument which enabled the Communist Party to defeat the Nationalists under Chiang Kai-shek and take over China. "Our principle is that the Party commands the gun, and the gun will never the allowed to command be Party," he stated, and this statement still applies today as China's forces compete with other sectors for the limited funds available for modernisation.

The PLA was born out of the communists' heroic Long March in 1934/35 and has remained a people's army designed to fight a people's war. Thus the PLA is an anachronism in this push button epoch of strategic and tactical, nuclear missiles, and chemical and germ warfare. Modernising the PLA will be an immense and staggeringly expensive task.

The Soviet Union, sharing a huge land border with China, is perceived as the enemy. The main tactic is not to oppose an attacker's advance but to draw him deep into China, force him to extend his communications and then smother him. Such tactics require enormous manpower and China's ground forces are the world's largest, totalling around 3.7 million men with about seven million more organised into an armed militia. But the troops lack firepower being armed with a large amount of obsolete weaponry. Though ground forces have a gamut of artillery from 152 mm howitzers, to anti-aircraft guns, to mortars and rockets, the Chinese went into the 1980s without, for example, the latest type of anti-tank weapons.

This deficiency and also the alarming obsolescence of Chinese armour leaves the country vulnerable to a tank-led invasion. China produces three types of tanks and its forces now have around 10,000 — but many are based on models which saw sterling service in World War II. Even the latest

Chinese main battle tank — the T59 —
would be no match for the T72 tank which
the Soviets already have in service on the
Chinese border. Its non-stabilised 100 mm
gun is weak by today's standards, and
there are no infra-red sighting devices for
night fighting.

Another major fault in the PLA is its
limited mobility. Chinese troops were some
of the last in the world to make regular use
of horses, mules and camels. They went
into war with Vietnam in 1979 by rail, and
when the railway stops they walk. Little
effort has been made to develop and build
armoured personnel carriers, essential
equipment in modern Western armies.

To offset equipment weaknesses, the
PLA is trained to remain in close contact
with the enemy. Extremely fit, highly
motivated and very skillful in traditional
infantry arts such as ambushes and night
fighting, the average Chinese soldier is a
splendid infantryman and one to whom the
bayonet is far from redundant. The
emphasis on defence and guerilla tactics
have produced major structural
weaknesses: The air force, which has no
part in guerilla warfare, has been woefully
neglected and the navy reduced to a
coastal defence role.

When China attacked Vietnam, its
forces went in with virtually no air support. This was not surprising. Though
China's air force is numerically the world's
third biggest, its combat planes are mostly
based on models that were flying in the
1950s. In keeping with the strategic stance,
aircraft are basically interceptors, there
being no modern strike aircraft as such.
Also many of China's warplanes lack all-
weather capability, attack radar systems
and sophisticated air-to-air missile
systems. Attacks in the face of modern
ground-air defence systems would be
simply suicidal. The best Chinese warplane
is the needle-nosed F7, derived from the
MIG 21. But the backbone of the airforce
are the F6s and F4s, modelled on the
venerable MIG 19 and 17. China has
purchased Spey aircraft engines from Britain's Rolls Royce, but development of

new aircraft has been slow.

With a strength of 300,000 men and
1,000 vessels, China's navy is second only
to that of the Soviet Union. But there the
comparison stops. The bulk of China's
fleet is for coastal defence — fast patrol
and strike boats, armed in many cases with
the near-pedestrian torpedo. By 1980 there
were 11 destroyers and nearly 20 frigates,
but in 1980 China still had no aircraft
carrier or a major helicopter carrier. Ship-
to-ship missiles were being developed, but
remained relatively primitive and easy
prey for modern electronic counter
measures such as those used by the Soviet
navy.

The shipbuilding industry, however, has
enormous potential and in the 1980s the
navy may get more attention. One
remarkable aspect of the ICBM test was the
navy's capability to adopt a blue-water
role. If official accounts are to be believed
an 18-ship flotilla travelled 8,000 miles
without any accidents or breakdowns to
police the target area. This flotilla included
a missile-launching destroyer and a space
event support ship bristling with domes
and saucers to monitor the rocket's
progress. This sortie to the Pacific may
prove China's debut as a blue-water naval
power.

The flotilla's success also raised the

"The Four Modernisations" programme was
initiated in 1977 to modernise four major
sectors of the Chinese economy: agriculture,
industry, science and technology, and defense.
It is primarily a "catch up" programme, aimed
at bringing China into the modern world, and at
best, raising it to the level of the major powers
— by the year 2000. Throughout China, people
are urged to use their resources to the fullest to
meet this goal. In Beijing, billboards (preceding
pages) exhort residents to support the Central
Committee of the Communist Party and
struggle to attain the Four Modernisations;
statuary (opposite) reminds them of the nation's
power through unity.

The military is woefully equipped to conduct
modern warfare. The 1979 action in Vietnam
demonstrated this quite clearly to both the
government in Beijing and the Western powers.
Tens of thousands of young men and women
who join the People's Liberation Army do so
not necessarily because of their interest in
defending the nation, but to improve their
economic and political place in society and to
take advantage of the perquisites of military life:
better quality food, higher meat rations and the
opportunity to travel.

Following pages: A high school student
practicing marksmanship; seemingly arrogant
P.L.A. soldiers ride through city streets in army
motorcycles with sidecars.

question of China's intervention capability. This, in the Asian context, is already enough to worry China's neighbours. Strategists say that China has the amphibious capacity to lift about 30,000 men (nearly three divisions) for a short-range strike and could, by making use of civil aircraft flown by the State-controlled airline, CAAC, airlift one division with light equipment.

There has been gradual and determined development of both the nuclear strike force and space capability. Since late 1964, China has tested about 25 nuclear devices. It now has a prototype ICBM, up to 40 intermediate range nuclear missiles and about the same number of medium range missiles. There is one nuclear submarine, possibly equipped with missiles. Nuclear test data show that China is developing a tactical nuclear weapon which would be extremely useful for defence of its immense border with the Soviet Union.

In 1964, China pledged it would "never be the first to use unclean weapons." But if the Soviets attacked, the riposte could be nuclear, either through an ICBM strike at Moscow or missile attacks on the Siberian railway and installations in the Soviet Far East. Already Moscow's anti-ballistic missile defences have been readjusted to take into account a strike from China.

The space efforts have been extremely vigorous. On April 24, 1974, Beijing sent aloft its first satellite which arched around the world broadcasting "The East is Red." Between then and 1980 it put up eight more satellites; at least three had firm military applications. By 1979 spacemen were in training in Shanghai. The ICBM's tested weighed about 200 tons and were similar in power to American rockets that launched the Gemini manned satellites. American specialists who have visited Chinese aerospace installations were deeply impressed and noted that the digital computers and solid state electronic equipment used was all Chinese made.

Other major interest areas for China are lasers and high-energy physics, two disciplines which provide the technology for the energy weapons of the future. An anti-satellite laser weapon for use against the several hundred Soviet satellites which overfly China each day seems a priority.

China started to look for new weapons abroad in the late 1970s. Primary interest has remained in the purchase of defensive equipment such as the Hot anti-tank missile and the Crotale air-defence system, both of which are being bought from France. Considerable interest was shown in the British-built Harrier — an aircraft capable of vertical and short take-off and landing. This sophisticated jet, though difficult to maintain, can operate from primitive forward airfields and would be suitable for defence of China's borders. China has expressed keen interest in anti-submarine equipment and all forms of transport, from helicopters to heavy duty civilian trucks, which would improve the PLA's mobility. Attention is also paid to radar systems, computers with military applications and a large spread of telecommunications equipment.

Some high school students receive military training (opposite). *A network of people's militia groups occasionally augments the police force and the P.L.A. in times of domestic troubles.*
   Above: *Soldiers travelling on business dress against the cold winter weather.*

China's defence budget is put at between US$35.5 billion and US$44.4 billion. This should be compared to American military spending which, in 1978, totalled around US$115 billion. Given the overall demands of modernisation, China cannot afford to purchase too much modern Western equipment at a time when a major warship costs US$1.5 billion, an aircraft US$ 25 million and a main battle tank around US$1 million.

There are of course pressures from the military for new equipment, especially following the costly, month-long "lesson"

Modernisation for China's rural sector (above) *may be the most difficult but the most vital task to carry out. More than 80 per cent of China's population lives in the countryside. Food production is not sufficient to feed the population, and basic foodstuffs such as grain, meat, oil and dairy products and rationed. The little machinery there is in the fields is old-fashioned* (opposite).

administered to Vietnam in 1979. China says that the Vietnamese lost 50,000 men killed and wounded and put its own dead and wounded at 20,000. But the 200,000-strong expeditionary force must have lost a considerable amount of equipment and this has had to be replaced. The invasion also revealed the weakness of China's forces, particulary their lack of fire power, faulty coordination and unreliable communications. The PLA's logistic services also came in for heavy criticism. But above all, the month-long campaign showed that the country's aging military commanders had failed to keep abreast of modern strategic and tactical thinking. Despite the lessons that the Chinese inflicted on themselves in Vietnam there has been no noticeable rush to acquire modern weapons, but there was a drive to eliminate antiquated military thinking by giving senior officers courses in modern warfare. The gerontocracy noticeable throughout the Chinese leadership is particularly marked in the military establishment where four marshals who sit on the powerful Military Committee are all over 80.

Purchases of advanced weapons systems from abroad will require considerable training for the PLA whose overall educational level is low. In early 1980, Chinese officials were stressing the importance of a modern revolutionary army and urging high school graduates to enroll in the country's 54 military institutes and schools. About 15,000 were attending these schools in 1980.

Despite this, officials seemed to be losing interest in military modernisation. When Chou En-lai first outlined the four modernisations in 1975, the military were listed third. But in late 1978, a visitor to the southern city of Guangzhou glimpsed a large and graphically illustrated wall poster. It showed four figures, each depicting one of the modernisations. The military programme had been ranked fourth and the soldier that symbolised it was substantially smaller than the other figures. Modernisation of the armed forces thus seems to be the last of the priorities in

China where the Communist Party still firmly controls the gun.

Modernisation's first battle is being fought on the land by the country's 700 million peasants. These long-suffering labourers, toiling in 50,000 communes, have for 30 years been the have-nots of the Chinese revolution even though they formed the sea within which Mao and his guerillas moved like fish.

For more than 2,000 years the survival of Chinese culture has hung on the precarious balance between food production and population growth. As Beijing officials like to remark, the Chinese communists are managing to feed about a quarter of the world's population with less than seven per cent of the planet's farmland. This is no mean feat and one that should be borne in mind by the knee jerk detractors of the Chinese revolution. What many people fail to realise is that only about 30 per cent of China is under cultivation as much of this vast land consists of mountain ranges and deserts. Already by the late 14th century, China was obtaining near maximum yields from its fields through the application of advanced, pre-industrial technology. Production increases could be achieved only by the opening up of new land, and by the 17th century the country had already begun to run out of readily cultivable terrain.

Agriculture faces other problems too. All farmers are dependent on the vagaries of the weather. But in China, nature is more fickle than elsewhere; rainfall is extremely unreliable and it is not unusual for farmers in one area to watch in despair as flood follows drought.

An American expert, Dwight H. Perkins, notes that China has managed to keep grain output approximately equal to population growth over the past six centuries by maintaining an average rate of increase considerably below two per cent. Modernisation originally aimed at an annual increase in grain production of four per cent. But by 1980 this was seen as one of the euphoric targets, and officials started talking of an output of 300 million tons

of grain by 1985.

Already about 70 per cent of land is double-cropped and, in the south, rice paddies are often triple-cropped. Much hope is placed in chemical fertiliser and China has spent US$650 million on purchasing from abroad 13 of the world's largest ammonia and urea fertiliser plants.

Storage and control of water is a necessary complement of fertiliser if yields are to be increased. China has been a pioneer of water control for centuries and today, in the south, irrigation has reached its optimum point. Little more can be done. But irrigation and water control on the north China plain, home of one in four Chinese and the country's wheat bowl, has been neglected or badly planned. Yields are low and unstable as rain brings floods and washes away precious top soil.

One of modernisation's most dramatic aims is to tame the Yangtze — the great river that has earned the name of "China's sorrow." Over the past 2,000 years it has flooded nearly two thousand times and one savage overflow in 1931 killed more than a million people. Among the modernisation projects is a massive hydro-electcic complex which will harness the river's power potential. It is also planned to pump some Yangtze water 700 miles north to irrigate the drought-plagued wheat belt and, by raising output, cut China's dependency on cereal imports.

Development of agriculture, particularly in the southern rice fields, will soon run up against the brick wall of diminishing yields although marginal improvement can perhaps be obtained by the development of new seed strains.

The greatest hope of China's farmers lies in specialisation, a part of the consolidation policies introduced in 1979 which is being energetically encouraged by the new leaders who have rid themselves of the Maoist food grain mania. This emphasis on food grain and the Maoist insistence on each commune being self-sufficent in grain produced some appalling catastrophes. The felling of forests wrecked rainfall patterns, and hastened erosion; lakes and fish ponds were filled in and fresh fish production declined dramatically; areas wrongly selected for irrigation went alkaline. The Communist Party newspaper the *People's Daily* has remarked bitterly: "There are regions where the pasture land was like an immense green sea; today hardly any grass grows, sand dunes cover the area and rats and insects devour what is left." As the drive to produce food grain developed, herdsmen — such as the Mongol descendants of Genghis Khan — were dragooned into abandoning traditional stock-raising activities. Mao, in his blinkered pursuit of higher grain output nearly ruined one of China's most precious assets — its 3,000 million hectares of grassland. These noxious policies were remedied as part of efforts to woo the country's non-Han minorities. Livestock raising is being firmly encouraged and production of meat, hides, wool and milk

"In agriculture, learn from Dazhai." This slogan (opposite) *once appeared everywhere, in the countryside and in the cities. Dazhai, a supposedly self-reliant commune in Shanxi province, where ordinary peasants were said to have built huge dams and terraced steep mountain hillsides, with their bare hands, was the Cultural Revolution model for agricultural development.*

In 1980, this model commune was exposed as a gigantic fraud and the resulting political ramifications reached right to the national leadership. Agriculture remains very primitive, even near the large cities like Beijing, where peasants are frequently seen harvesting grain by hand.

Transportation and communiction links throughout the country are primitive. This will undoubtedly affect the speed of modernisation, especially in agriculture and industry.

This major Shanghai dock (top, right) is too small and out-moded for the efficient and rapid transfer of increasing numbers of goods between China and its foreign trading partners. Several container terminals are planned for the near future, and a container manufacturing plant, built with foreign technology and expertise, opened outside Guangzhou in 1981. In the meantime, hundreds of barges continue to ply these same waters day in and day out bringing scarce raw materials to this industrial heartland of China.

The rail network is undeveloped. Few lines are double tracked; there is a shortage of boxcars and tankers; and fuel is limited. Most trains are run by coal-fired steam engines, (bottom, right) though diesel engines operate on some major long-distance routes. French-made engines powered by electricity are in trial operation. Even if workers such as this tailor in Hefei (opposite) increase their production, the problem of distributing their goods even a few hundred miles from their workshops wil be a difficult one.

Low productivity and factory mismanagement plagues almost all of China's industry. Part of this is institutional; workers usually spend two or three non-productive half-days a week in political study sessions. Workers commonly take sick on the slightest pretext. Workers themselves complain of frequent mechanical breakdowns and the lack of spare parts and skilled technicians that hold up repairs for days and weeks (here, a silk textile factory in Hangzhou).

are climbing fast. A necessary accompaniment to the new policies will be development of refrigeration facilities and railcars to enable meat and milk to be shipped to the cities where vegetables and cereals still form the basis of the people's protein-poor diet. Wool is also a vital input for light industry which, as will be seen later, is based heavily on textiles. The growing of other industrial inputs such as silk cocoons, cotton, sugar beet, peanuts, oil seed plants, fruit and tobacco are being vigorously encouraged. By 1980, peasants were being allowed to raise silkworms as part of their private, or sideline, production and cocoon production was expanding by around 14 per cent a year. This has helped to make China's raw silk and silk textile exports the major hard currency earner after oil.

Efforts to expand cotton output for the country's voracious textile mills have been less successful. It is proving difficult to lift production off a plateau of around 2,000 million tons a year. The reason is interesting: Peasants remain extremely wary

about growing cotton when they could produce food. They point out that during the frequent political upheavals of the last 30 years food production and distribution often broke down. The peasants remark that one cannot eat cotton.

In terms of manpower, China's farms are extraordinarily inefficient: In the United States, one farmer feeds 10 people, but in China it takes five peasants to feed one urban dweller. At one stage mechanisation was seen as the answer to China's agricultural problems and in 1976 it was forecast that 70 per cent of agricultural tasks would be mechanised by 1980. But this prediction was made before the difficulties of modernisation were correctly assessed. American experts say that there is no really appropriate technology for China's labour-based agriculture. For example tractors — although a floating type does exist — are of little use in a flooded paddy.

Also officials began asking what they would do with all the surplus labour once

agriculture had been modernised. An unchecked rural drift would drown already over-crowded cities, compounding the problems of unemployment, housing and social services. By 1980, enthusiam for mechanisation had been quenched. It would have proved a mammoth task anyway. Tractor factories have always been the butt of Chinese jokes. One of them in Guangzhou produced 7,000 machines in 12 years. But they were of such poor quality that not a single one worked properly. Communes which have tractors often lack complimentary equipment and have to hitch up their old ploughs. For this reason peasants came to call the tractors "panting behind the plough" because they have to trot behind it, holding the plough's handles. Zhao Ziyang, when he was party chief in Szechuan province, remarked that it was pointless to produce tractors when peasants seemed to use them — not in the fields — but for transport: "It would be better to give than lorries," he wisely observed.

For 30 years the two rival schools in the Chinese party have argued about the best way of increasing agricultural production. The Maoists believed that ideological bullying, tight controls by party officials and commune bosses — who are often woefully ignorant of farming — was the best approach. But today's pragmatic officials have opted for another and simpler way of spurring the peasants onward: They pay them more. In 1979, Hua recognised that agricultural production was languishing and was insufficent either to feed the people properly or provide the necessary inputs for light industry. He announced that prices paid to farmers for state quota production of 18 commodities including grain, oils, cotton, meat, eggs and sugar would be raised by between 15 and 26 per cent. This rise for the farmers, which has been so long postponed, boosted rural incomes by around US$5,000 million. Further income is also flowing to the country areas following the lifting of price controls on 10,000 items, many of them food products or articles produced by peasants

To rebuild worker confidence in the system, many factories have recently been permitted to give productive workers incentive pay and additional bonuses. In addition, supply and distribution offices are being reorganised so that supply more closely follows demand, and marketing and sales offices are being encouraged to advertise products on radio and television, billboards and newspapers.
Above: *a worker in Hefei.*
Opposite: *Diesel engine on passenger route.*

and small rural workshops.

Also the production team — often made up of around 20 families and the smallest unit in the commune organisation — has been given a dominant voice over the running of the fields. No longer can arrogant officials tell them when and what to plant. The peasants are encouraged to make maximum use of their private plots — often about five per cent of the commune's overall land area — to grow cash crops and produce that they can sell profitably in the markets.

Agriculture is, at it has been for two millenia, China's crucial sector. The emphasis that the leadership has put on progress in the fields, pastures and paddies means that more resources will have to be allocated to agriculture. Further triple-cropping will mean more pumps and more electric power for the pumps; agricultural machinery and repair facilities will have to be made available and there will be a growing need for fertilisers. This means that there will be less resources available for development of light and heavy industry, energy, transport, communications and social overhead spending that modernisation and the improving of the nation's quality of life requires.

This attempt to slice the revenue cake more evenly is only justice, given the sacrifices that Chinese peasants have made for the revolution. Mao always held that in China's case it was the peasants who would provide the revolutionary impetus with the countryside encircling and then taking over the towns. This theory had made Mao a communist heretic early in his career as he scorned the Soviet dictum that a revolution could not be staged successfully unless it was spearheaded by an urban proletariat. But, in 1927, an uprising by communists in Shanghai had horrendous consequences as Chiang Kai-shek used it as an opportunity to turn against them and stage a bloodbath with brutality that was to be rivalled only by the Kampuchean leader Pol Pot half a century later. Chiang had communists thrown into the boilers of locomotives as he virtually

destroyed the workers' movement in China's largest city.

When the Nationalists were defeated and China — as Mao put it — had "stood up," the urban workers and heavy industry took over again. Steel exercises deep fascination on young revolutionary nations; it seems to symbolise strength and self fulfillment. Perhaps also socialist artists find steel workers easy to paint with their muscular torsos glistening with sweat outlined against the Dante-esque glare of th furnaces. China also fell victim to this fascination and investment policies ensured that heavy industry grew nearly five times faster between 1949 and 1978 than light industry. When modernisation was first outlined in some detail in 1976, steel again obtained star billing and it was forecast that output would be doubled to 60 million tons by 1985. This has proved one of the wildly over-ambitious targets. Many reasons vitiate against industrial targets being achieved, including the high cost of importing foreign technology, a shortage of energy, the low education standard of Chinese workers and rank bad planning. One glaring planning error occurred in Wuhan where a complex steel plant, complete with the best West German and Japanese machinery and computerised controls, was set up. Power came from hydro-electric stations along the Yangtze, but the planners had failed to take into account the effects of severe drought. When, in 1979, the level of the river fell drastically, the power stations could not produce the necessary electricity and the magnificent plant was crippled.

Another example is the mammoth steel works at Baoshan, on the coast north of Shanghai. Expensive plant and equipment was bought from Japan. But, in 1979, construction was briefly frozen after it was found that some of the equipment was not only too expensive but sub-standard. Also it was noticed that ways of supplying the plant with the necessary high-grade iron ore had somehow been overlooked. The waters of the estuary on which the plant stands were found to be too shallow to

Shanghai is a huge industrial megalopolis *(opposite) and has many of the problems we have come to associate with such a large urban sprawl — high noise and pollution levels, unemployment, overcrowding and juvenile delinquency.*

It is also the most modern and sophisticated city in China. As the number of television sets, radios and foreign tourists increase, many people, especially the young, are learning more about the West than they've ever known before — and finding their own country lacking by comparison. This train engineer (left) has seen many visitors embarking at stations on his route.

allow the berthing of large ore-carrying ships. So a separate iron ore port had to be built a full 130 nautical miles south. There the ore is off-loaded and taken to the plant on small coastal vessels.

It was errors such as these that convinced Chinese leaders grouped around Deng to demote capital-intensive heavy industry and put the major thrust of industrial modernisation on light industry, oil, energy, communications and also tourism. What Beijing seeks is the maximum fastest return on the smallest possible investment. The purge of heavy industry was launched in late 1979 and enterprises that were unprofitable, badly planned, inefficiently run or energy guzzlers were told brutally to shape up or close down.

To achieve its modernisation goals, China needs to purchase advance equipment from abroad which economists consider with other investment could involve the spending of some US$600 billion. Beijing's credit rating is one of the world's highest and after China signalled that it was ready to seek loans, Western bankers queued up to offer billions of dollars on the best terms available. Membership of the International Monetary Fund in 1980 has also made more funds available to China. But as many ambitious developing nations have found, debts have to be serviced and eventually repaid. At the same time, in China's case, imports will have to be maintained at a high level to supply both industry and agriculture. Already about one of every four dollars that China spends abroad goes for the purchase of such materials as iron ore, steel, copper, aluminium, nickel, chrome and cobalt. China also loads its import bill down with massive purchases of commodities. A third of China's sugar has to be imported and, by 1980, its purchases were disrupting the market. Cotton purchases from the United States amounting to more than 2.25 million bales sent prices sky-rocketing in 1980 and Beijing's purchases have also been a major factor on the wheat market. China bought around 10 million tons of grain — mainly from the United States

and Australia — in 1979.

China's imports in 1979 — nearly 30 per cent greater than the previous year — totalled US$ 16.2 billion while exports were up 26 per cent to US$ 14.1 billion. This left China with a trade deficit of more than US$2 billion and there was little hope that it could be greatly reduced in the immediate future. By 1980, with modernisation only a few years old, economists were shaking their heads over China's balance of payments problem and suggesting that it would have to eventually consider devaluation of its currency, the Renminbi. Nothing could perhaps symbolise better China's reliance on the Western economies than devaluation.

Four main sectors have been earmarked for an export drive to balance increasing purchases from abroad — oil, coal, textiles and light industry. In this epoch of spiralling oil prices, crude petroleum is Beijing's bright hope. Most experts believe that China has about 4,000 million tons of oil waiting to be tapped on shore and about as much again off shore in southern waters and the Northern Bo Hai Gulf. The Soviet Union had laid down the basis for China's oil industry with some expert survey work, and between 1965 and 1975 — which are known as the 10 Great Oil Years — annual production growth hovered above 21 per cent. But by 1979 the oil burst had slowed and the growth rate dropped sharply from 11.1 per cent in 1978 to a meagre two per cent in 1979 for a total output of 106 million tons.

The oil industry was languishing on a dangerous plateau and foreign specialists were increasingly sceptical that the 1990 target of 400 million tons would be met. One problem is that the country's main offshore field, Daqing (Taching Oilfield), had already reached a production peak in 1976 and Shengli (Victory Oilfield), the second onshore field, had started to peak by late 1979. It is not an exaggeration to say that China's economic future — and thus political future — hangs heavily on development of its offshore fields. In 1980, American, French, British and other

Western firms completed seismic surveys in six offshore blocks extending from south-west of Taiwan to the western side of Hainan Island in the Gulf of Tonkin. It will take more than a year to process and thoroughly interpret the miles of data and tapes obtained from the surveys and only then will it be known whether Beijing can expect an oil bonzana from its southern waters.

By 1980, Beijing was exporting its first substantial amounts of oil to Japan, the Philippines and Thailand and also to Europe and Brazil. There were prospects of sales to the U.S. West Coast. Much depends on oil exports but there were clear signs in 1980 that all was not well in this key sector.

Yu Quili, a pioneer of the oil industry, was dismissed from his post as president of the State Planning Commission which is masterminding modernisation. Communist sources laid his downfall squarely on his over-ambitious plans for the oil industry. It was Yu, they said, who had boasted that China would establish 10 Daqing-size oil fields by 1980. In a move typical of over-ambitious and hasty decisions which have marred the modernisation programme, Yu advised purchase from abroad of large amounts of sophisticated oil machinery and equipment, but it was found that Chinese workers did not have the skills necessary to use it.

A similar shortage of skilled workers also affects the coal industry. Mechanisation of China's pits is vital if the target of doubling coal output to about 800 million tons is to be reached by 1987. At present China, which has verified coal reserves of around 600,000 million tons, ranks with the United States and the Soviet Union as the world's leading coal producer. But the industry's potential has not been realised because of serious under-investment. But by 1979, growth had almost petered out and production was almost stationary at around 600 million tons. This production setback underlined that large scale investment in new, mechanised shafts and the opening up of strip mines was necessary if

the coal industry — which furnishes more than 65 per cent of China's primary energy — is to advance.

Chinese miners are still very much at the pick and shovel stage. A mine in Shanxi set a new national record in labour productivity when it turned out 2.70 tons of coal daily per miner. This may sound a lot of coal until it one notes that the average productivity of an American miner is around 12 tons per day. Modern equipment would boost output, but it could prove difficult to absorb smoothly.

Coal remains crucial, not only for industry and exports but for millions of urban dwellers. They use it for domestic fuel as a view of China's soot-smeared, smog-choked cities will testify. Coal is earmarked to remain the principal energy source with oil being exported or used in the petro-chemical and other industries. China wants to avoid the energy transition that has marked the modernisation process of other large nations — from wood to coal and then from coal to oil as a leading fuel.

Stonecutters fashion granite slabs by hand in Beijing (opposite). *A rare sight — a welder who wears protective eyeglasses on the job* (above).

As it hovers on the brink of modernisation, China is haunted by fears of a major energy crisis. Already some industries — particularly in the coal-poor Guangzhou region — have to shut down sporadically because of power cuts. China's water resources are second to none but hydropower accounts for only 17 per cent of energy. The south has plenty of rivers but the rugged terrain makes construction of hydro-electric facilities extremely difficult. The problem is not so much a shortage of energy as waste. Consider for example that, in 1978, only 28 per cent of the energy that China used was converted to useful ends and that 72 per cent was wasted. In contrast, Japan's energy conversion efficiency is 55 percent and the American figure is 50 per cent. To ensure that available energy and raw material supplies go to enterprises essential to the export drive, non-essential plants have been closed down. This happened for example in Zhejiang one of the centres of the textile industry, a major modernisation

For decades, women have formed the majority of workers in the textile industry (above, opposite), *and more recently, women have made themselves a place in heavier industry, as in this machine tool plant* (right).

locomotive. Hua has stressed the two main credentials that make textiles an elite sector: "It requires relatively small investment and brings quick returns."

Textiles was the largest industry in pre-communist China, and in the decade up to the 1980s it was expanded away from its narrow, traditional silk and cotton base toward woollen goods and synthetic materials. In the country's industrial line-up, textiles look the winner. Apart from a long-standing expertise which goes back centuries, there are now 4,500 mills, dyeing plants, and other factories, and textiles and finished garment exports earn about 20 per cent of China's foreign exchange. Silk, China's traditional luxury export along with tea, remains as popular as it was in the distant days of the romantic Silk Road. Such lines as raw silk, Zhejiang's beautiful silk brocades and dramatically designed silk prints from Shanghai were earning around US$300 million a year in the late 1970s. China seeks also to pay for modernisation with sales of light industrial goods, including products from a rapidly expanding electronics sector. China hopes to become the bargain basement of the world for radios, casette recorders and pocket calculators. It is meanwhile selling a wide variety of products including leather items, canned goods, building materials, silverware, crockery and flashlights. Investors, mainly Overseas Chinese, but also including Western firms, have established joint ventures with China in the light and heavy industrial field, often on a compensation trade basis under which China pays back the original investment and also purchases advanced technology provided by the foreign partner with actual production from the factory.

To improve light industry, officials are calling for a revamping of the vital machine tool sector. Official media complains that the machine tool plants are often 30 years behind the West, workers are poorly trained and management elderly and unimaginative.

Much of China's potential wealth, as

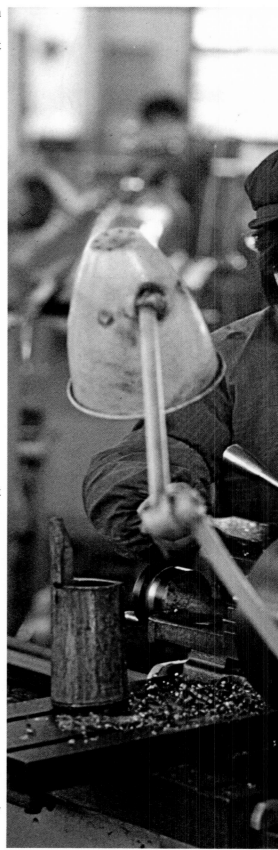

团结起来 为建设社会主义的现代化强国而奋斗

Each person seems to have his own opinion about whether life is better in the countryside or in the city. Some city-dwellers will talk wistfully about the peace and quiet of a farm village, and some will say with envy that the peasant can build his own home.

But the city continues to be attractive to tens of thousands of people. The government in Beijing has strict rules as to who is eligible to move to a city from a rural area, who may transfer from one city to another and, until recently, who should leave an urban centre to resettle in the countryside.

These rules are meant to ease some of the problems that exist in the cities, one of which is a chronic housing shortage. As the government promises more benefits to city workers and gives them more cash, they expect a better standard of life, with larger living space, more food, and a better variety of consumer products. These demands, in turn, create even more pressure on the government.

Opposite: *Life in the city also means more variety in entertainment.*
This page: *Worker housing* (top) *and a new high-rise hotel* (bottom).

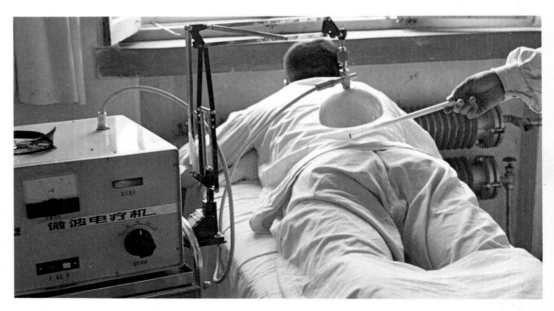

has already been seen with oil and coal, lies underground; the country is one of the world's treasure houses of ferrous and non-ferrous metals. Minister of Geology, Sun Daqing, said that the country's deposits of tungsten, antimony, tin, iron and copper are among the largest in the world. China has substantial deposits of 130 useful minerals — including considerable amounts of gold and silver — and a wide spread of valuable rare earths. Deng Xiaoping has underlined that China intends to sell its rare metals to finance modernisation. But again, before China can cash in on its minerals, the yawning technological gap must be bridged. Experts hold that China's metallurgical sector is probably about 20 years behind the rest of the world.

This technological chasm exists in almost all branches of China's industry and it can be partly blamed on the total breakdown of the country's educational system and research programmes during the Cultural Revolution. One example that explains the mining industry's handicap: an institute dealing with rock mechanics produced no graduates at all between 1966 and 1977. Deng and other leaders are well aware of this educational collapse. Talking with visiting scientists in 1979, Deng remarked: "The greatest difficulty that confronts China is the low level of

technological training." Zhang Longxian could have confirmed this. Nearing 70, he is vice president of Beijing University and a professor of bio-chemistry.

Like thousands of other scientists, technologists and experts, Zhang suffered from the scorn and suspicion that marked Mao's attitude towards all intellectuals. When the Cultural Revolution erupted, Zhang was taken from his laboratory and sent to the countryside. There he learned to build houses and farm rice, ending up as manager of a rice mill.

China's scientific development simply screeched to a halt as Red Guards swarmed throughout the land dispatching the nation's educated élite for sometimes fatal re-education in the countryside. Nuclear scientists and experts who maintain the country's unique earthquake alert service seemed to have been among the few to have escaped. As the slogan "better red than expert" echoed throughout China, more than 80 national science societies failed to meet for a decade and it was only in May 1978 that the four principal departments of the Chinese Academy of Sciences were re-established.

Now the scientists are back in their laboratories. Hu Yaobang, General Secretary of the Communist Party told 5,000 of them gathered at the first scientific congress for a decade that "China's

The fourth modernisation, science and technology, is beset with serious problems as well. China has lost the intelligence and skills of two generations of young people, first through the Cultural Revolution when most schools and universities were closed and students roamed the country in the name of revolutionary politics. Some of those students have reached their mid-thirties, an age when they should be reaching their optimum period of contribution to society.

And students in elementary and high schools today are paying the price of the Cultural Revolution. Although they may try as best they can to study, they may be held back because skilled teachers and up-to-date textbooks are not available.

Because there was so little activity in the sciences for more than a decade, scenes like this demonstration (above) of a heat machine in a Shijiazhuang military hospital might be staged, having been specially set up for show purposes only, to Chinese and foreign visitors alike.

The shortage of doctors is severe. The success of the barefoot doctor (opposite), perhaps one of the Cultural Revolution's best reforms, is also being questioned.

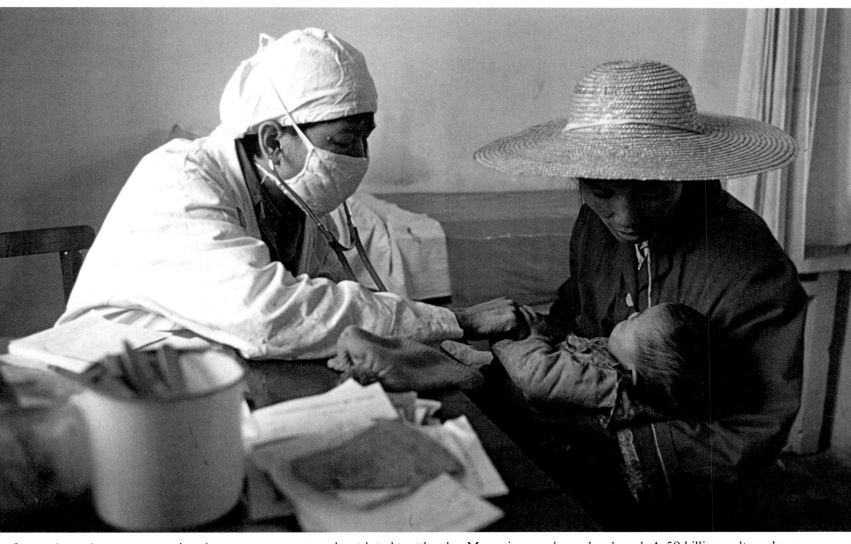

future depends on our grasping the most advanced science and technology." Intellectuals are being given party membership, declared Labour Heroes and told that, after all, they are members of the working class.

Between 1976 and 1979, more than 160,000 scientists and technologists got their former jobs back. But there were still thought to be thousands languishing as storemen, farm workers and administrators. In one classic case it was found that a group of highly-skilled radar specialists were toiling in a brewery.

Western experts put the total number of China's scientific and technological personnel at a mere 1.2 million. Also, most of the laboratories are primitive by Western standards with homemade, obsolete equip-ment and outdated text books. Magazines are being republished to propagate interest in the sciences and societies are being set up in many fields from mathematics to optics to futurology. Large and even small enterprises have set up their own research and development sections. The immediate concern of leaders is to obtain inventions and new techniques which can be promptly applied to increasing the output and profitability of agriculture and light industry.

Achievements, such as the ICBM test — show that in some fields, the Chinese are maintaining their reputation for being some of the smartest people on earth. As has been already seen, laser technology is advanced. In Shanghai, the latest telecommunications technique, optical fibres, has been developed. A 50 billion volt nuclear particle accelerator is being developed at a cost of around US$100 million with help from the United States, and this will help push China to the frontier of high-energy physics.

Science is therefore another critical area, and a new generation has to be produced fast. In 1980, the *Beijing Evening News* remarked: "China is at present the youngest country in the world: 60 per cent of the population is under 30. However the age of scientists and technologists does not conform to this pattern."

It noted that nearly 80 per cent of 1,500 delegates attending a scientific and technological conference were over 50 years of age. Less than one per cent were under 35. The newspaper claimed that more than 99 per cent of China's scientists had passed the best age for invention, and added: "The ship of China's science and technology has started its voyage, but the captain, first mate and helmsman have greying hair." It said that these aging scientists could no longer produce the inventions that China needed and leaders should now seek new talents in the country's schoolrooms.

Mao regarded China after the revolution as a blank sheet of paper on which he could, with his undistinguished calligraphy, pen what he wished. His design for education may have left China with an unsurmountable handicap. The educational system was simply shut down as he launched the Cultural Revolution and used millions of high school pupils and university students as his ideological cannon fodder. No nation can afford such a folly and expect to advance.

In 1971, universities began to splutter back to life but Mao demanded a simpler curriculum and a damaging mix of work, study, and Maoist indoctrination. Students were selected not for their academic abilities, but on their political credentials and background, preferably working class.

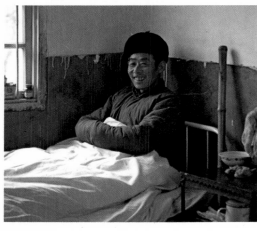

Health care in hospitals on agricultural communes: to have a well-stocked western-style pharmacy on the commune is very rare.

Students were dispatched to the countryside for lengthy periods and given menial tasks. One student at Beijing University, jewel of China's higher educational crown, recalled that "we spent those years teaching English to pigs."

Now the Cultural Revolution is described by leaders as an appalling catastrophe. It certainly was for education. Teachers say that the whole level of general knowledge among schoolchildren has fallen. The few students who managed to finish Mao's truncated three-year courses are now considered inadequately educated. Among the country's workers, seven out of 10 have educational levels well below high school level.

So a crash education policy is part of modernisation. Most of the country's universities and colleges had reopened their doors by 1980. The curriculum is once again focused on academic studies and in 1980 more than 3.3 million hopefuls sat reintroduced university entrance examinations. Knowledge of the once-hallowed canons of Mao's Little Red Book no longer counts; only academic excellence wins a seat in the lecture halls. They, however, are extremely limited, with about 300,000 places available in universities and specialised institutions.

For those who fail to enter, the future is grim indeed — years in a humdrum oc-

cupation that a worker is expected to keep for the whole of this working life lie ahead. There is no such thing as labour mobility in China and advancement up the industrial ranks is painfully slow. In 1979, students who were not awarded university places paraded through Beijing shaking their fists and shouting "We want to go to college."

Student rejects will join China's lost generation, the millions who, as youths, were summarily dispatched from the cities for what must seem a hundred years of solitude in the communes or on the state farms. And there are the other members of this generation — the millions whose chances for education were wrecked by the Cultural Revolution. The fury they feel for the so-called "Gang of Four" is deep and real. One encountered in Guangzhou told of his deep hatred of them. He was 30 years old and had never had a proper education. He had no hopes for a better life.

In China today, the three paths to the top and a privileged life-style are the party, the army and the university. Part-time education is booming as people try to improve their positions. About 30 million workers are receiving further training, a vital necessity if they are to be able to cope with new technology. A third TV channel for education was started in 1979 and was

soon teaching mathematics, physics, chemistry and English to about 700,000 viewers.

China, which perfected public exams for administrators under the Sui dynasty 1,500 years ago, has long had an educated élite — the mandarins who were probably first trained to deal with the complicated administrative problems posed by China's canal transport system widely developed by Sui dynasty engineers. Today, as it faces the unusually complicated tasks of modernisation, the mandarins are being reborn. Mao spurned university degrees as an encouragement to individualism, but now they are to be re-introduced. About 40,000 students are being sent abroad to study in the United States, Japan and Western Europe, Deng's son among them. Foreign experts are summoned to Beijing to give lectures.

The brightest Chinese children are enrolled in a special class set up in 1978 at the country's Science and Technology Institute. The 29 super-brains admitted for the six-month course in 1979 all got over 90 per cent in their physics and mathematics examinations. They are the leading scientists and technologists of the future.

But the greatest educational process launched in China is outside the classrooms and lecture halls; an attempt to do away what the Dengians call "ossified thinking," to break the ideological shackles of Maoism and to learn truth — not from theory and the Little Red Book — but from facts. The success of China's gigantic endeavours will depend on the modernisation of a billion minds.

Most of the facts that the Tengians want people to recognise are economic. They are driving to improve managerial efficiency and say that China must accept the basic laws of a market economy and do away with the notion that a good communist does not seek to maximise profits. A newspaper in Heilongjiang once put it this way: "Modernisation is the means and getting rich is the goal. Modernisation is for the sake of getting rich," it said, noting

China's future may depend on its children and on the education they receive. With educational reforms begun in 1977, these children (right) may have a better chance than their older brothers and sisters. The State now funds selected "key" universities and institutes, and their feeder high schools and elementary schools as well. Some children, especially the offspring of officials and other well-placed parents, will be able to start their college preparation even earlier than elementary school, in state-run nurseries and kindergartens.

that some cadres and workers were worried about the relationship between getting rich and modernisation. This confusion is understandable given 30 years of ideological stop-go and as one official remarked: "Some comrades still consider that material incentives are revisionist."

But this is the path that Deng and his allies have chosen — material incentives and a better quality of life. Newspapers press the view that only by providing people with more material benefits will they be willing to work for modernisation. And they say that the old Maoist way of doing things, without material rewards, was "like spurring a horse to race without feeding it."

Better rich than red? Not yet perhaps but almost, with management in hundreds of factories given a free hand and told to maximise profits. These enterprises are allowed to pay bonuses, but by 1980 the maximum annual bonus payable was still a niggardly US$70 or only 15 per cent of the average workers' salary. The new policies, however, have breached the twin dams of price and wage controls. In 1978, millions of workers got a pay rise and, in 1980, another rise was handed out to 40 per cent of workers who were judged by their colleagues to have been the most hard-working and reserving.

Out of favour now is what Maoists called the "iron rice bowl philosophy" under which a worker kept his job and received full wages no matter whether he went to work or not and regardless of his performance on the factory floor. Now, workers can actually be fired while those who work harder get paid more. But price increases threaten to wipe out the wage creases and bonuses. In 1979 prices for food, including such staples as meat, poultry, milk, eggs and vegetables, were increased up to 30 per cent.

China in the 1980s is negotiating that most hazardous of economic minefields — a mixed economy, where state concerns and private enterprise exist uneasily side by side. Large numbers of unemployed youths have been enrolled in what are

University entrance examinations were reinstated in 1977 to select the best students. This change came after more than a decade of a policy aimed at giving priority for university places to students of worker, peasant or soldier background who also had the proper political qualifications.

Professors, teachers and other intellectuals are being summoned back from almost every corner of China where they were sent either in the first purge of intellectuals in the early 1960s or during the Cultural Revolution. Some of these people are going overseas to study, do research and to update their knowledge with current developments in their disciplines.

Right: English is the most popular foreign language in the schools.

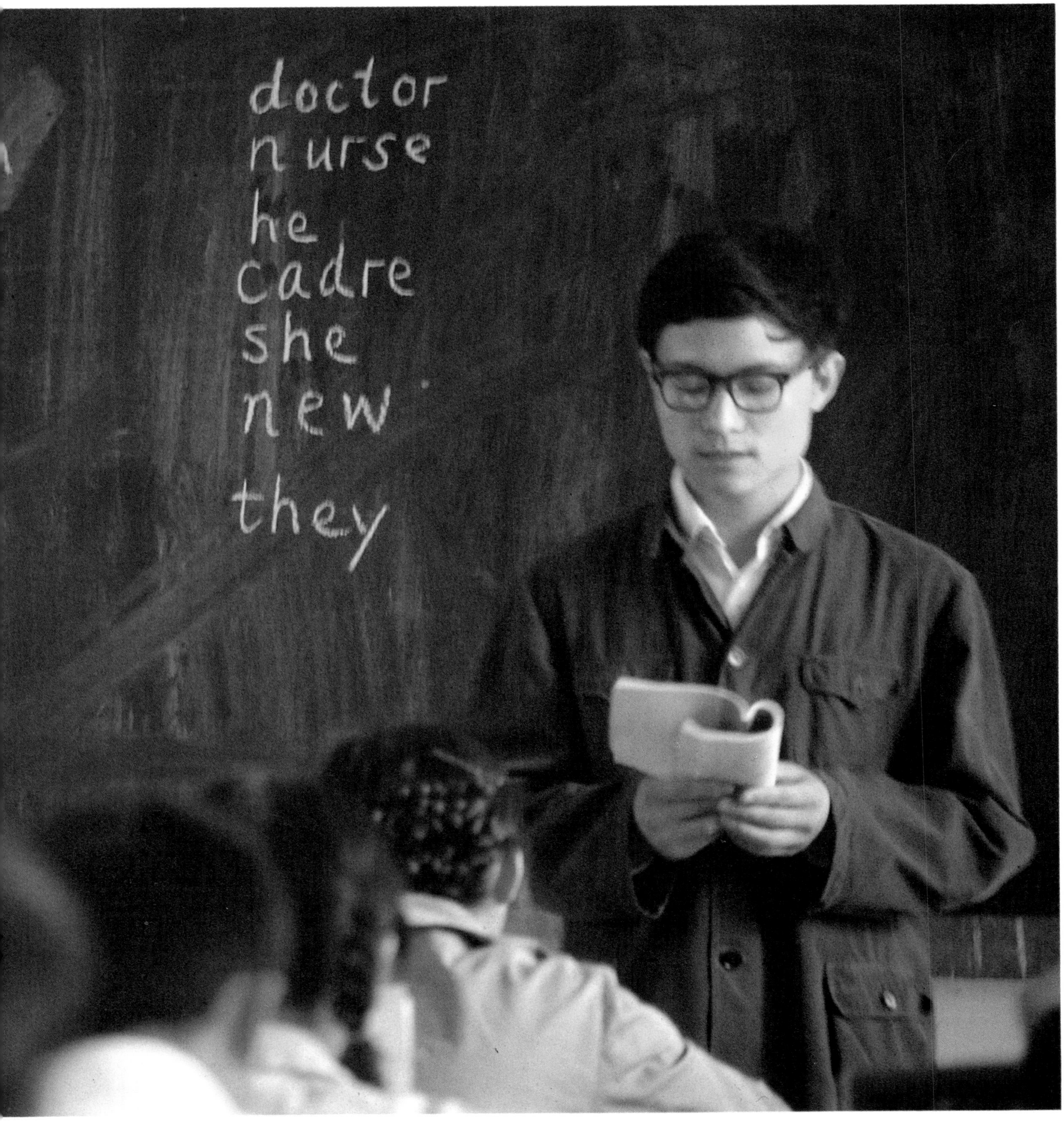
doctor
nurse
he
cadre
she
new
they

known as collective enterprises. These are mainly small organisations such as shops, snack bars, or service firms providing household repairs, scrap recuperation and shoe repairs. They are allowed to distribute some profits to their workers and wages are essentially the same — if not higher — than in the state concerns. Meanwhile, as they chase higher profits and bigger bonuses, state-run enterprises push up prices, often illegally. By 1980, officials were seriously worried by a wave of speculation and profiteering. The party Central Committee warned that unless inflation was checked it could endanger political stability and undermine the prestige of the party — or at least the Dengian leaders of it.

In the cities, a nascent consumer revolution is taking hold. Demand surged for consumer durables, and between April 1979 and April 1980, the number of TV sets per 1,000 families rose from 15 to 26. In Shanghai, there was one TV set for every four households, a national record. There was a rush for such products as digital watches, small-wheeled leisure bikes and the most sought-after items — casette recorders and pocket calculators. Promised were washing machines, refrigerators, air conditioners and even micro-wave ovens.

The problem with any revolution in expectations is that it can generate frustrations. Sharply rising deposits in banks — where interest rates are a miserly 0.51 per cent — were a sure sign that too much money was chasing too few goods. Chinese consumer durables industry enterprises will be hard put to meet rising demand, specially from rural areas. With the rise in farm produce prices and increasing sales at markets, many peasants have — relatively — more to spend. In the countryside, consumer horizons broaden; formerly the peasants yearned for the three rewards: wristwatch, bicycle and sewing machine. Now they are seeking more radios, electric fans, expensive liquor and synthetic as opposed to cotton materials. As materialism engulfs Maoism, so the young start to drift from the austere revolutionary path. In homes and parks, young people dance to the disco beat or the pop music cassettes smuggled in from Taiwan and Hong Kong. Women queue to buy perfume. In the streets some wear a trace of lipstick and the baggy, unisex Liberation Suit is being replaced by gaily patterned skirts and blouses. But shortages remain serious. People who want to buy a good pair of shoes can queue up for hours while young couples setting up home and seeking a set of furniture have to register for it six months in advance.

Unfulfilled expectations encourage black marketeering. In Beijing, Shanghai, Guangzhou and other big cities, street-corner dealers do a roaring trade in cassettes. They are smuggled in from Hong Kong or brought in by Chinese visitors who are allowed to give them as presents to relatives (who often promptly sell them).

To finance some of the modernisation programmes, China badly needs foreign currency. Tourism is one industry that is being tapped for dollars, pounds and francs (opposite, at the Summer Palace in Beijing). *Above, children are introduced to electronic calculating through a large educational display.*

Modernisation, to some, means adopting the ways of the West — a trombone, a suit and tie, and individual salesmanship — anyone want to buy a bottle of soda?
Even an international advertising agency (opposite) *is not averse to advertising itself, and boasting of its own friends all over the world.*

Raising the quality of life in China is an awesome task. Vast areas need attention and heavy spending. Housing is primitive and in the cities pitifully inadequate. Pollution is rampant, despite official threats to close down the worst offending enterprises. New schools, leisure facilities, libraries and hospitals have to be built. The Dengians will have to provide these services if they are to keep the people happy. But above all, if China is to pull off its modernisation gamble it must succeed in efforts to control the growth of population.

All China's economic gains may be negated if population growth is not checked. At the end of 1980, a vice premier, Kang Shien, admitted for the first time that the population had passed the billion mark. The target for population growth was set at 10 per thousand for 1979, dropping to five per thousand in 1985 and reaching zero growth by the year 2,000.

To reach that goal China seeks to convince parents that — as the slogan on the giant billboard said — "one child is better." To implement the policies, strong pressure is put on parents and procreation is being literally penalised for the first time in history. Provinces are in charge of population policies and, in some areas, parents are harshly sanctioned if they have a third and fourth child. These big families will become the outcasts of the Chinese revolution as, for example in Anhui province, five per cent of parents' total income is deducted to pay the welfare expenses of a third child.

In contrast, families who pledge to have only one child are hailed as national heroes, and at mass meetings to push the restricted families idea, one-child volunteers have huge red flowers pinned to their tunics. There are also more concrete advantages: Free schooling and medical treatment is now provided in many areas for only children; one-child families are also entitled to the same amount of living space as a family of four and an only child will get priority admission in schools and, later, in factories. In Sichuan, parents who promise not to have a second child get about US$3 a month in subsidies.

Pressures on couples who ignore the new policies are far from subtle. Often they are lectured and hounded until the woman agrees to have an abortion. Couples who continue to have children despite the pressures are often virtually forced to submit either to the sterilisation of the wife or vasectomy for the men. Despite some successes, such as Shanghai's in the first quarter of 1980, the policies will prove difficult to implement. It should be noted that in 1979 the rise in the national birth rate exceeded the target of 10 per thousand by two points. The only child runs up against a long-standing Chinese tradition of large families, particularly in rural areas where more children mean more people to work the fields. There is also a preference for boys who — besides being better suited to agricultural tasks — could in the past alone perform the sacrifices to the ancestors. This preference for boys persists and couples who produce a girl at their first attempt are more than likely to have a second child and — in the rural areas — continue having children until they produce a boy.

In a country where filial loyalties remain strong and tradition calls on children to care for aged parents, there is also concern for what will happen to old people in a one-child society where families are often separated. A system of pensions will probably have to be introduced for peasants. Another fear is that by placing restrictions on population growth, China may produce a "generation of brats" — pampered children who are unsuitable raw material for communism.

But Deng and the men around him are prepared to take that chance. They know that if population growth is not checked, China's hopes could be drowned in a sea of people. Deng and his close companions are old men who have survived a long and often bloody revolutionary struggle only to see the best years of their lives wasted in bitter idealogical struggles with successive purges that eliminated the brightest of their generation and twice tore the economy to shreds. In the years left to them they seek to lock China on a development trajectory as sure as that which took the country's first ICBM to its landing zone in the Pacific. If they succeed it would mean that their successors — like opposition parties in many Western democracies today — will inherit a solidly structured economy and, perhaps more important, a psychological climate of long-term expectations which would make radical economic and social change for political reasons an extremely hazardous exercise.

A young woman takes a lesson on how to ride a bicycle (opposite), *while in Guangzhou* (above) *passers-by see an advertisement for* Mobaolu *cigarettes.*

LIAO CHENGZHI

China's principal links with the millions of Chinese people living abroad have long been the responsibility of Liao Chengzhi, a colourful and dashing revolutionary figure, who just qualifies as an "Overseas Chinese" himself, having been born in Tokyo in 1908. His father, a student supporter of Sun Yat-sen, "father of the Chinese revolution," was assassinated in Guangzhou when Liao was 17 years old.

Liao's credentials as an expert on Overseas Chinese affairs are enhanced by the fact that he is Cantonese — like huge numbers of the Chinese people who have emigrated abroad. He was educated in Shanghai and Guangzhou, returning to Tokyo's Waseda University for a year's study shortly after the death of his father. He was deported from Japan for demonstrating against Japanese military intervention in Shandong province.

Taking ship from Shanghai, Liao spent the next three or four years trying to organise strikes of Chinese seamen in major European ports, going to jail at least twice in Holland and Germany. After a visit to the USSR (then still the bright, hopeful citadel of revolution), Liao threw himself into underground work and revolutionary intrigue in Shanghai — the "paradise of adventurers". Falling foul of

the Kuomintang police, he was arrested but later released, and joined Mao's Long March as the Red Army passed through the western province of Sichuan.

At the Communists' new base area in the northwest, Liao worked on propaganda and journalism, until he was sent with an important mission to Hong Kong — where he stayed for four years up till 1941, when the Japanese overran the British Colony. Escaping from the Japanese, he was captured and imprisoned for three years by the Kuomintang authorities, being released in 1946.

By that time the Party had shown its gratitude for his work and suffering by electing him in absentia to the Central Committee. For the next few years he carried out political assignments in Shanghai, Hong Kong, Guangzhou and Beijing and at age 40 was appointed to organise the Communist youth movement which was set up following the fall of Beijing and the establishment of the People's Republic.

The versatile revolutionary spent almost a decade on youth work, travelling in the newly Communist countries of Eastern Europe to attend congresses and meetings. But he was also occupied with other work in journalism and the drafting of the new Chinese Constitution, as well as the work which would later make him famous —

relations with the Overseas Chinese, a field in which his widowed mother, He Xiangning, was also active.

In the 1950s and 1960s, Liao devoted himself to diplomacy and to the care of Overseas Chinese who had fled persecution in Indonesia and settled again in China. He was also named head of the Overseas Chinese University in Fujian province.

In 1967, the Red Guards denounced him as a "revisionist" — but he bounced back not long afterwards, and was particularly active in China's burgeoning relationship with Japan following mutual diplomatic recognition in 1972. After Mao's death and the purge of the "Gang of Four", he turned again to Overseas Chinese affairs — and his experience was badly needed because of the flood of more than 200,000 ethnic Chinese who were forced to return to China from Vietnam. His role has been further enhanced by the new policy of soliciting development funds from the Overseas Chinese business communities, and restoring the privileges and facilities which Chinese people born overseas can enjoy in the People's Republic if they return.

In Beijing (opposite), *adjacent billboards promote Chinese athletic equipment to the city's many foreign business travellers, and electronic products to the local residents.*

In Guangzhou (this page), *P.L.A. soldiers ride past an advertisement for* Kekou Kele. *Except for a few items like radios, televisions and wristwatches, the foreign products available in China are sold only to foreigners. Even so, the company that introduces its products into China must be careful about the way in which its brand names are translated into Chinese. Because of variations in the spoken language, most names that are pronounced a certain way in Beijing, where people speak the national dialect, mandarin, are pronounced differently in Shanghai or in Guangzhou. For instance, the Chinese characters for Coca-Cola in mandarin sound similar to the English name, but in the cantonese dialect they are pronounced as "houhao houlok."*

Children with a head start: a youngster whose family can afford fancy jackets, sunglasses and a camera (this page, top); teenagers in organised spare time activity (this page, bottom).

An average worker must save several months' wages to afford to buy a foreign television set (opposite). Following pages: flashcard display depicting industrial modernization at the Beijing workers' stadium.

The Physical China

Margaret Spackman

The creator of the universe, according to Chinese legend, was a being called Pangu. Assisted by a dragon, a unicorn, a tortoise and a phoenix, Pangu laboured 18,000 years moulding the earth into its present shape. Then he died and his body underwent a transformation as marvellous as his creation. His flesh became soil. His blood became rivers and his sweat rain. The hair of his body became trees and other plants. His breath turned into wind and his voice thunder. His left eye became the sun and his right eye became the moon.

Every major culture has a traditional story of creation but the Chinese version of the universal impulse in man to describe the earth's beginnings animates the land and the elements with a special spirit that is both human and divine and places this planet in harmony with other heavenly bodies from the start. Pangu was a being with supernatural powers, but also flesh and blood. When his great work was completed it was barren until he was absorbed into it, starting cycles of animal and plant life, flowing rivers, fire and all other elements and the march of the seasons.

Long before civilisation arose, before language was written, ritual was formalised and legends such as that of Pangu became part of folklore, the ancestors of modern Chinese people and many other peoples around the world saw the earth itself as sacred, inhabited by a spirit that animates all created things, manifested even in phenomena such as wind, thunder and earthquakes.

In China, however, more than in any other great nation, this initial mystical concept endured and led to many natural features of the landscape being preserved for fear of upsetting some guardian spirit.

Much of China's landscape is among the most sublime in the world. There are areas so richly covered in vegetation that they seem to be carved from imperial jade. There are terraced fields and paddies that create a masterful mosiac of nature's colours, mist embraced mountains, gentle lakes and grassy foothills and savannahs. The wild beauty of Guilin's unique domes — towers and cones of chalk, the bizarrely shaped outcroppings of limestone extending for hundreds of miles — has inspired poets and painters since the Song dynasty. In song, painting, prose and poem, stretching back to the birth of their civilisation, Chinese have celebrated their land, its rich diversity of animal and plant life, its seasons and moods.

The contrasts of its landscapes and climate are extreme. In winter, when the north country as described in a Mao Tse-tung poem is a "thousand miles sealed with ice . . . ten thousand miles of swirling snow," China's regions south of the Tropic of Cancer are covered with carpets and canopies of green jungle. In the poetic terms of an anonymous modern geographer in Sichuan (Szechuan) Province "moso bamboo covers some mountains like a green sea." When the sun rises over the Yalu River separating China and Korea in the east, the Pamirs in the far west near Afghanistan, are still dark. In this land of nearly 9.6 million square kilometres almost six million square kilometres are areas where camel caravans and survey teams can travel for days and not meet a single human.

Yet, it is the most populous nation on earth, home to almost 1,000 million people. Because of its vast territory the average population density is just over 80 people to the square kilometre. Most of them live in the southwest where all of the major cities are located. Over ten of these have populations of more than one million. Close to 11 million live in the bustling municipality of Shanghai while the capital, Beijing has eight million. These figures contrast sharply with the northwest where settlement is so sparse that in Xinjiang (Sinkiang) Uygur Autonomous Region, which occupies about one-sixth of the country's territory, there are about five persons to the square kilometre. However, the population there is growing steadily as the area becomes more developed.

China is the largest single nation in Asia, the third largest — after Canada and the Soviet Union — in the world. In terms of natural diversity, it is probably the grandest. The little known western mountains, soaring to heights of 7,000 metres and more, are actually part of the Himalayas, its peaks being amongst the highest in the world. In the northwest, China features one of the lowest spots on the earth's land surface, the Turfan Depression, 154 metres below sea level. The land between the cloud-wrapped peaks permanently capped in snow and the depression contains plateaux and steppes, plains and savannahs, deserts and jungles, rivers, streams and lakes. Off-shore are 3,415 islands.

Within her borders all of the soils of the Eurasian continent but tundra are represented, 32,000 species of higher plants and more than 4,500 species of animals and birds. Many, including the giant panda and ginko tree of Sichuan, are not found elsewhere. In the thick forests of the cold north roam tigers, bears, sables, moose and deer. Game birds like hazel grouse, ring necked pheasants and Daurian partridges abound. Gazelles, wild horses and camels are found in Inner Mongolia and Xinjiang along with grey wolves and kit foxes. While the Roof of the World, the Qinghai (Chinghai)-Tibet Plateau, is home to snow leopards, bears, yaks and antelopes, at lower levels live Rhesus and golden haired monkeys, large Indian civet cats and takins or ox sheep. Asiatic elephants are found in Southérn Yunnan.

China's land frontier of 22,800 kilometres borders with Korea in the east, the Soviet Union in the northeast and northwest; Outer Mongolia in the north; Afghanistan, Pakistan, India, Nepal, Sikkim and Bhutan in part of the west and southwest and Burma, Laos and Vietnam in the south. The mainland coastline stretches 4,000 kilometres giving onto vast areas of shallows and swamps, river estuaries and fine deepwater ports.

In most areas with rocky coastlines the mountains run down to the sea. The continuous pounding of the waves against them has formed cliffs with steep faces. In the Fujian (Fukien) and Zhejiang (Chekiang) provinces the mountain ridges lie at an angle to the coast and the action of sea swells into valleys has formed triangular harbours. Some coasts are jagged with rocks protruding out as capes, like the Chengshan Cape in Shandong (Shantung) Peninsula. This type of seacoast has zigzag lines, with big, deep bays and

It would take weeks of continuous travel to view all the various attractions of China's geography. One of the most beautiful scenic areas is in Guangxi province and western Guangdong. This region of limestone outcroppings, jutting hundreds of metres up into an otherwise flat landscape, has been described in poetry and paintings for hundreds of years. The poet Libo:

The fields are chill; the sparse rain has stopped
The colours of spring teem on every side.
With leaping fish the blue pond is full
With singing thrushes the green boughs droop.

149

good natural harbours as well as numerous islands and is considered to be strategically important.

As China stretches across some 5,000 kilometres (60 degrees of longitude) from east to west and has numerous high mountain ranges, the moisture laden summer monsoons from the Pacific and the Indian Oceans cannot penetrate deep into the northwest hinterland. As a result the annual rainfall in the northwest is the lowest in the country and increases gradually to the east, the south and the southeast.

Both altitude and terrain strongly influence the climate. Generally with the rise of every 1,000 kilometres the temperature drops five or six degrees. In the snow-clad, mountain-encircled Qinghai-Tibet Plateau, which stands at 4,000 to 5,000 metres above the sea, the temperature fails to touch 10 degrees celsius in the summer month of July.

But elsewhere during the summer months most of China is hot. The temperature however varies to an extraordinary degree during winter when all of the country north of the Huai River and west of the Chinling Mountains registers temperatures below zero. It is so cold that rivers and even the oil-rich Bo Hai Sea freeze over. In the northernmost parts of Heilongjiang (Heilungkiang) and Xinjiang average daily temperatures range between −20 and −30 degrees.

Not surprisingly there are vast areas hostile to habitation. In all, perhaps only 10 to 15 percent of the entire land surface can be used for farming. The rest is too steep, too dry, too high or too exhausted. For thousands of years certain regions have undergone tragic cycles of famine and flood and for centuries the silt-laden Huaihe (Yellow River) has been known as "China's Sorrow." Year after year people toil along the banks of this river raising its dykes against overflow. When floodwaters breach the mounds disaster follows as tens of thousands of square kilometres of precious cropland are engulfed.

According to records spanning the

2,000 years before 1949 the lower Yangtze River broke its dykes and flooded over 1,500 times and changed its course 26 times. In its upper course the river flows slowly and irrigates 1,000 hectares of good fields with clear water as it loops through Inner Mongolia. After it turns abruptly southward the river becomes a raging torrent and its water the colour of mud as it surges through gorges in the Loess Plateau. The amount of silt brought down from this area every year to its lowest course totals 1,600 million tons — the most of any river in the world. A great deal of this is dumped in the Yellow Sea but much of it is deposited on the river's bottom as the current slows when the river crosses the North China Plain. This causes the river bed to keep rising every year. Now it is an astounding ten metres above the surrounding countryside and is only kept on course by dykes that are continually strengthened. Steps have been taken to reduce the amount of silt carried by the river through carrying out extensive conservation projects in the loess highlands in the hope of preventing the soil erosion.

Down the river efforts are being made to use the silt to improve surrounding soil conditions. For instance, peasants have directed river water into low-lying sandy land to let the silt precipitate and then channelled its waters into canals to irrigate cropland. In this way large bodies of barren alkaline land have been transformed into fertile fields. Officials believe that the danger of the river breaching its banks have been removed through the building of flood detention locks on the Tungping Lake in the Yellow River's upper reaches at Shandong (Shantung) and through the widening of the river's bed in several places from one kilometre to four. A large number of regulating systems have also been built which play an important part in controlling floods and ice floes.

The Loess Plateau through which the Yellow River passes stretches across Shaanxi (Shensi), Gansu (Kansu) and Shanxi (Shansi) provinces and is one of

The country is drained by rivers emptying into the China Sea. These waterways are the lifeblood and the scourge of millions of people. The Yellow River, called "China's Sorrow" because of its periodic flooding of thousands of square kilometres, passes through four provinces covering an area as large as England, before draining into the Bo Hai Sea.

The Yangtze River, third largest in the world, begins in the mountains of Qinghai and crosses almost the entire country before opening up into the Yellow Sea. It too caused unalterable changes in China's geography through more than 2,000 years of flooding.

Today, both river systems are pretty well controlled by extensive flood control programmes. Recently scientists have announced that Shanghai, at the mouth of the Yangtze, is slowly sinking.

East China has a relatively humid climate and consists mostly of plains and hills. It's divided roughly into four sections by the Yellow and Yangtze Rivers, and the loess plateaux of Shanxi.

Northeast China, north of Beijing, is a fertile basin of rich black soil, excellent for wheat growing. The steppes of Inner Mongolia (this page, top) and the northernmost part of the area formerly known as Manchuria experience extreme variations in temperature and are unsuited for agriculture. But areas of Inner Mongolia provide rich grazing lands for horses and sheep.

South China begins south of the Huaihe River, which flows through five southern provinces before joining the Yangtze north of Nanjing. Left and opposite: scenery in and near Guilin.

China's earliest cultivated areas. The loess layer varies in depth from 50 to 80 metres and in some places exceeds 200 metres. This yellowish soil is rich in nutrients and minerals and is easily tilled. Along the terraced banks of the Yellow River and its tributaries years of cultivation have produced a mature layer of soil, loose and porous, which at the same time retains water. Known as the "cotton and grain country" the region produces wheat, maize, cotton and tobacco. This Yellow River valley is regarded as the cradle of ancient civilisation and is where agriculture began to develop 5,000 years ago. Big ancient water conservation works were carried out on the Yellow, the Yangtze and other rivers, the Grand Canal, the Dujiang Dam Irrigation System, and the Ling Canal being the most famous.

A number of canals, including the Ling, were built during the reign of the Qin Dynasty emperor, Qinshihuangdi, who succeeded to the throne in 246 BC. The canal is 30 kilometres long and links the Li River, a tributary of the Pearl River, the main artery of the South, with the Xiang Jiang River, a tributary of the Yangtze.

The canal thus opened up a vast inland water transport system that enabled goods to be carried more easily from the southern to the northern provinces and vice versa. The canal was completed in 214 BC but it was not the main construction task carried out during the reign of Qinshihuangdi.

His major achievement was the building of the 1,400 mile long Great Wall which traverses the Yellow River valley, the North China Plain and ends in the Liaodong Peninsula. This wall, five to 10 metres high, is dotted with lookout towers and campsites. It was built by conscript labour mobilised on a tremendous scale. The terrible suffering and loss of life among the conscripts added to the discontent rising against the Qin Dynasty and led to its overthrow in 206 BC — four years after the death of Qinshihuangdi.

In modern times one of the most remarkable achievements involving mass labour was the building of the Red Flag Canal. It lies in northwestern Henan (Honan), a province lying north of the Yellow River and winds its way through the peaks of the Taihang Mountains and leaps across their valleys and ravines. The major work on the project was completed

in June 1969, after ten years of hard struggle. It entailed cutting through 1,250 hilltops, drilling 134 tunnels and building 150 aqueducts. The main and three trunk canals and auxilliary channels total 2,500 kilometres in length. The canal was built because, although there are several rivers in Linxian county, where the canal is, they were dry for most of the year. As a result people there had to carry water great distances. The small water conservation works built after 1949 were not sufficient to solve the problem. So the Communist Party Committee of Linxian County decided in February, 1960 to cut through the Taihang Mountains and lead the water of the Changhe River which flowed in nearby Shaanxi Province into their county. They organised tens of thousands of workers from 15 communes in the area to build a dam across the Changho, dig the canals and cut tunnels through the hills. The main channel, 70 kilometres long, eight metres wide and 4.3 metres deep was completed in April, 1965. Work was then begun on the three trunk canals and hundreds of subsidiary channels. The canal has brought tremendous changes to Linxian county. The once-parched region

is now criss-crossed with irrigation ditches flowing with clean, clear water irrigating 40,000 hectares of fields.

The Yangtze is China's largest river. It has a total length of 6,300 kilometres and ranks after the Amazon and the Nile as the third largest in the world. Rising in the Koko Shili Mountains in western Qinghai Province the Yangtze traverses Tibet, Yunnan, Sichuan, Hubei (Hupeh), Hunan, Jiangxi (Kiangsi), Anhui (Anhwei), and Jiangsu (Kiangsu) to enter into the East China Sea at Shanghai. It drains a basin of 1.8 million square kilometres — about 19 percent of the country's total area. This drainage basin is rich and fertile and is inhabited by about 300 million people. Since ancient times the river has been a great artery for transport, linking the east to the west and, through the Ling Canal, the north with the south. Along its lengths are rich metallic and non-metallic mineral deposits.

But the Yangtze also has the reputation of being one of the fiercest and most savage rivers in the world. Its potential as a source of electricity is virtually untapped but this situation will soon change. A multi-purpose hydraulic project consisting of a 2.56 kilometre dam and two hydro-electric power plants with a combined generating capacity of 2,700 megawatts is now being built in the middle reaches of the river. The biggest ever hydro-engineering project to be carried out in China, it marks the first major step to harness the Yangtze.

The majority of China's rivers flow to the Pacific, the Indian Ocean and the Arctic Ocean. These are of two types. Those in the north have great seasonal variations in their drainage volumes, a large flow in summer which dwindles to quite a small flow in winter when they freeze over. Most of these rivers carry large amounts of silt so that the lower courses fill up and they tend to flood. Rivers in the south, however, carry heavy volumes of water all of the year round. Unlike those in the north they never freeze and carry little sediment. Other rivers in

southwest China, such as the Nujiang and the Lancang are different. They rise in the Qinghai-Tibet Plateau and gush down narrow gorges between towering mountains. They are spectacular to look at and have an enormous flow. They are ice free and have great potential for hydro-electricity generation.

The highest river in the world, the Yalutsangpo, flows from west to east across the Qinghai-Tibet Plateau. It is fed by glaciers and its river bed averages 3,000 feet above sea level. It flows eastward through the deep gorges of the Himalayas and the Kangkar Tesi Mountains until it reaches about longitude 95 degrees east, where it cuts through the Himalayas, turns southward and flows across India and Bangladesh to empty into the Bay of Bengal.

Inland rivers are mainly found in the arid northwest and drain one third of the country's total area. They are fed by glaciers and snow and these determine their volume and length. They flow intermittently and frequently dry up. Many of them contribute to the vast underground reservoirs of water that lie beneath the wide stretches of desert in the northern and northwest hinterland of China. Their area covers more than one million square kilometres. Most of them consist of shifting dunes and Gobi.

Sixty percent of their area is in Xinjiang (Sinkiang) Uygur Autonomous Region. The rest are in Gansu, Qinghai, Inner Mongolia, Ningxia (Ningsia), Jilin (Kirin), Liaoning, Shaanxi and Heilongjiang. The Taklamakan in Xinjiang is the largest, covering some 327,000 square kilometres, while the Badan Jiryn in northwestern Gansu has the biggest sandhills. The natural conditions vary but most are to be found in plateaus and in basins at high altitudes.

The Taklamakan is in the Tarim Basin that is surrounded by the Tienshan Mountains in the north, the Kunlan Mountains in the south and the Pamirs in the west. Covering about 800,000 square kilometres, the basin is the biggest of its

The plateau between the two rivers (previous page, opposite) *is of yellow loess soil, rich in nutrients and minerals. It's one of China's earliest cultivated areas, the land having been worked for more than 5,000 years. It produces wheat, maize, cotton and tobacco.*

Rainfall varies considerably from year to year, resulting in regular announcements in the Chinese press of drought conditions and crop failure in one part of the country or another. In winter and spring, weather systems move in from the north and west, bringing freezing temperatures from Siberia and dry winds from the Gobi Desert.

Above: *The dry, difficult soil of western Hebei.*

The land slopes gradually down to the sea from the mountain ranges in the west — the Himalayas in Tibet, dominated by Mount Everest (called Mount Chomolungma by the Chinese), and the rows of sharply ridged mountains of Sichuan which are the source of the Yangtze River. In the northwest lies the Xinjiang Basin, the nearly 4,000-metre-high Tianshan mountain range, and the sandy plain of the Gobi Desert. In this isolated spot sits China's nuclear research facility of Lobnor.

Preceding pages, opposite: The Li River, which flows into the Xi Jiang (Western) River hose many forks form the Pearl River Delta in southern Guangdong. Guangzhou's Pearl River is actually one of the larger forks of the Xi Jiang.

type in the world. Its average elevation is 1,000 metres above sea level. Its name in Uygur means "converging rivers" and it a place to which a large number of rivers, with headwaters in ice-capped mountains, flow.

The underground water supply created by these rivers has assisted the great efforts which have been made in recent years to stop the spread of the deserts. In Minchin County in Gansu Province on the southern fringe of the Tyngeri desert, for example, the people fixed the sand dunes by covering the surface with soil in which they planted grass and trees. The county has now afforested some 500,000 acres and set up a large number of shelter belts which have kept the sand from shifting and protected farmland. Their example was followed in other areas, and it has led, among other things to cultivatible land being reclaimed from the Gobi and other desert land in the Xinjiang Uygur Autonomous region.

China has a considerable number of lakes scattered throughout the country but only 370 of them are of any considerable size and these are mainly found in the Middle-Lower Yangtze Plain and the Qinghai-Tibet plateau. The largest freshwater lake is the Poyang in northern Jiangxi province just south of the Yangtze. During the flood season it has an area of 5,100 square kilometres but during the dry season it is more like a river with many branches. This impression is given by its indented shoreline. Beautiful scenery surrounds most of China's lakes and many of them are ornamented with decorative pagodas and bridges. On most of them wildlife abounds. Many of the lakes in the northwest of country are salt and those in the northeast, southeast and southwest are fresh.

On the eastern edge of the Tarim Basin in Xinjiang is Lake Lop Nor, the biggest salt water shifting lake in China. It covers some 2,570 square kilometres and in the past 2,000 years the lower Tarim River changed its course three times causing the lake to shift backwards and forwards between latitudes 39, 40 and 41 degrees north. Its area and shape still change continually as does its depth and water volume. Around the strange lake are numerous sand dunes and white salt crusts, which hinder transport and agriculture. The lake, however, yields saline and alkaline compounds which are useful to the chemical industry.

The biggest surface rock-salt bed, however, is Charhan Salt Lake covering 1,600 square kilometres. It is in the centre of Tsaidam Basin in the northwest. Two or three hundred million years ago the whole of the basin was a huge lake. Then the western part gradually rose and the surface area of the lake shrank, leaving some 5,000 salt lakes. *Tsaidam* is a Mongolian word meaning "salt marsh." Apart from salt the area has ample deposits of coal, oil, asbestos and various kinds of metallic ores and Tsaidam is often referred to as the "treasure basin." The highest lake is the Namu which lies north of Lhasa in Tibet. Its basin is rich in wildlife and the scenery there is spectacularly beautiful.

One of the most fascinating lakes however is the Hongzehu in the northern part of Jiangsu (Kiangsu). It has an average depth of less than four metres and the bottom of the lake is higher than the surrounding ground. Hence it is referred to as the "hanging lake." Another lake in the province which attracts a great deal of attention is the Taihu which has some 90 islets inside its 2,213 square kilometre

Summer weather patterns spread over eastern China from the south, so that temperatures even in northerly Harbin can reach 20 degrees centigrade. With the tropical weather come heavily laden clouds that dump more than 250 mm. of rain around Guangzhou (opposite), 165 mm. in the central plains (top), but less than half that as they finally reach Beijing.

Below the Tropic of Cancer in Yunnan province, weather conditions are suitable for the commercial cultivation of oil palm and rubber trees. This area (below), bordering Burma, Laos and Vietnam, is peopled mainly by the Dai, an ethnic minority related to the people of Thailand.

The best-known tea- and silk-producing area is around Hangzhou (opposite). These two commodities were key factors in opening China to trade with the barbarians from the West, who built the ancient "Silk Route."
Above: *On the Li River.*

area. The surrounding district contains many famous scenic spots.

China's major rivers and lakes all provide excellent grounds for fish farming and their waters are exploited to the fullest. The present output of Hubei (Hupeh) Province alone of 150,000 tons is equal to that of the whole of China in 1949. The country has over 800 species of freshwater fish of which 250 are considered to be of high economic value. The black carp, the silver carp, grass carp and "big head" are all peculiar to China but they are now found in the waters of more than 30 countries in Europe and Latin America where they have been introduced to strengthen local breeds.

The seas surrounding China are also rich fishing grounds. China is fortunate that her seas are relatively shallow and that the coastal waters come under the influence of the warm Taiwan current and the cold East China current at the same time. Where the two currents meet both cold water and warm water fish types are to be found in large shoals. For over 430,000 square nautical miles, the sea's depth reaches less than 200 metres. Most of the shallow water fishing grounds are in the warm temperate and subtropical zones. The Chousan Archipelago off Zhejiang in the East China Sea is now China's biggest fishing ground. It is visited by both cold and warm currents and fish come there in search of the nutritious food washed down by the Yangtze and Chang Jiang Rivers. This fishing ground has an area of 150,000 square nautical miles and fishing vessels can operate in it throughout the year. There are other famous fishing grounds in the Yellow and Bo Hai Seas. The area around China's southern islands is also important. The islands are made up of coral reefs. Owing to their proximity to the equator, the climate is hot and wet, with a mean temperature of over 24 degrees celsius. Typically tropical, they abound in flora and fauna as well as marine resources. Fish, including tuna, mackerel, snapper, garoupa, and golden banded caesios, are found in great numbers as well

as lobsters, giant turtles, sea cucumbers and sea weeds.

Greater attention is to be paid to modernising fish breeding methods during this decade in addition to other aspects of agriculture. The major cash crops are cotton, flax, soya bean, peanuts, sesame, sugar cane, sugar beet, sisal hemp, tung oil, silk and tea. China is one of the major cotton producing countries and in 1975 the production amounted to 2.16 million tons. Cotton requires sunshine and heat for its growth and it is grown in practically every part of the country but the main production areas are the North China Plain and surrounding districts and the Yangtze delta, the middle and lower Yangtze Plain, the Sichuan Basin and the Yunnan-Guizhou Plateau. Hebei Province is the biggest cotton region in China, accounting for one-fifth of the total cotton acreage.

Tea has been grown in China for more than 5,000 years and along with silk has long been one of the most important sources of foreign exchange. The earliest gardens were established in the provinces of Sichuan, Hunan and Guizhou (Kweichow), on a mountainous plateau on which some of the oldest trees in existence are still producing tea. If allowed to grow unpruned a tea "bush" may grow into a tree of up to 25 metres in height and at least one metre across the trunk. Several trees in Sichuan today are dated as being 800 years old. Tea plantations have now spread north into Shandong and large plantations have been established in Guangdong and Hainan.

To geographers of the ancient world China was known as Serica, Sera and Seres — "the land of silk" — a title it can still lay claim to. Samples of the silk exported to the far-flung empires of Rome and Carthage and Babylon have been unearthed along the ancient silk road which threaded its way through high mountains and deserts across some of the most inhospitable country on earth. The road was generally closed to foreigners and among the first Westerners to journey

The Great Wall (opposite, at sunrise) *may have formed a barrier against invading Manchus, but it's never stopped the dust storms from sweeping across the Gobi Desert to Beijing. At least, that's what Beijing residents have believed about the winds that rise up in the west at the end of April and sweep loose, yellow sand across the city. When the winds come, nothing escapes the dust which finds its way into homes through the most tightly shut windows.*

Recently, some Chinese researchers claimed that these dust storms are of local origin — that the wind from the west picks up loose soil only as it nears Hebei province, whose lands are poor and suffer from centuries of neglect. It is hoped that an extensive reaforestation programme will help control the sand and wind.

Tea and rice are the dominant crops of the Hubei-Hunan-Jiangxi (top) region. Although the Yangtze River flows here, most power is generated by coal-burning hydroelectric stations. As in ancient times, the river is used as a waterway. Nanchang, the capital of Jiangxi, is a key transportation centre, and a diversified manufacturing city with major cotton textile mills, oils- and fats-processing factories and lumber and paper mills.

Further down the Yangtze is one of China's leading agricultural regions. Here (bottom, Suzhou), more than 50 per cent of China's total land mass is arable. This is also an area where fish farming abounds in the hundreds of shallow lakes and rivers, and where deep-sea fishing is an important industry.

The area has traditionally been the leader in light industry, especially cotton and silk textiles, processed foods, paper and chemicals. With the emphasis on heavy industry after 1949, machinery and equipment manufacturing took over the industrial base in Shanghai (opposite) and its surroundings. In 1980, economic policy shifted back to light industry, and the Shanghai government announced it wanted to develop more "clean" industries for the city, such as electronics.

across it were the Genoan merchantmen, Marco Polo and his brothers, in the thirteenth century. The stories of their experiences at the court of Kublai Khan excited the Western world of that time and created a great deal of scepticism. Silk samples dug up along the road include delicate slippers as well as remains of bolts of embroidered cloth. Some of them have been dated as being more than 2,000 years old. The silk they were made from comes from some of the same places where silk is produced today. These are in Jiangsu, Zhejiang, Guangdong and Sichuan.

The cultivated worms are fed on a traditional diet of mulberry leaves but efforts have been made to raise them on castor oil plants which take less time and labour to grow. In addition, silk is also obtained from wild silkworms fed on oak and ash leaves in Shandong and the Liaodong Peninsula.

Tobacco is grown in many parts of the country but chiefly in Sichuan, Henan and Shandong.

China is a major grain growing nation and her northern plains are given over to enormous fields of wheat. Winter wheat is grown extensively south of the Great Wall on the Yangtze River Basin which is the main wheat belt of China. Spring wheat fields extend up to the northwestern regions of Inner Mongolia. But rice is the main crop and vast areas of the countryside are given over to its cultivation. Approximately one-third of the arable land is under paddy. In the fertile southern regions as many as three crops are harvested each year.

Soyabean, peanut, grape seed and sesame are the all important oil crops with soyabean being the most important. It has a long history of cultivation in the country where the main growing areas are in the northeast. The province producing the largest harvest is Heilongjiang.

In the cultivated areas of China, where the bulk of the population is to be found, almost all of the suitable land is used for arable farming so that pasture hardly exists. The only livestock raised in these

China's population is densest in the middle and lower Yangtze regions where there are upwards of 1,000 people per square kilometre. Similar overcrowded conditions exist around Guangzhou and along the coast of Guangdong and Fujian provinces. In the north, the density is a high 300 persons per square kilometre. The country as a whole has a density of 80 per square kilometre.

About 75 per cent of China's population lives in 15 per cent of its land; most of the people live in a belt running north-south parallel to the coast.

Above: *A mountain stream near Lushan.*
Opposite: *Along the Gui River.*

parts for food are pigs, chickens, ducks and geese, and some occasional buffaloes, though these are mainly kept as draught animals. China's pig population is said to number some 230 million, or about 34 per-cent of the world's total. In the northeast and northwest there are vast areas of rolling grasslands that have been home for centuries to nomadic herdsmen. The bulk of these lands are in Inner Mongolia which accounts for sixty percent of the total grassland area of the country. There are also extensive grasslands in Xinjiang, Qinghai and Tibet that extend into Gansu, Sichuan and Yunnan. The principal animals reared are sheep, cows, goats, camels and yaks. In some parts open-range deer farming is being undertaken. In most of these grazing areas communes, brigades and army farms have set up stud farms and breeding stations to improve the herds.

Life on these vast plains is not easy. The grazing areas are subjected to bitter temperatures during winter. Sudden snow storms and blizzards have long been the

biggest threat to the flocks and they are protected from the worst of it by winter shelters. The worst temperatures recorded on grazing lands in Xinjiang this century were registered in 1968 when ther-mometers plummetted to −40 degree celcius. Not suprisingly the strains of sheep found in these areas are particularly hardy and have good thick coats. Their wool has been improved through cross breeding. One of the best of the new strains is the large Xinjiang breed which produces high quality meat as well as long-staple wool. One of the sturdiest breeds of all is the "purple" Tibetan sheep which is noted for its ability to withstand the cold. It is raised on pastures 4,000 metres above sea level where the temperature never rises to much more than nine degrees celcius. The plateau on which it lives is surrounded by snow-capped mountains and glaciers.

China is rich in minerals and it is the country's good fortune that its road, rail and water transport systems all remained very much under-developed until the latter part of this century because reserves of

China is rich in mineral resources that haven't yet been significantly developed. It could become one of the leading suppliers in the world for iron, copper, tungsten, aluminium and other minerals. Several major oil fields have been discovered in the past two decades. Off-shore oil exploration is underway in the South China Sea and the Gulf of Bo Hai. The mining of coal has been stepped up. Major hydroelectric power projects are planned, including the Liujiachang complex south of Chengdu. Although several major oil fields have been discovered in the past two decades, and the mining of oil and coal, iron, copper and other minerals is underway, China's rich mineral deposits haven't yet been significantly developed. Many of today's scenic spots (left, Guilin; above, Yangshuo) may have to give way to the country's economic development needs.

Despite the advances made in this century, under the rule of the Kuomintang and the Chinese Communist Party, many parts of the country remain isolated or difficult to reach. People's lives have changed little in these decades, and village traditions continue.

The words of the Tang dynasty poet Bo Zhuyi, writing more than a thousand years ago, evoke these parts of contemporary China for us:

So far from the town, government affairs
    are few,
So deep in the hills, man's ways are simple.
Each family keeps to its village trade.
Grey-headed, they have never left the gates.

these natural resources are still pretty much intact. Over 140 kinds of useful minerals been found in all parts of the country and surveys have established that China is one of the leading countries in the world in deposits of iron, copper, tungsten, tin, aluminium, antimony, maganese, zinc, lead and mercury. The country also has large deposits of coal and oil. These reserves are vital to China's plans to modernise her agriculture and industry as well as to her overall policy of increasing productivity in all areas by means of more advanced technology, machinery and equipment.

Before World War II the most important industrial centres for light industry were Shanghai and Tianjin (Tientsin) and for heavy industry the province of Liaoning which is part of the area that used to be known as Manchuria. This area and the coastal provinces accounted for more than 90 percent of the cotton looms and 80 percent of the heavy industrial output. That has now changed and industrial development has taken place in various parts of China notably at Baotou in Inner Mongolia, Lanzhou in Gansu, Xi'an in Shanxi, Zhengzhou in Henan and in the environs of Beijing, as well as in the south in Guangzhou (Canton), Kunming in Yunnan and at Liuzhou in Guangsi. New industrial zones have been established in areas around Hong Kong and Macau.

China is now in the first phase of an economic revolution with targets set at completely modernising its agriculture, industry, national defence, science and technology by the end of this century. The current ten-year plan (1976-1985) calls for an annual increase of four to five percent in agricultural output and an annual increase of over 10 percent in industrial production. The key objectives of the plan are the development of heavy industry, with the metallurgical, fuel, power and machine building industries being specifically identified; a rapid increase in the production of iron and steel, coal, crude oil and electricity; and the development of more sophisticated industries such as petrochemicals and electronics.

Opposite, above: *Tranquil rural scenes of everyday life in Guangxi.*
Page 178: *The wild beauty of limestone crags.*
Page 179: *Rice ripening on the banks of the Grand Canal.*
Pages 180, 181: *A canal in the centre of Kunming. Situated on a plateau at 2,000 metres altitude, the city enjoys probably the most pleasant climate in China, similar to that of California, with the same mix of palm trees and stands of evergreens.*

XIAO LIUMANG

Xiao Liumang — literally, "the little vaga-bond" — is the way in which novelist Liu Xinwu refers to a juvenile delinquent whom he knew during his work as a schoolteacher in Beijing.

"Little Vagabond" was the son of a penniless woman without a husband who could barely earn enough to keep the two of them, let alone supervise his behaviour when away from home. He played hooky from school — and the other pupils were glad, because they were afraid he would beat them up or disturb the order of the classroom if he had to stay at his lessons.

The boy hung around with a street-gang who were interested in graduating from rocks and sticks as their weapons in fights with other gangs, by obtaining knives. They had heard of something called a "Tibetan knife" — and "Little Vagabond" boasted one day to other gang-members that he had one at home. "Why don't you bring it round tomorrow then?" they chorused.

"All right, I will!" he promised — then went off with some friends to worry about where they were to find such a knife.

"Let's go to Tibet and get one!" someone suggested, and all agreed. They went on a spree picking pockets in buses, and collected enough money — so they thought — for their tickets to Tibet. But at the railway station people told them you could not go to Tibet by train, as there was no railway.

The "Little Vagabond" had vaguely heard of Inner Mongolia — which, he knew, was an "autonomous region" like Tibet. What he didn't know was that they were 2,000 miles apart. So they went to the ticket counter and shouted and fussed until the clerk gave in and sold them tickets to Inner Mongolia — a day's train ride away.

On arrival at Huhhot, the capital of Inner Mongolia, they found the weather cold. Some local people took pity on them and lent them sheepskin coats. Then they went charging off downtown to find their knife. Of course, there were no Tibetan knives in Mongolia, so they settled instead for a razor-sharp Mongolian herdsman's knife, and caught the train back to Beijing.

At Beijing Railway station the weather was mild, so they dumped the valuable sheepskins by a lamp-standard, and wondered what to do next.

One of them could read just enough to make out the destination "Zoo" on a bus-sign. So they climbed aboard to go to the Zoo, picking a few pockets again on the way. When they got there, they bought a pile of expensive candy, and fed it to the bears.

Tiring of this, they stole a grip from an out-of-town visitor, and made off with it. Alerted, the Zoo police picked them up and gave them a dressing-down. But they were quite unconscious of having done anything wrong: they had no concept of right and wrong, and simply did as they pleased.

Author Liu blamed this state of affairs on the Cultural Revolution and the Red Guard turmoil, which he says encouraged young people to ignore their elders and do as they please.

The "Little Vagabond" was not ignorant or stupid, either. He had heard of Paris and the Champs Elysées, and planned to go there one day for a holiday. It was just that he had not learnt about society and discipline. You couldn't call him bad. But if he went on the way he was going, he would soon end up in a youth detention centre, and graduate from there to "labour-reform" camp and perhaps prison. His case is by no means unique.

CHEN YONGGUI

One of the notable casualties of the political infighting in China in the late 1970s was the national model peasant, Chen Yonggui, whose coarse, lined features and inseparable white head-towel made him the symbol of Mao's policies in agriculture.

In 1979 Chen was withdrawn from the national limelight he had enjoyed since the early 1960s, and the Dazhai Production Brigade which he had built up as a shining example to all China's peasants fell into obscurity and semi-disgrace.

Chen, who was born into a poor peasant family in 1915, in the harsh climatic conditions of the northwestern province of Shanxi, was a hired labourer from the age of eleven. Little is known about his youth, but when he was in his late forties he was named a model agricultural worker, and never looked back for the next 15 years.

The Dazhai concept was one of Mao's favourites — standing as it did for full socialisation of production, and arduous struggle to terrace barren mountain sides and grow grain on them, to build up a self-reliant, prosperous peasant economy. The peasants of Dazhai "voluntarily" gave up the private plots on which they had

previously grown some vegetables or tobacco or raised a pig for sale to the state butcheries. They lived in identical rows of little brick houses, spent much time on studying the works of Marx, Engels, Lenin, Stalin and Mao, and rigorously denied themselves anything but the barest diet required for good health and hard work. The gap in incomes among various families was levelled out as far as possible.

Soon people from all over China were flocking to Dazhai, which became a living museum as much as a production unit. In 1964, Chen was picked to represent Shanxi province at the Third National People's Congress in Beijing. When the Cultural Revolution burst on China in 1966, the symbol of Dazhai was an effective means of urging the peasants on to greater efforts in growing crops, while industry and education in many of the cities ground to a halt amidst increasingly violent factional battles.

Unlike most people who rose to positions of power in the 1950s and early 1960s, the turbanned Chen kept his job through the upheavals, and in 1970 was appointed leading administrator for Xiyang county, where Dazhai is located. In 1973, when the radical clique around Mao swept all before them at the Tenth

Congress of the Communist Party, he rose to the august rank of Politburo member, as a totem figure for the prevailing leftist policies in agriculture.

But the days of Chen's glory were numbered. When Mao died and his widow and supporters were swept aside by the veteran Party bureaucrats and army generals, the Dazhai experiment came in for close scrutiny on suspicion of being an elaborate fiction devised by the "Gang of Four" and their supporters. Over-reporting of crops and acceptance of aid from the State and the armed forces were alleged, rendering almost meaningless Dazhai's claim to have achieved high grain yields through nothing but its own efforts.

Chen and his model brigade were let down lightly, however — perhaps because Chaiman Hua had associated himself closely with the Dazhai experiment before Mao's death. But it was stated bluntly that other communes and villages should only learn from the reputed *spirit* of Dazhai — hard work and fair treatment for all — rather than trying to put its "progressive" measures into operation nation-wide. Chen and his fellow-villagers will now be able to haul wheelbarrows in peace and quiet without floods of inquisitive visitors.

The Minorities

Dr. Hugh Baker

With an area of nearly 9,583,000 square km China is considerably larger than the United States of America or Western Europe. In such a vast area there is of course an enormous variety of climate and physical geography, and these have an effect on the ways of life of the people living there.

By far the majority of China's population of 1,000 million are Han Chinese, that is people who consider themselves to be of fully Chinese descent. The name Han is taken from the title of the dynasty which ruled the country for over four hundred years between 206 BC and 220 AD, a period which saw great progress in China's civilisation. It is important to realise that this name is not a "racial" but rather a "cultural" term, because although it is true that the Han Chinese all subscribe to one common overall culture, it is not the case that they are all of one racial type or that they all speak the same language or that they observe a uniform set of customs — they are as varied as the country in which they live.

Probably much of the variety of type found amongst the Han is to be laid at the door of the minority peoples who have either influenced or been aborbed by the Chinese. Certainly it is not possible to understand China's historical development without reference to the non-Han.

The agricultual character of the Chinese was already formed by about 2500 BC when the rich loess lands of the Yellow River basin were thickly studded with farming settlements. A true civilisation with centralised political control, specialisation of occupation, urbanisation, writing and bronze technology had set in by the earliest historical Chinese dynasty, the Shang-Yin (1600-1050 BC approx.). It covered much of the central plain of China, the area of fertile soil which is now Henan, Hebei and Shandong provinces.

The Shang-Yin were eventually overcome by the Zhou, who were their neighbours to the West. The Zhou appear to have been of Turkic stock, probably pastoralists who learned from and then conquered the superior culture, dividing the land into a number of feudal dependencies. In course of time, these became virtually independent states, and one of them finally bested the others to found the short-lived Qin dynasty in 221 BC.

By now the standard of civilisation reached was markedly higher than that of any neighbouring people, and it became necessary to protect the wealth of China from covetous "barbarian" tribes, particularly the Mongols, the Tibetans and the Turkic peoples who lived to the north and west. The building of the Great Wall at this time did not just show the state boundary, it divided the civilised settled Chinese world from the primitive nomadic wilderness. The criterion for being Chinese became the living of the civilised life within the wall; it was not a matter of racial origin, for the Chinese were already of mixed Turkic and Mongoloid blood.

The threat posed by the northern barbarians was to remain right through history, colouring Chinese attitudes to national and cultural security. From time to time the threat was translated into action as marauding tribesmen found their way round the wall or through its gates. The Xiongnu, a confederation of slave-owning nomad tribes, harried the frontier throughout the Han dynasty, and when the Han collapsed in 220 AD large numbers of Xiongnu came into China on the side of one of the contenders for the throne. They remained for four hundred years.

From 220 AD to 580 AD barbarian tribesmen followed each other into the Chinese homeland in a steady stream. Xiongnu, Mongols, Toba, Xianbi, Tibetans — each group conquered, settled and then turned to a Chinese life-style. Chinese culture, it has been said, just like an ocean turned every river that ran into it salty.

The Chinese Sui dynasty which came to power in 581 AD was brought down by ruinous wars with invading Turkic peoples, and the glorious Tang dynasty which succeeded it came to power with Turkic help in 618. Three hundred years later it too fell to Turkic hordes.

The next Chinese dynasty, the Song, lasted from 960-1279, but it had to co-exist first with the (Mongol) Khitan rulers of the north and north-east, and then with the (Tungus) Juchen, who conquered the Khitan in 1125. In 1279 all China was overrun by the irresistible Kublai Khan, whose Mongol Yuan dynasty ruled until 1368. The last dynasty of Imperial China, the Qing, was founded in 1644 by Manchus from China's north-east frontiers, and lasted until 1911.

This constant contact with northern neighbours did not merely result in loss (and perhaps subsequent enrichment) of Chinese blood. It had a backwash effect as Han culture was carried home by returning conquerors and by captured Chinese taken back as slaves. And when the Chinese state was strong and prosperous it was sometimes led to conquer territory beyond the wall. But its expansionist attention was more often turned southward, for that way lay vast tracts of fertile land, while to the north neither climate nor terrain was suited to Chinese agriculture. And when the Chinese state was weak and vulnerable to attack from the north, it was only to the south and south-west that the Han could flee.

But this area was not empty of people. The Yangtze River region was the homeland of Tai people, much as the Yellow River was of the Chinese. The coastal areas and hill regions supported Austronesian tribes, while in the west and south-west were Tibetan (Tangut), Tibeto-Burmese and Austro-Asiatic tribes.

The Tai people were settled river-valley farmers of rice and were relatively advanced culturally. This meant that their lands were the most attractive to the Chinese, but it also meant that they were themselves ripe for take-over by Chinese culture, and the result was that once overrun they quickly became assimilated. Those who were unwilling to be absorbed were forced either further south-westwards into South-east Asia (notably Thailand and Vietnam) or into the higher less productive ground, or to areas where climate and disease proved unattractive to the Han.

The other southern and western peoples were mostly inhabitants of regions which were unsuitable for the Chinese, and they were in much less danger of colonisation or assimilation. Unlike the northern barbarians they were neither

numerous enough, nor developed enough, nor organised enough to be a major threat to the Chinese way of life.

Before the Qin dynasty the whole of south China was dominated by the Tai peoples, the Chinese having contacts with the area but no control over it. The Qin and after it the Han sent military expeditions to conquer the south, but climate and geography made the area hard to hold. Many Chinese fell victim to disease, those who survived were ill-supplied over the difficult land routes, and the distance from central control bred ideas of revolt and independence in their generals — the kingdom of Nan Yue, founded by one such general, flourished in Guangdong, Guangxi and Guizhou until 112 BC. For a thousand years the most successful form of colonisation in the south was the military settlement, in which a garrison was expected to be self-supporting, up to 80 percent of the men being assigned to agricultural duties when no actual fighting was to be done. The need for such settlements indicates the "spotty" and nominal nature of Han control — most of the territory was still in barbarian hands.

In the 4th century AD the invasion of the Wu Hu Tartars from the north caused the deaths of hundreds of thousands of Chinese, and an estimated 60 to 70 percent of the population fled to the south of the Yangtze River, where they soon merged with Tai rice farmers and turned that region into a permanent part of the Han cultural sphere. The Tang dynasty and the Song continued to expand southwards and westwards out of the Yangtze plain, using the old military settlement pattern, and with the collapse of the Song before Kublai Khan's armies there was again a massive movement of refugee Chinese who took up whatever suitable cultivable land there was in the southernmost provinces, previously only sparsely settled by Han culture.

The process of expansion south and west has never really come to an end. Chinese control over parts of Yunnan province, for instance, was only fully exerted after World War Two. In the 20th century there has been a large movement of Han Chinese into Yunnan into the southwest, into Tibet in the west, into Xinjiang in the north-west, into Inner Mongolia in the north, and into Manchuria in the north-east.

Throughout the entire expansion process from the Yellow River basin to the extremities of modern China, non-Han peoples living in geographical conditions suitable for traditional Chinese agriculture seem to have been absorbed without difficulty into the Han cultural sphere because their life-style was in any case predisposed in that direction. Remnants of non-Han origin may still be seen in variant customs, in unusual place names or localisms, and probably more than anywhere else in dialect differences, but all these are so heavily outweighed by the general subscription to Han culture that they cannot be said to have significance in marking off minority groups. More important, the people with these variant features would themselves deny any suggestion that they are not Chinese.

A case in point is that of the Hakka people. Hakka (Mandarin *Ke-Jia*) means "guest families", and the name appears to be justified in that the Hakka are widely scattered through south China without having a true homeland area. Research has shown that they probably originated in Henan province in north China. It has been said that their language has a few similarities to Tai, though these may be no more than linguistic borrowings. Hakka women never bound their feet, and appear to have had a greater degree of equality with their menfolk than did most Chinese women. Differences of dress, architecture and customs are quite marked, and physical differences from other Chinese have even been claimed by some observers. The Hakka are often settled on higher, less fertile land than the other Chinese people amongst whom they live and, although this is easily explained if it is assumed that they migrated to south China only after the better land had been taken up by earlier settlers, it has been

Of China's nearly one billion people, five per cent are distinct ethnic minorities, some with their own languages, customs and manner of dress.

The largest separate nationality groups are the Tibetans, the Mongols (preceding pages, girls riding bareback on the steppes of Inner Mongolia) and the Uygurs in northwestern Xinjiang. These three groups in particular developed their own complex civilisations complete with written languages and religions.

This old man (opposite) lives in Xi'an, a crossroads of China's east and west. Xi'an, once the nation's capital, is the major westerly city of China and attracts Uygur and Kazakh people from the Xinjiang region who come to the city for business, shopping or a holiday.

Above: *A young woman from Suzhou.*

While countries all over the world are grappling with "minority problems," China seems to have found a sophisticated formula for dealing with minorities, at least here (these pages) in Inner Mongolia.

The Mongolians get preferred entry to schools, employment in factories and admission to government positions, in a sort of quota system.

Under communist rule, Mongolians and other ethnic minorities are exempt from population control, and are encouraged to raise as many children as they wish.

The government has also assisted in developing a dictionary for the Mongol language and a Mongol-Han dictionary of terms.

Opposite: *A Mongolian schoolteacher, Mongol script on the blackboard behind him.*

This page: *A Mongolian herdsman.*

One of the most ethnically diverse areas in China is Yunnan province in the South. The most important ethnolinguistic group is the Tibeto-Burman ethnic family, which includes the Yi, Lahu and other peoples.

The Thai family is related to the people of Thailand and Cambodia (Kampuchea) and encompasses the Dai (opposite) of southern Yunnan who speak their own dialect of the Thai language and who maintain many of the traditions still found in some rural areas of Thailand. This page, clockwise from top left: Yao, Miao, Aini, and Yi minority peoples.

suggested that they have a *preference* for higher land because they are of hill-tribe, non-Han stock. Yet it is undeniable that the Hakka have a culture which is fully within the range of Han-type culture, that their language is basically of Chinese type, and that they unreservedly consider themselves to be Chinese. Whatever their origins may have been, they cannot now be counted as a minority people.

Similarly, the south China coast has a large boat-dwelling population known to the land-people as Tanka (Mandarin *Danjia*), which means "egg families." There is reason to suppose that the Tanka were originally related to the Yao and other Austronesian tribes, yet they now speak the same Chinese languages as the people from whose shores they work, are probably heavily interbred with them, and their dress, physical appearance, religious observances and other customs show no greater degree of difference from other Chinese than is consistent with their water-borne way of life. They resent any inference that they are not Chinese, and do not recognise the term Tanka at all, referring to themselves as *shui-shang-ren* or *shui-mian-ren*, both of which mean "water-folk". Again, they are not counted as a minority people.

Chinese culture can be seen to have a high tolerance level, and this is perhaps not surprising in a country so vast. Many of the existing variants of the Chinese language are mutually unintelligible; some areas traditionally practised a form of marriage where it was preferred for a man to be wed to his mother's brother's daughter, while other areas did not recognise the custom; the Buddhist deity Guan Yin was represented as a male in some parts of China, but a female in others; northern Chinese eat lamb, most southerners cannot abide it; and so on.

Yet despite this tolerance there are all over China non-Han peoples who have managed to maintain their separate cultural identities. Where this is the case it seems that the decisive factor has been the geographic one. Those who live in condi-

tions unsuited to Chinese-style agriculture have developed their own cultures in ways which are greatly at variance with Chinese civilisation, and that contrast has combined with the unattractiveness of their domains to keep the Han at bay. Quite simply, nomad pastoralists, slash-and-burn agriculturalists and settled farmers have not been eager to appreciate or welcome each other's cultural values. The minority peoples, then, are to be found in the hills, on the high plateaux, and in unrewarding steppe-lands and deserts. They range in size from isolated pockets of a few hundred to major groups over a million strong. Each is an island in the Chinese sea which the still rising tide of Han population has not covered.

Precise figures are hard to come by, but Chinese sources have for many years put the minority nationalities population at six percent of the nation's total. On this basis there would be some 60 million non-Han inhabitants of China in 1980 — a figure which is probably higher than the true one. Many of them live in remote border

Opposite: *A group of schoolchildren, with the regular features of the Han Chinese.*
Above: *A young girl dressed in fanciful costume.*

The Chinese say that the preferential treatment given to minorities is compensation for the extra hardships which they suffered before 1949. Not only were the minorities exploited along with the rest of the people, but they claim they were also discriminated against because of their minority status.

Life indeed has been hard. This fact is etched dramatically on old faces and old bodies. The smooth unblemished complexion of this Shanghai woman (this page, bottom right) will change in a few years because she now lives in Inner Mongolia as a ''resettled youth'' where she will be exposed to the harsh extremes of climate in that wind- and sand-swept land.
Opposite: in Sichuan.
This page, left: in Yang Shuo.
This page, top right: in Xi'an.

regions which support life only with difficulty, a picture made startlingly clear by the fact that this six percent of the Chinese population occupies well over 50 percent of the territory of China.

Fifty four different minority peoples are officially recognised by the Chinese government. Table A shows the major areas of settlement of each of the peoples:

National Minorities	Major Areas of Distribution
Mongolian	Inner Mongolia Autonomous Region, Lianoning Province, Jilin Province, Heilongjiang Province, Gansu Province, Xinjiang Uygur Autonomous Region, Qinghai Province, Hebei Province, Henan Province, Yunnan Province
Zhuang	Guangxi Zhuang Autonomous Region, Yunnan Province, Guangdong Province
Uygur	Xinjiang Uygur Autonomous Region
Miao	Guizhou Province, Hunan Province, Yunnan Province, Guangxi Zhuang Autonomous Region, Sichuan Province, Guangdong Province, Hubei Province
Hui	Ningxia Hui Autonomous Region, Gansu Province, Henan Province, Hebei Province, Qinghai Province, Shandong Province, Yunnan Province, Anhui Province, Xinjiang Uygur Autonomous Region, Liaoning Province
Tibetan	Tibet Autonomous Region, Qinghai Province, Sichuan Province, Gansu Province, Yunnan Province
Yi	Yunnan Province, Sichuan Province, Guizhou Province
Korea	Jilin Province, Heilongjiang Province, Liaoning Province
Manchu	Liaoning Province, Heilongjiang Province Jilin Province, Hebei Province, Beijing, Inner Mongolia Antonomous Region
Bouyei	Guizhou Province
Dong	Guizhou Province, Hunan Province, Guangxi Zhuang Autonomous Region

Much of life in China is conducted in the streets and hutongs of the towns. When someone decides to build a bird cage (opposite, left) *the neighbours all know; or when someone else buys a couple of ducks at the market, his friends can see that he's planning to cook a duck or two soon.*

Many of the elderly can pass their last years in comfort, relaxing with their friends in the afternoon sunshine and smoking a familiar pipe (this page, top); or taking a stroll by a river (this page, bottom) and perhaps bringing home a special treat for the family from a shop on the way. Others, who do not have family members to look after them or whose political backgrounds are not good, must continue to work until the end because the state does not provide institutional care for old people.

Yoo	Guangxi Zhang Autonomous Region, Hunan Province, Yunnan Province, Guangdong Province, Guizhou Province
Bai	Yunnan Province
Tujia	Hunan Province, Hubei Province
Hani	Yunnan Province
Kazakh	Xinjiang Uygur Autonomous Region, Gansu Province, Qinghai Province
Dai	Yunnan Province
Li	Guangdong Province
Lisu	Yannan Province
Va	Yunnan Province
She	Fujian Province, Zhejiang Province, Jiangxi Province, Guangdong Province, Anhui Province
Gaoshan	Taiwan Province
Lahu	Yunnan Province
Shui	Guizhou Province
Dongxiang	Gansu Province
Naxi	Yunnan Province
Jingpo	Yunnan Province
Khalkhas	Xinjiang Uygur Antonomous Region
Tu	Qinghai Province
Dour	Heilongjiang Province, Xinjiang Uygur Autonomous Region
Mulao	Guangxi Zhuang Autonomous Region, Guizhou Province
Qiang	Sichuan Province
Bulang	Yunnan Province
Salar	Qinghai Province, Gansu Province
Moonan	Guangxi Zhuang Autonomous Region
Gelao	Guizhou Province, Yunnan Province, Guangxi Zhuang Autonomous Region
Xibe	Xinjiang Uygur Autonomous Region, Liaoning Province, Jilin Province
Achang	Yunnan Province
Pumi	Yunnan Province
Tajik	Xinjiang Uygur Autonomous Region
Nu	Yunnan Province
Uzbek	Xinjiang Uygur Autonomous Region
Russian	Xinjiang Uygur Autonomous Region
Ewenki	Heilongjiang Province
Benglong	Yunnan Province
Baoan	Gansu Province
Yugur	Gansu Province
Jing	Guangdong Province
Tartar	Xinjiang Uygur Autonomous Region
Drung	Yunnan Province
Hezhe	Heilongjiang Province
Manba	Tibet Autonomous Region
Laba	Tibet Autonomous Region

Little is known about some of these groups, but an indication of the range of diversity is given by the following brief summaries which include most of the most numerous and a few of the smaller peoples.

Bai. The Bai are a Tibeto-Burmese people, and most of their population of 700,000 are found in the Dali Bai Autonomous Prefecture of Yunnan province. They are efficient valley-rice cultivators, but have probably been saved from Han swamping by the remoteness of their domain — close to the border with Burma and some 7000 feet above sea level. Traditionally they lived in stilt-houses near or over water. Bai women were considerably more free than were Han women, both in having high status in the family and in having sexual freedom before marriage; footbinding was never practised. Bethrothal was marked by the couple pouring water over each other. The Bai were fond of tattooing, a custom said to have been introduced only after the Han dynasty by immigrating Tai peoples. Bai religion recognised many gods (including ancestors and those of Buddhism and Taoism), and there was a belief in sorcery and in the turning of men into animals. An old Chinese name for them was "Gold-teeth barbarians" because of the practice of capping the two front teeth with gold. The Bai language has no written form.

Ewenki (Evenki). The Ewenki are a Tungus people numbering about 10,000, most of them living in Heilongjiang province. They were (and still in modified form are) nomadic herdsmen, moving with their flocks of sheep or herds or reindeer through the grasslands and forests. They lived (and still do) in tents of wooden poles covered with reed mats or skins. Most Ewenki were also huntsmen, obtaining furs and antlers for the Russian and Chinese markets, and supplementing their diet of

Many traditional customs have been changed because of the needs of modern society. Elaborate and expensive funerals, though sometimes seen in the rural areas, are officially discouraged. Mourning for one's dead is usually marked by wearing a black armband on one's sleeve or fastening the portrait of the dead person on one's bicycle (opposite).
Above: A fan has not outlived its usefulness

Life in China does not move at a fast pace.
There is no feeling of haste even in the largest
cities. All work stops during the almost standard
two-hour lunch break, when the major activity
is sleeping after quickly eating a simple meal.
Opposite: *A pipe smoker in Yangshuo*
Centre: *A Hefei knife grinder*
This page, top: *An old man relaxes near the
great wall.*
This page, bottom: *A young railway worker.*

domestic meats and milk. The prime religious belief was in nature spirits and demons, and female *shamans* doubled as priests and doctors, seeking the advice of spirits in curing sickness.

Hui (Hui-hui, Moslems). There have been Moslems in China from the 7th century AD. The first major group consisted of 4000 Arab mercenaries who fought in government armies during the Tang dynasty. They were allowed to settle in China and keep their faith. The Yuan dynasty with its widespread Mongol empire connections saw the introduction of many more, and Moslem communities sprang up all over the country. Inter-marriage has made the Hui indistinguishable physically from the Han, but in matters of diet and custom they have remained apart. Pork, the most important Chinese meat, they will not touch, and they observe the Ramadan fast. A few words of Arabic are sometimes used in greetings and ritual matters, but very few Chinese. Circumcision is not universally practised, nor are daily prayers the norm. Moslem women are not in *purdah* and wear the same dress as Han women. There are mosques in many Chinese cities, and most large cities have Hui restaurants where Moslems may eat without fear of breaking dietary prohibitions.

It is clearly not on religious grounds alone that the Moslems have come to be considered a special group, for Chinese Buddhists are not counted as a minority people, and nor are Chinese Christians. The distinction probably lies in their historial identification as self-contained communities based on the mosques. This has marked them off from other Chinese who only practised congregational religion in the form of ancester worship, and who otherwise did not have the potential for group action based on religion. Ancestor worship was tied into Confucian state orthodoxy, but the state could not be happy with organised religion which recognised a supreme authority beyond itself. The Moslems tended to stick together more as they grew more numerous, and they preferred where possible not to inter-marry with other Chinese. This clannishness was viewed with suspicion by the state, persecution resulted, and the Moslems in turn rose in revolt at times.

When the Chinese Republic was set up in 1912, the new national flag consisted of

Above: *Relaxing in a Yangshuo park.*
Right: *One more satisfied customer for this* **sugar cane seller in Guangzhou.**
Opposite: *A waddle of ducks, some of which may soon grace a lucky diner's table as the famous dish Beijing Duck.*

Life is open to public view. Everyone can see who is taking what goods to market by bicycle (opposite, top left, dogs) *or shoulder pole* (opposite, rattan baskets and trays); *who is eating* (opposite, top centre); *where a heavily-laden cart of straw* (opposite, top right) *is headed; and what romances are in bloom* (above).

Peasants come in from the countryside to sell their produce at free markets in the cities. Many villages have organised themselves so that the most productive farm workers don't have to spend the time to go into the cities, and have arranged to sell their vegetables, eggs and meats through middlemen.

Generally, people find that the produce in the free markets is fresher than in the state-run stores so they are willing to pay the higher prices that the peasants charge.

five horizontal stripes — yellow for the Han, red for the Manchus, blue for the Mongols, black for the Tibetans, and white for the Moslems. This inclusion in a set of racial groups provided the pattern for posterity, and with Moslems securely classified as a minority people Islam has been able to exist where other religions have been branded as evil superstitions.

The census of 1953 gave the Hui population as nearly 3,600,000 and figures issued in 1979 showed 4,480,000. If these numbers are correct (their accuracy is very difficult to assess), then the rate of growth

Above: *A young official who rose to a prominent position in Shanghai during the upheaval of the Cultural Revolution.*
Opposite: *Relaxing in the winter sun in some rare free time.*

210

of the Hui population has lagged some way behind that of the Han Chinese. It seems likely that a proportion of Hui youth has been affected by the atheist ambience, has deserted its religion, and has been swallowed up in the mass of the population from which in essence only its religion distinguished it. This marginal nature of the Moslems' minority status makes the group particularly vulnerable to absorption in the wider community, and the future may well see a decline in numbers. (It is worth comparing them with a similar though smaller group, the Chinese Jews' who, after surviving for at least eight hundred years, sold their last synagogue early in the 20th century. They had been merging with their surroundings long before that, and were Jews in name only by the 1930's, certainly not candidates for minority status.) Meanwhile, Islam is certainly not dead, and the first Chinese pilgrims for nearly two decades went to Mecca in 1979: Four men from Ningxia Hui Autonomous Region made the journey in February, and another small party went in November.

Koreans. Over a million Korean people live in the three north-eastern provinces of Liaoning, Jilin and Heilongjiang, most of them in the Yanbian Korean Autonomous Prefecture. The Koreans began to move into the area about three hundred years ago, perhaps to fill the vacuum left by the Manchu descent on China, and the migration continued into the 20th century. They are mostly farmers, and have tended to remain apart from other peoples in the area, speaking and writing standard Korean. Their religion leaned heavily towards placating the evil spirits which were thought to swarm everywhere. They also practised ancestor worship and Buddhism. Confucianism was a great influence on Korea, and the Koreans in China brought with them a sense of family and of respect for age which was at least as strong as that of the Chinese themselves.

Manchus. To the north-east of China, beyond the Great Wall, lay the area known to the West as Manchuria and to the Chinese simply as "the Northeast." For many centuries it belonged to the peripheral Chinese world, being partly settled by Chinese, partly grazed by Mongol pastoralists, and partly the domain of rather primitive hunting and fishing Tungus peoples. There had been much intermarriage between the groups and there was a general acceptance of the superiority of the Chinese culture and state to the south. In the early 17th century Nurhachi, a Tungus tribal chieftain, began to weld the various peoples into a powerful military alliance which quickly threw off such control as the failing Chinese Ming dynasty had and threatened China itself. By 1644 this Manchu alliance had tricked and fought its way to the throne of China, and the dynasty lasted until China became a republic in 1912.

The Manchus (the name itself seems to date only from about 1635) were a mixture of peoples and included urban merchants trading in furs, pearls and ginseng, agriculturalists, nomadic herdsmen, hunters and fishermen. There was a common Manchu language (belonging to the Ural-Altaic group) and a script which had been borrowed from Mongol and then adapted. Once ensconced in China the Manchu rulers made efforts to further their own culture and to avoid the fate of absorption which had befallen previous conquerors. It was in vain. No native Manchu literature developed, the Manchu language was little spoken after the mid-18th century, the Manchus in China were physically similar to the Han and were quickly sinicized, and the Manchu homeland, now added to Chinese territory, become swamped with Chinese settlers.

The 1953 census reported a total of nearly two and a half million Manchus, but there is considerable doubt about this figure. One recent Western estimate puts the number as low as 200,000 living in pockets in Heilongjiang province. It is difficult to discover what now distinguished the Manchus since their language, culture, dress and way of life have all been assimilated into the Han. Probably this

The physical characteristics of many of China's designated minority peoples are indistinguishable from those of the Han Chinese. They differ only in custom and traditions. For instance, the Hui people, who are of Moslem background, continue certain dietary customs such as not eating pork, but otherwise are not easily identifiable.
Opposite: *In Beijing.*
Centre: *A tea-picker in Hangzhou.*
This page top and bottom: *Hilltribe women of Yangshuo*

minority is defined historically rather than by any contemporary features.

Miao. The two and a half million Miao are divided into many different tribes, some of which are very small, and some of their languages are mutually unintelligible. They appear to be of Austronesian origin, but have been greatly mixed with other peoples. They live in high land, mainly in Guizhou, Hunan, Yunnan, Guanxi and Sichuan provinces, and practise slash-and-burn agriculture, producing corn, millet, beans and a little rice. They keep some pigs, cattle and dogs, all of which are used for food. In less remote areas much of their land has traditionally been rented from the Chinese or the Yi. Agriculture was supplemented by hunting and gathering. The groups lived in villages, usually in stilt-houses, and the family was the work unit. They practised ancestor worship and shamanism. They have no written language.

Mongols. The Mongols have a population of about one and a half million, most of them living in Inner Mongolia. They were essentially a nomadic people, living off their flocks of sheep and goats and herds of cattle, horses and camels. These provided milk, meat and skins. Felt or skin-covered tents were the normal form of housing, and hunting was both a form of recreation and a means of varying diet. The extended family was the main unit of social organisation, and all animals were owned in common by the family, but there was a recognition also of tribal authority. Buddhism was the major religious influence, but like other northern people the Mongols also practised shamanism. The Mongol language is written in a script derived from Aramaic through Uygur.

Tibetans. About 90 percent of the nearly two million Tibetans live in Tibet itself, but there are scattered groups in other provinces too. There are many different types of life-style practised, from settled agriculture to nomadic pastoralist. Principal crops are wheat, barley, peas and potatoes, and domestic animals include sheep, horses, yaks, donkeys and cattle.

Designated minority areas can be as large as provinces (these are called autonomous regions, like Tibet, Xinjiang and Guangxi) or as small as one commune in size. These so-called autonomous regions and prefectures (counties) are found in all parts of the country, from the Koreans in the North to the Dai in areas bordering Vietnam, Burma and Laos.

Many of China's resettled youth used to be sent to these areas to give a hand in their rural and industrial development. They often joined the contingents from the army and experienced administrators from the major cities who were already there.

Opposite: *Mongolians are very adept at handling horses, a tradition developed by hundreds of years of nomadic life on the steppes of a land now governed by three nations, China, Outer Mongolia and the U.S.S.R.*

Dairy products are much used. Women had a high position in Tibetan society, and monogamous, plural wife and plural husband forms of marriage were all quite common. Lamaistic Buddhism was the greatest religious influence, and many men entered monasteries for at least some of their life. At any one time up to one third of the male population were in monasteries, and until 1959 the Dalai Lama was both the secular and the religious head of the Tibetans, giving the church great power.

Uygurs. The Uygurs are a Turkic people living mostly in the Uygur Autonomous Region of Xinjiang province. They number about three and a half million. A thousand years ago they were nomadic, but they became settled agriculturalists, probably under Chinese influence. Wheat and corn are grown, and sheep-farming is also common. The family was the main unit of social organisation, with a few families dominating as major landowners, but unlike the Chinese the Uygurs did not combine their families into extended families or clans. Islam was their recognised religion, but there existed also a strong belief in evil spirits and sorcery. Their language is written in a form of Arabic script.

Yi. The Tibeto-Burman Yi are known by many other names, including Lolo, Losu and Nosu. They number about three and a half million, with a major concentration living in Liangshan in Yunnan province. The Black Lolo were an aristocratic group owning large numbers of slaves, mostly Niao or captured Han. Between these two groups came the White Lolo, freed slaves in a serf relationship with their Black lords for whom they worked and fought. Serfs and slaves could intermarry, but the Black Lolo were forbidden to marry outside their class on pain of death. The Yi lived in a low wooden houses surrounded by bamboo stockades. Agriculture was somewhat primitive, and the poorer quality high land was farmed on the slash-and-burn principle, being abandoned as soon as the soil was worked out. Rice, buckwheat and corn were grown, and they raised sheep,

cattle and horses where the land and climate permitted. The Yi were divided into clans, and clan unity was strong, but leadership was not institutionalised, devolving upon whoever was felt to be most suitable. Women had complete sexual freedom from puberty through marriage until the birth of their first child, after which they were expected to be faithful to their husbands. Religion was strongly influenced by a belief in good and evil spirits which were controlled by *shamans*. Sorcery was practised. The Yi have a non-phonetic writing system distinct from Chinese.

Zhuang. The Zhuang are the largest of China's minorities with a population of 12 million, more than 90 percent of whom live in the Guangxi Zhuang Autonomous Region in south China. They are a Tai people who have been in the area for at least 2000 years practising agriculture, principally wet-rice cultivation, and keeping some cattle and water-buffalo. Other products are bananas, mushrooms, tung oil, bamboo and timber. The Zhuang lived in stilt-houses and were famous for their weaving of brocade, painting, song and dance. They practised tattooing. They had a clan system and worshipped their ancestors. They resembled the Han too in their belief in many different gods and spirits. Zhuang women were free to choose their own husbands, though the bride traditionally stayed with her parents until the birth of her first child cemented her marriage. Their language has no written form, and some Zhuang have for many decades spoken Cantonese, written Chinese and preferred to consider themselves as Han people.

In 1951, shortly after the founding of the People's Republic, Institutes of National Minorities were set up in Beijing and other cities. They were to train students from the minorities to be administrators, doctor, teachers and technicians, and they were also to act as centres of research into the history, social organisation and languages of the various minorities.

Above: *A Mongolian girl pouring millet tea from a kettle.*
Opposite: *A Lahu minority girl from Yunnan province.*

The Constitution of the People's Republic of China adopted at the first National People's Congress in 1954 stated that:

The People's Republic of China is a single multi-national state.
All the nationalities are equal. Discrimination against, or oppression of, any nationality, and acts which undermine the unity of the nationalities are prohibited.
All the nationalities have freedom to use and foster the growth of their spoken and written languages, and to preserve or reform their own customs or ways.
Regional autonomy applies in areas where people of national minorities live in compact communities. National autonomous areas are inalienable parts of the People's Republic of China.

The same Congress set up a Nationalities Committee to deal with minority problems, and some five-sixths of the committee members were themselves from minority peoples.

The policies which were implemented in the early days of the People's Republic remain today: to give regional autonomy to those areas where minorities predominate; to train cadres from the minorities so that it is unnecessary to have Han Chinese administering in minority fields; to protect the freedom of the minorities to use and develop their own spoken and written languages; to respect the customs and ways of life of the minorities; and to give aid to the minority areas in their economic and cultural development.

In pursuance of these policies over a hundred autonomous areas have been set up. There are five Autonomous Regions, which are equivalent to full provinces, 29 Autonomous Prefectures, and 69 Autonomous Counties or Banners. Most of these have been in existence since the late 1950's. They qualify for extra development funding from the state, and are allowed to keep back a small proportion of state taxes to be spent on local projects.

All 54 minority peoples (even the Hezhes of Heilongjiang, who number less than 1000) are represented by deputies at the National People's Congresses, which has the effect of giving over-representation to the non-Han, the 6 percent minority peoples sending nearly 11 percent of the deputies. Clearly the Chinese government does not ignore the minorities — never before has there been such a thorough-going and systematic attempt to bring all the peoples of China into the government system or to treat them as equals.

Previous attempts at handling minorities involved either crushing or absorption or a kind of state vassalage, where the peoples on China's borders sent tribute to the Emperor as acknowledgement of his supremacy. The border peoples (Tibetans, Mongolians, Manchus, Uygur, etc.) are no longer vassals, their territories are "inalienable parts of the People's Republic

Above: A woman of Penglung minority. The Penglung people are not designated as an official minority.
Opposite: The Mongolians have very strong faces, with high cheekbones and straight noses.

of China." There has been no evidence of extermination of minorities. The International Commission of Jurists, in its report on Tibet in 1960, decided that there was a *prima facie* case of genocide against China, but the Chinese refute this and recent Chinese figures insist that the population of Tibetans in Tibet (the Xizang Autonomous Region) has risen from 1,190,000 in 1959 to 1,630,000 in 1979. Birth control policies have been applied less strictly to the minorities than to the Han, which does not indicate a desire to exterminate them.

Absorption of minorities (swamping by Han people), however, is still going on as an answer to problems which might be caused by minority peoples. In particular this applies to those border regions which are politically sensitive. There have been reports that there are now more Han in Tibet than there are Tibetans, and even if these are exaggerated, there is no doubt that a policy of organised population transfer has planted major colonies of Han Chinese in areas previously inhabited more or less exclusively by minorities. Zinjiang, Manchuria Tibet and Inner Mongolia have all seen heavy immigration from China proper — Zinjiang has now probably less than 60 percent minorities population, Manchuria and Inner Mongolia only about 10%, and Ningxia Hui Autonomous Region about 30 percent. In the context of these population movements the increase in numbers of a minority people may be insignificant. The 1.19 million Tibetans of 1959 represented over 90 percent of the population of Tibet, but the 1.63 million of 1979 was almost certainly nowhere near 90 percent of Tibet's total.

On the one hand minorities are given "autonomy," but on the other they are diluted with Han settlers: How can these policies be reconciled? Or is the autonomy merely a cynical euphemism? The answers lie in the ultimate aims of the Chinese leadership. Those aims are the achievement of a classless Communist state. Minority versus majority is considered to be a matter of class, and both minorities

and majorities therefore have to be eliminated if Communism is to be attained. Han and non-Han alike must in this sense give way to Communist Man.

Obviously there are existing inequalities which have to be rectified, and many minority peoples, being illiterate and economically disadvantaged, have further to travel on the road of progress than the more civilised Han. To force them to travel it at the same pace as the Han would be difficult and would provoke or revive fear and hatred of Han domination. The creation of autonomous regions and of special minority status, then, allows a certain leeway for minorities to progress under their own leaders at a speed suited to their more primitive state. But progress they must, and that progress must be towards the same aim as Han progress: their autonomy is strictly limited.

Some Han Chinese have been guilty of "great Han Chauvinism" in their attitudes to the minorities, but there seems no reason to doubt the genuineness of the government in its declared belief that "all the nationalities are equal." Nor is there any doubt about the sincerity of the policy giving the nationalities freedom "to use and foster the growth of their spoken and written languages." New scripts for Miao,

Bouyei and Li, and improved scripts for the Dai and Yi languages were devised within the first decade of Communist rule.

But the minorities do not have freedom to "preserve or reform their own customs or ways" except within the strict limits set by the socialist aims which have been laid down for all Chinese. They may preserve only those of their customs which do not get in the way of progress towards Communism. Language, dress, hair-style, dance, diet and architecture are among the outward trappings of cultural difference which may remain to give an illusion of separate identity. But serfdom in Tibet, landlordism among the Zhuang, slavery among the Yi — these like the power of the Family Head among the Han have had to go. Religious practices too have necessarily been reduced or done away with — *shamans* and priests are as rare among the minorities as among the Han.

The preservation of national minority identities is something to which China's policies are sincerely dedicated, but the minority peoples are not reserves of traditional custom and ways of life any more than the Han Chinese are preservers of their traditional life-style. The separate identities of China's peoples are becoming more and more superficial.

Occasionally one sees a Hui minority person with distinct western features (opposite) *though most, like this old man* (above left), *do not differ from the Han people* above, right *they live amongst. Islam may have arrived with Arabs who were brought to China during the Tang dynasty, and then gained a stronghold during the Yuan dynasty. The Huis generally observe some Islamic food customs.*

Simple pleasures bring a smile to one's day: having one's picture taken by a foreign visitor (this page, top left); *hitching a ride on the back of daddy's bicycle* (this page, top right); *learning that one is studying well in school* (this page, bottom); *and strolling confidently with one's parents on a city street, knowing that any call of nature can be answered by quickly squatting on the sidewalk and letting one's specially designed split pants take care of the rest* (opposite).

Above: *A Dai woman takes out her finery for special holidays celebrated only by those of her nationality. In this instance, it's the annual Water Splashing Festival, once a spring fertility rite and now an occasion for the entire village. Her belt is made of silver, and her teeth are filled with gold.*
Opposite: *Early morning relaxation in Beijing's imperial garden.*

CHEN JINGRUN

China's most brilliant mathematician of the younger generation is Chen Jingrun, who was born into the family of an impoverished mailman in the southeastern province of Fujian (Fukien) in 1933. He grew up to the sight and sound of atrocities committed by the invading Japanese armies. He was weak and sickly, and even at primary school he was intimidated and bullied by his classmates. He sought refuge in algebraic equations gleaned from the maths teacher, and whatever books he could lay hands on.

When he was a teenager, a teacher explained to Chen's class about the "Goldbach Conjecture" — an 18th century problem which sought to prove that all large numbers were the sum of only two prime numbers. He laughed at the class's boyish attempts to prove the theorem.

Chen eventually impressed his teachers enough to be sent to the University of Xiamen (Amoy) at the age of seventeen. He was given a teaching job in a Beijing secondary school on graduation, but failed to control his pupils, and gave himself an ulcer on top of his existing problem of tuberculosis. Luckily, an eminent scholar had him transferred to a research post at Xiamen University, and at age 23 he went back to the Institute of Mathematics in Beijing. He took a full ten years to write his most famous treatise on the Goldbach Conjecture — having taught himself to read seven foreign languages in order to explore all the relevant mathematical literature.

Only a few months later, the Cultural Revolution engulfed China, and Chen was denounced by the Red Guards as a "bourgeois" and a "parasite." He managed to escape extreme persecution, and ensconced himself in the library reading foreign mathematics journals. He worked persistently on a monograph — with the deceptively simple theme of (1 + 2) — actually an acute problem of logical method. His monograph was published in Europe and acclaimed.

Chen's case is of particular interest because it shows, on the one hand, how a few brilliant scientists and intellectuals were able to hide themselves away from the lunatic fanaticism of the Cultural Revolution; and on the other hand, because his life was made so hard and lonely by the shifting winds of politics that his talent expended itself on a single monograph, and he never did any serious teaching. On the threshold of middle-age, his health was broken, and hardly anything has been heard of him since his biography was written up in the English-language journal *Chinese Literature*.

Name-lists for the Fifth National People's Congress held in 1979 named him as a deputy, and he was confirmed as a research fellow of the Institute of Mathematics. There is no evidence that he has ever been abroad, though he is believed to have met some foreign mathematicians visiting China. The science-and-technology orientation of the post-Mao leadership has perhaps come too late for him. But to other Chinese scientists he remains a symbol of intellectual integrity and persistence.

The Great Cities

Daniel P. Reid

Modern China is a land of contrasts, a land where jarring juxtapositions of old and new confront the visitor wherever he goes. Nowhere is this contrast more evident than in the cities of China. Scanning the sky-line of any Chinese city, you'll notice the exquisite, picture-book outlines of ancient temple roofs, city gates, and graceful pagodas etched against the sky. And inevitably you'll also see the blunt, tubular forms of filthy factory chimneys jutting up above these delicate sky-lines, belching forth clouds of noxious fumes. Sleek black "Red Flag" limousines bearing important "foreign guests" or ranking party cadres plough through thick traffic or bicycles, rickshaws, human-drawn carts of all sizes and descriptions, and a sea of cotton-clad pedestrians. Your spacious, comfortably appointed hotel room — designed and built in the now-extinct grand imperial style of the '20s and '30s — may boast a brand-new Japanese colour TV and mini-refrigerator. But there is usually nothing but static to view on the television, and the refrigerators are usually bare.

Perhaps the most glaring contrast of all is the appearance of the world's boldest new social experiment taking place amidst the ancient settings of the world's oldest civilization. Peasants wander wide-eyed through the fabulous halls and palaces of the Forbidden City in Beijing, where once only the Son of Heaven and his entourage of eunuchs and concubines were permitted to set foot. At Hangzhou's (Hangchow's) West Lake, formerly the haunt of poets, scholars, and officials in search of pleasure, you now see PLA troops on manoeuvre next to throngs of factory workers strolling leisurely along the garden paths. Many old temples have been converted to primary schools, where portraits of Chairman Mao and Chairman Hua have replaced the old icons, and the grand old mansions of the mandarins are now hospitals and sanatoria for ailing labourers. The old social structures and social stereotypes of imperial China have vanished since the revolution, but their great achievements in art and architecture are everywhere in evidence. Even more ironic is the fact that the intrinsically courteous, good-humoured, easy-going, earthy, and optimistic character for which the Chinese people have been known throughout their long history remains intact in modern socialist China.

The cities of China generally appear run-down and worn-out to Western eyes. The dominant colour is dull grey, there are no modern buildings, no chrome-and-glass storefronts, little colour or variety in either the clothing or houses of the people. But by any standards in the world Chinese cities are faultlessly clean and orderly, and this urban cleanliness is the first major impression to strike the new visitor to China. It is virtually impossible to find a cigarette butt or a fallen leaf on any Chinese street or alley, though everyone smokes and most streets are tree-lined. From dawn to dusk every day, teams of street sweepers, armed with sturdy brooms of bamboo and straw, sweep the streets of China spotlessly clean. They even sweep up and collect the dust! Miscellaneous items around houses and work sites are always neatly stacked, and garbage is never left lying around for long. Flies and mosquitoes, once the bane of Chinese cities, are few and far between today. All over Asia people have the habit of coughing up and spitting out phlegm, but only in China are spittoons provided for this purpose in every office, hotel, restaurant, and other public place, as well as along the sidewalks. The city dwellers of modern China are highly conscious of public hygiene, and in this respect Chinese cities put New York, London, and Paris, not to mention other Asian cities, to shame.

After their cleanliness and orderliness, the most singular trait of Chinese cities is the slow, relaxed pace of life. Absent is the frenzy and compulsive rush so prevalent in Hong Kong, Singapore, Taipei, and Tokyo, as well as in Western cities. The population of China is so great that many jobs are deliberately over-staffed in order to provide sufficient employment for everyone. Most factories in the big urban areas run round the clock in three eight-hour shifts. Since the shifts are staggered, there are no morning and evening rush-hours, and at any time of day or night most of the people in the streets are at leisure, not on their way to or from work. More significantly, in a society where public co-operation is placed high above personal competition, where the basics of food, health, clothing, and shelter are guaranteed to all but extra individual earnings are strictly limited, and where money is not the determining social factor, it makes no sense to drive oneself to distress and disease on the job, as people so commonly do in the West. Modern China, as much as any other developing nation, is a work-a-day world, but the pace of work is slower and the style of life far more relaxed than in any Western or modern Asian country.

By comparison to the West, modern technology is glaringly absent in the cities of China, being reserved exclusively for use in vital areas of the economy. Wherever possible, man power is used and motor power saved. The only motor vehicles you see on the streets are public buses, antiquated trucks delivering goods and workers to and from factories or communes, and hired sedans whisking "foreign guests" about town. There are no privately owned automobiles in China. The primary forms of transportation are bicycle and foot. The overwhelming majority of goods, especially produce from surrounding rural areas, are transported around town in dilapidated two-wheeled carts of ancient design, to which men and women are harnessed.

In all the cities of China and in all areas of the economy, man power is far cheaper and in far greater evidence than motor or electric power. This feature of urban China contrasts directly with conditions in the mechanised West, where the cost of having anything done by man, from laundry to haircuts, has become almost prohibitive. Asked why a jackhammer wasn't brought in to break the concrete on a road where half a dozen men were laboriously chipping away with hand-picks, a guide in Beijing gave a two-fold explanation: "Then there would be no work for five of those six men to earn their food. And besides, such machines are expensive in China and are only used for special jobs." The China Travel Service guides, well trained and fluent in the language of the visitor, are available for only two yuan (US$1.20) per hour, while taxi rentals cost five or six times that amount. In the West, trained linguists demand at least ten times the fee of their Chinese counterparts, while motor power remains relatively cheap. Similarly, a large bag of dirty clothes may be sent out for hand laundering and pressing in your hotel and returned the same day for less than the price of a phone call between Beijing and Shanghai. The limited stocks of motors and machines available in China are generally quite old and out-dated by Western standards; yet the Chinese give them the utmost loving care and keep them in top working order, to be used only when man power is impractical or impossible. China's greatest energy resource remains her vast population.

Despite this apparent paucity of technology, the inexorable march of industrial progress is everywhere to be seen in and around the cities of China today. Since the fall of the Gang of Four, industrialisation has become the top priority on the Chinese agenda. Every tour organised by China Travel Service includes numerous visits to factories, which more often than not operate with machinery pre-dating World War II. Yet these factories are the pride of modern China. The Chinese are often surprised and puzzled when foreign visitors express the greatest delight at the sight of a water buffalo or ancient hand drawn well, but ignore a new tractor in the fields or a mechanised irrigation project. Or when tourists insist on stopping the bus to watch free-market blacksmiths working with hammer and anvil, then groan with disappointment at the prospect of visiting yet another tool factory. The urban Chinese are very self-conscious about their country's technological backwardness and are just beginning to glimpse the dark side of large-scale, haphazard industrialisation.

The Chinese have rid their cities of flies, mosquitoes, and dirt only to find new, more ominous forms of pestilence creeping up on them — smog and general environ-

mental pollution from their factories. The problem is just beginning, but already some city dwellers are clearly unhappy about it. A common request put to visitors from the West these days is, "Tell us about pollution." A young factory worker relaxing with his colleagues in a temple tea-house in Suzhou made his complaint against industrial pollution with a characteristically Chinese culinary twist. He said, "The factories dump oil and wastes into the rivers, which ruins the taste of our river fish." River fish are one of Suzhou's specialties. Now as ever, food is the most important pursuit of the Chinese, all of whom are to some extent gourmets, and anything which ruins the taste and quality of their favourite delicacies is a serious threat indeed.

Smog is rapidly becoming a common denominator in all of China's cities and is already a serious problem in the big industrial centres such as Tianjin, Shanghai, Wuhan, and Guangzhou. On bad days, many Chinese can be seen wearing gauze masks to protect their lungs. There are three major factors which make smog an increasingly serious hazard in Chinese cities. First, most big factories run 24 hours a day, spewing foul fumes into the atmosphere round the clock. Second, most of China's industrial plants are very old and the machinery is far from fuel-efficient. Finally, with the current drive for modernisation in full swing, factory managers are unable and unwilling to install costly pollution-control devices which slow down production and increase costs. This is a great pity, for while China has managed to preserve its purity and integrity from "decadent" Western influences of all types, it now risks absorbing one of the Wests's most salient evils — the systematic pollution of air, water, and land by industrial wastes and chemicals.

Historically, China has been a highly decentralised, provincial country, where local dialects, customs, and manners flourished in the far-flung provinces. Today, Chinese cities still reflect this provincial flavour, identifying more closely with the local province than with the nation at large. Cities, especially provincial capitals, distill the essence of their province's culture and traditions and offer the cream of the crop of the provinces's produce for sale. As in the past, provincial pride is still very strong in China, and one of the true joys of travelling to the widespread cities of China is discovering the local colour unique to each city. Within a few hours of arriving in a new city, you'll no doubt be told what famous general or poet was born there, how the city excelled through history, what foods, wines, and

232

other products it's famous for and what the character of the inhabitants is. Despite the prevalence of Mandarin in official discourse, residents speak freely amongst themselves in the local dialect of the city. In each city you'll also find a few local beers as well as a wide array of local wines, cigarettes, and other items produced exclusively in that province. Most of them are quite good. Most charming of all, each city has its own individual personality, which is reflected both in the different architecture and scenery as well as the unique provincial character of its inhabitants. Contrary to common misconceptions, China is not a monolithic entity where uniformity is strictly enforced: national conformity is only required in politics. Beyond the political realm, China is a collection of at least a dozen different geographic, ethnic, culinary, and cultural traditions, each of which proudly maintains its identity and unique flavour within the nation at large. These regional differences are condensed and well reflected in the cities.

If you have epicurean tastes and like Chinese food, you will not be disappointed with the food served in the best restaurants of China. With the sole exception of Guilin, which for some unexplained reason serves up some of the worst food in China, Chinese cities consistently serve some of the best food in the world. With the "Gang of Four" out of the way and tourism on boom, the great chefs of China have once again appeared on the scene, and the culinary arts have regained their traditional place of respect. Most of the chefs currently supervising China's kitchens were trained in the traditional ways well before Liberation, and their cooking reflects it. Unlike Singapore, Hong Kong, and Taïpei, where Chinese food is good but overdone with spices and flavouring agents to account for more jaded palates, the great traditional dishes served in China's cities still maintain their original identities and pristine flavours. They are prepared without short cuts according to the ancient methods and are presented to

please the eye as well as the palate. The old chefs are now training young cooks in the old ways, and today competition for jobs in the culinary field is fierce.

Restaurants in Chinese cities always have a special "VIP Room" for use by foreign travellers as well as important Chinese guests. Here, lavish banquets are prepared with great pride, featuring the local and seasonal specialities, as well as the great wines and liquors, for which the city has always been famous. Prices are very reasonable by world standards. Since kitchens in China do not have freezers, everything served is fresh that day. Major banquets (6-12 persons) can be organised by calling the restaurant at least half a day in advance. It is advisable to simply state the number of people in the party and the price per person you are willing to pay; let the chef choose the menu. You can also go in alone or with a few friends and order excellent meals à la carte. The foreign traveller in China will quickly discover that eating and drinking is the most gratifying, consistently good, and characteristically Chinese form of entertainment available in urban China today.

The Chinese people are early birds — early to bed and early to rise. Along the Bund in Shanghai, in the Cultural Park in Guangzhou, on the banks of West Lake in Hangzhou, in the parks and along the river banks of every Chinese city, people young and old gather before dawn to practice *Tai Qi Chuan*, Chinese *kung-fu*, swordfighting, jogging, and other exercises. This continues until shortly before 7:00 AM, when everyone starts heading to work. It is well worth rising early a few times and getting out of your hotel in time to watch this mass display of physical culture, for it is surely one of the most admirable aspects of city life in modern China.

To be sure, the early-bird syndrome probably owes as much to the singular lack of entertainment in Chinese cities as it does to healthy habits. Touring the cities of China and speaking with the residents, one does not get the impression that people are generally unhappy with their lot, but one

The chaotic urban style of old Shanghai (pages 228, 229) contrasts sharply with the planned development of industry and housing in Beijing's suburbs (pages 230, 231). In downtown Beijing, stark, modern, high-rise developments coexist with the beautiful and stately Imperial Palace of former emperors (opposite).

Although most new buildings are architecturally unimaginative, a few (above) demonstrate that a decade or two ago, Chinese architects were interested in combining the two styles, by using traditional roof designs and material for modern concrete structures.

This page, top: *A vista overlooking the well-preserved Bund of Shanghai.* This page, bottom: *The lack of refrigeration and food storage facilities is evident in the pile of frozen animal carcasses which have simply been dumped alongside this modern-style housing development.*
Opposite: *Buildings in Shanghai's former British Concession being restored.*

does get the impression that they are uniformly bored during their long leisure hours. There is very little to do in China but work. The few movies shown draw packed houses and there are never enough tickets. There are no daytime and few night-time television programmes, and even when there is a show, there are so few television sets in China that only a fraction of the populace ever sees them. The New China Bookstores found in every city offer very limited selections of entertaining, non-political materials, and the staid, highly-political *People's Daily* is the only newspaper. About the only thing to do by day in Chinese cities is wander in the many exquisite old parks and gardens of which every city is justifiably proud. Or sip tea and gossip in a temple tea-house. Or sit by a river-side and smoke cigarettes. An accident, an incident, or a group of "outlandish" (the literal Chinese translation for "foreign") tourists instantly draws a large crowd of gawkers — not because people are simple and unsophisticated but because they are starved for entertainment and visual stimulation.

If leisure life in Chinese cities is boring by day, it becomes absolutely languid by night. Parks and gardens usually close at 5:30 PM. The masses' restaurants start closing around 7:30 PM, as do tea-shops, stores, and other public facilities. Most cities don't even turn on their street lights at night, unless some special event is in progress, and those that do promptly turn them off again before 9:00 PM. Needless to say, there are no discos, night-clubs, bars, amusement parks, 24-hour coffee shops, or other forms of Western night-life. By 9:00 PM all is dark and quiet in Chinese cities, and there is little to do but go to bed.

Nevertheless, the main boulevards of the big cities are packed with people at night as well as day, especially during the intense heat of summer. With most factories running round the clock in three eight-hour shifts, at least a third of the urban workers have no choice but to take their strolls and seek amusement during the evenings. The only evidence of these milling crowds at night is the orange glow of thousands of cigarettes being smoked. With not even a single street lamp burning, there is not enough light to play cards or dominoes, or to read. These idle night strollers are thus confined to cigarettes and conversation for entertainment. The problem is especially acute for young couples, who must be both ingenious and furtive in order to find place for a few moments of privacy together. If the municipal authorities of China are to be faulted for anything, it should be for their failure to provide even the most rudimentary entertainment facilities for their residents, especially the restless young. Crowds of bored, energetic, young people wandering along darkened streets and river fronts form fertile ground for many of the social evils China is trying so hard to avoid — prostitution, black-marketeering, theft, vandalism, and other crime. It is surprising that the otherwise enlightened Chinese authorities have so far failed to realise the vital importance of adequate entertainment to the human spirit, especially in crowded urban environments.

In light of the general austerity and boredom of Chinese city life, the question which often occurs to foreign visitors is this: "With all these tourists running around the cities of China flaunting their fancy clothes, expensive cameras and tape-recorders, stylish *coiffures*, and other luxuries, riding around in special cars and air-conditioned buses while the Chinese walk, eating in VIP dining rooms, and spending the equivalent of a Chinese worker's monthly salary on a simple souvenir, won't the Chinese people become envious of the foreigners and dissatisfied with their own lot?" The Chinese authorities who finally approved foreign tourism in China no doubt had this question in mind, too, and their inscrutable answer was probably something like this: "Some will, some won't, but in the long run foreigners will have no influence on our people."

Why? Because despite the massive urban populations one encounters in such cities as Shanghai (the world's largest),

Barges ply Suzhou Creek (opposite), *which cuts through Shanghai.*

The Beijing Hotel, crossroads of East and West. This modern section (above) *opened in the mid-1970s. The oldest section* (furthest left on following pages) *was built after the original hotel, in the old Legation Quarter, was destroyed during the Boxer Rebellion.*

Beijing, Guangzhou, and others, city and town dwellers represent only 20 percent of China's total population! Less than half of these reside in cities, or parts of cities, open to foreign tourists, which cuts down to less than 10 percent of the population the number of Chinese citizens who could possibly even get a distant glimpse of foreign tourists. And the only Chinese who ever get close enough to tourists to actually be influenced by them, namely travel service, hotel, airline, restaurant, and trade personnel as well as the handful of pedestrians able to speak English and bold enough to accost a foreigner, represent at most one percent of China's population — a mere drop in the bucket. The Chinese government no doubt feels it can risk this miniscule exposure to "Western decadence" in light of the great financial and public relations benefits it realises from foreign tourism. And since this exposure is confined to certain cities, far from the mainstreams of Chinese society, it is easy to contain. Travel and hospitality staff who show too obvious signs of Western influence would no doubt soon find themselves back in the boondocks weeding rice paddies. Historically, Chinese civilisation has always absorbed foreign

influences and sinified them beyond recognition, and this is still the case today.

Indeed, it is the foreign visitor who is most influenced by the experience of travelling in Chinese cities, not the Chinese residents. He sees a society radically different from his own, with none of the luxury, variety, and personal privilege with which Western societies are pampered, but also without the social chaos, economic uncertainty, rudeness, insecurity, crime, and psychological malaise which plague contemporary Western societies. He enters an absolute Communist dictatorship where he finds the people are uniformly friendly, consistently courteous, enviably relaxed, and, in the final balance, happy. The convulsive political changes experienced by China during this century have not altered the physical face of China: The historical monuments, sculpted gardens, temples, art, the exquisite beauty of China are still there. Nor have these political changes influenced the basic good nature, polite attitude, practical optimism, and quick humour of the Chinese people. The basic lesson of the Chinese city as it exists today is this: There is a viable alternative urban system to such chaotic, jumbled Asian cities as Bombay, Calcutta, Jakarta, and Manila on the one hand, and such hectic, commercial, over-developed, and expensive Western cities as New York, London, Paris and their Asian imitators Hong Kong, Singapore, Taipei, and Tokyo on the other.

Following are brief descriptions of seven major Chinese cities which are open to foreign travellers: Beijing, Shanghai, Suzhou, Hangzhou, Xi'an, Chengdu, and Guangzhou. These cities offer a representative cross-section of the major cultural traditions, geographic conditions, and people which constitute both historical and contemporary China.

Beijing (Peking) — "The Northern Capital"

In the far north of China proper, just within the Great Wall, lies the capital city of Beijing. First built by the Mongols as

Beijing rooftops and city streets in winter. Very little snow falls in Beijing.

*Much of Beijing's city centre is scheduled for
redevelopment. Old one- and two-storey shops
and residences lining this street that leads to the
Drum Tower north of the Imperial Palace
(opposite)* are sorely in need of major repairs.
*The newer sections of the city are
characterised by wide tree-lined streets and
developments of five-storey walk-up flats or
high-rise apartment buildings with elevators
(left, top and bottom).*

their capital when they conquered Song China and established the Yuan dynasty in the 13th century, it was further developed and expanded by the succeeding Ming and Qing dynasties. It has been China's political nerve centre for 700 years, and its fabulous Forbidden City has been home to 24 Chinese emperors.

Beijing is famous for its magnificent imperial architecture and monuments, which still lend the city an ambiance of imperial grandeur. Everything appears to be built on a grand scale. During a visit to Beijing shortly before his death, S.J. Perelman observed, "Beijing is a city built by giants — for giants!"

The boulevards of Beijing are among the widest in the world. When the Mongols originally laid out the city, they made sure that the streets were built very wide and very long so that they could careen through town on their ponies at a full gallop. Today, bicycles have replaced the ponies, and what they lack in speed they make up for in sheer numbers. These broad boulevards are direct contrasts with many Chinese city streets, which are often quite narrow and crowded. They contribute to the general impression of immensity which Beijing evokes.

The architectural and historical centre of Beijing is the Tienamen Square and the Forbidden City. This square is one of the biggest public plazas in the world, occupying a total area of almost 40 hectares. It takes its name from the huge gate on the North, which forms the imposing entrance to the Forbidden City. To the South is the Chairman Mao Memorial Hall, to the West the Great Hall of the People, and to the East are the Museum of Chinese History. In the centre stands a tall granite obelisk, which is the Monument to the People's Heroes. More than any other spot in China, the Tienamen Square gives the foreign visitor a feeling for the sheer size of China and for the grandeur of its imperial past. While the label "socialist" has replaced "imperial" in contemporary China, one still senses the aura of power and mystery which surround the secluded

Chinese leaders.

Without a doubt, the Forbidden City is the most magnificent historical structure extant in the world today. Built over 500 years ago by the third Ming emperor Yung Le, it has housed every Chinese emperor since then. Protected by a wide moat and high wall, it occupies an area of 100 hectares and contains over 9,000 rooms. The various palaces and pavilions, halls and anterooms are connected by an elaborate maze of walk-ways, steps, bridges, and gates and contain a wealth of ancient Chinese art and furnishings. In the gardens are rare trees, sculpted rock formations, ponds, and paths that reflect the four seasons and were the delight of emperors and their consorts for centuries. The huge bronze animals that guard the gates and platforms are among the best examples of bronze-casting in the world.

Within the city limits are many other monuments and structures reflecting China's past imperial splendour. The Temple of Heaven, which emperors used to ascend to invoke the blessings of Heaven, is a marvellous contrast of size and simplicity. Beihai Park, where people stroll under shade-trees in summer and ice-skate in winter, is a classic example of Chinese gardening arts, complete with winding paths, subtle rock and flower arrangements, exquisite pavilions, and fish ponds. Even the Beijing Hotel is an architectural wonder, built in three stages: The first wing was built during the early part of this century and reflects a strange combination of traditional Chinese imperial and old European baroque styles. The second wing was built with the aid of Russia in the 1950's in the heavy, large-scale, "socialist-realist" style of the day. The third wing, larger even than the first two, was built more recently in the "modern" style. The three together offer a stylised chronology of China's recent history.

Outside of Beijing lies the world's greatest engineering feat and the only man-made structure visible from the moon — The Great Wall of China. Started 2,200 years ago by the first emperor of China, it

snakes its way 3,600 miles across the sharp mountain ridges which separate China proper from Mongolia and Manchuria. It was designed to keep the barbaric Mongols, Manchus, and other Northern tribes out of China. Thousands of soldiers were permanently garrisoned in the Great Wall along its entire length. Like so many historical structures in and around Beijing, the vast scale and grand ambition of this project overwhelm the first-time visitor, Chinese and foreign alike.

Two other sites well worth visiting near Beijing are the Ming Tombs and the Summer Palace. The tombs of 13 Ming emperors are built into the rolling foothills north of the city. Their splendour is no less than that provided for living emperors. Rows and rows of huge stone-sculpted animals guard the approach to the tombs, each of which is a palace complex in itself, with gardens, pavilions, ponds, and monuments. Only one tomb, that of the Wan Li emperor, has been opened, and visitors may tour it.

The biggest traffic problem in every city is the control of thousands of bicyclists, especially during the rush hours.

The Summer Palace was the final splurge of the Qing imperial court. Totally rebuilt and expanded under orders from the infamous Empress Dowager Ci-Xi in the late 19th century, it features an elaborate solid marble boat set by an artificial lake. It was built with funds allocated for construction of a modern Chinese navy. The Summer Palace boasts some of the loveliest settings in China. A long, covered walk-way with carved balustrades runs the entire length of the lake, the friezes and ceilings of which are decorated with colourful, highly detailed enamelled paintings depicting famous myths and stories of China. The Listening to Orioles Pavilion has been converted to a restaurant which serves excellent food.

The people who inhabit Beijing and surrounding provinces are called "North-side people" by the Chinese. Northerners are taller and stouter than their southern cousins and tend to be somewhat moon-faced. Their stronger constitution is attributed to the harsh environment of the north and to a staple diet of wheat rather than rice.

Throughout history the people of Beijing have been known for their courtesy and hospitality. This is still true today. As residents of the great capital, they regard both foreigners and visitors from other Chinese provinces as their honoured guests. In fact, the streets of Beijing are jammed with Chinese on their first visit to the capital. Many are simple peasants from the country-side who mill through the streets gawking more at displays of modern products in store windows than at famous historical monuments. By tradition, the residents are extemely courteous and helpful to all visitors to their city, which is certainly not the case in most capital cities of the world.

"North-side food" is based on a staple of wheat rather than rice and features a wide variety of breads and buns, pan-cakes and *crêpes,* stuffed dumplings and noodles. It is generally more filling than the fancier southern cuisines. Though not one of China's *haute cuisines*, the simpler

The Forbidden City stands as an artistic and cultural monument to the glory of the Chinese empire. The present structure dates from the third Ming Emperor, Yong Le, under whom the palace reconstruction was completed in 1420.

The roofs are of yellow porcelain tiles, individually hand-laid. The creatures perched in a row on the uppermost rooftop are always found in odd numbers and are there to keep away tyrants and other evils.

Shanghai, covering an area of 9,300 square kilometers, and having a population of more than 11 million people, is probably the largest city in the world. It was opened to foreign trade after the Opium War in the mid-nineteenth century, and grew rapidly with the designation of special territories for foreign traders. The British, French and Japanese held the largest of these concessions, with the Americans, Italians and Germans also holding large blocks in the city. The architectural influence of this era is one of the most attractive features of Shanghai.

At the turn of the century, it was the most sophisticated and modern city in China, and the financial, industrial and entertainment centre of the Orient.

flavours and more conventional ingredients of northern food seem to have great appeal to Western palates. The capital's most famous dish is, of course, Beijing Duck, and this specialty may be sampled any time at a huge, relatively new restaurant appropriately named "The Beijing Duck."

Beijing has an ambiance of great power and importance. The weight of history and the awesome responsibility for the world's largest nation hang heavy in the air. The buildings and streets are so big and broad that they dwarf man. Sometimes the only sound to be heard is the whish and wail of Mongolian winds blowing down from the North. Beijing is a serious city, and after the initial impressions of historical grandeur wear off, it is time to move on to the more light-hearted cities of the south.

Shanghai — "On the Sea"

Shanghai is China's most sophisticated city. With 11 million residents and over 10,000 factories, it is also the largest city in China, and the world. Located near the mouth of the Yangtze River on the East China Sea, the port of Shanghai is the most vital trading link between the vast interior of China and the outside world.

Ironically, it was foreigners who finally brought Shanghai to its greatness. Prior to the 19th century, it was nothing but an insignificant little fishing village straddling the mud-flats of the Yangtze and Huangpu Rivers. After the Opium Wars and the Unequal Treaties signed with European powers in the mid-19th century, Shanghai was one of the minor ports opened up to foreign interests.

The Europeans went right to work on the place, gradually building up the city and port to its present-day dimensions. Today, the architecture and ambiance of Shanghai still retain a distinctly European flavour. The famous Bund, where once the dynastic commercial families of Europe held meetings and enjoyed afternoon tea in palatial European mansions, hasn't changed a bit since the heyday of economic imperialism, though the former

residents have disappeared. Today, these extravagant examples of 19th century European architecture house the Shanghai municipal authorities, government trade associations, the People's Bank, and other government entities.

One of the most charming structures along the Bund is the Peace Hotel, where most foreign visitors prefer to stay. Formerly called the "Palace Hotel" and owned by the Sassoon family, this wonderful old hotel has been well maintained by the Chinese. The rooms are large and airy, with the high ceilings, wooden floors, and old furnishings of former days. The eighth-floor dining room commands a fine view of the Bund and, happily, serves excellent food as well. On the second floor is a billiards room with two very old and very well kept tables and a set of solid ivory balls, tinged yellow with age. A stay at the Peace Hotel is a step back into the graceful style and service of another age.

The entire city is full of elegant and sometimes eccentric examples of classical European architecture. The huge Sassoon residence, surely one of the world's most elaborate and expensive private mansions, has been preserved and converted to a "Children's Palace," where gifted children attend special classes to develop their individual interests and talents. Most of the biggest and best shops are located on Nanjing Rd., where fancy window-displays remind one more of Europe than China. Here you'll find the Mediterranean-style Dong Hai Cafe, which serves the best meringue pies in China. A visit to this old cafe offers a clear view of the unique blend of old and new, Chinese and Western, cross-currents which define Shanghai.

There are of course purely Chinese sights to see in Shanghai, but they are not as impressive as elsewhere in China and sometimes even seem out of place, tucked away as they are among European structures. The most characteristic and charming Chinese scenes in Shanghai are to be found on and along the Yangtze and Huanghe Rivers, where river-life still retains a timeless Chinese flavour. The

Modern Shanghai opposite is China's industrial core, and the trend-setter for today's youth. During the Cultural Revolution, some of China's most radical political leaders had their base in this city. With their recent demise, cafes and teahouses flourish again, and young people dare to try new fashions in clothing, hair styles and music.

A haze of mist and pollution renders a warm glow to the sky over the Chang Jiang River, (following pages).

variety of vessels, from steamers and tug-boats to sampans and junks, is incredible. Entire families still move up and down these rivers, providing goods and services to riverside residents as they have for centuries.

Shanghai has always maintained an independent, sometimes arrogant attitude towards the rest of China. It is a city which savours superlatives. In the heyday of capitalism and decadence, Shanghai became the most capitalistic and the most decadent city in China. During the days of radical revolutionary zeal, such as the Cultural Revolution, Shanghai became the most radical of Chinese cities. Today, with the "Four Modernisations" as the current national guideline, Shanghai has once again pushed to the forefront by becoming the most modern in all four areas. The Shanghainese have a reputation in China for cunning, business acumen, and relentless practicality.

Part of this reputation may stem from envy. Shanghai is by far China's wealthiest city (another superlative) and is a very desirable place for urbanites to live. There are far more stores than elsewhere in China, and they are better stocked with a wider variety of goods. The women wear more colour in their clothing and more style in their hair. Living conditions are better and opportunities for advancement greater. And there are more movies, televisions, and books available to wile away the leisure hours.

In order to stem the growth of the city's population, Chinese authorities no longer permit new residents to move into metropolitan Shanghai. If a Shanghainese woman marries a non-Shanghainese man, the couple gets transferred out of the city to another location in China. Shanghainese men, however, may marry brides from elsewhere and still maintain residency in the city. The net result of this curious law

is that Shanghai girls, highly desirable for their looks, education, jobs, and other benefits, are "hard to get." To maintain their residency, most Shanghai girls reject suitors from outside the city limits.

Shanghainese cuisine has a justifiably good reputation in China. Located on the sea, the city specialises in a wide range of sea-foods. When in season, the jumbo prawns steamed whole in the shell are among the best in the world. There are numerous good restaurants which cater to foreign visitors, and they offer a great variety of foods and flavours.

Shanghai is the Chinese city least likely to throw the Western visitor off balance. Not only will he recognise the architecture but also the attitude of the city. It is very much business-oriented and lacks the frank friendliness and relative naiveté of other Chinese cities. It is, perhaps, a model for what the rest of China may become if current trends continue.

Suzhou (Soochow) — "District of Soo"

One hour due west by train from Shanghai lies the 3,000-year-old city of Suzhou, one of China's loveliest cities. The King of Wu founded the city as his capital in the fifth century BC. Throughout history this charming city has attracted artists, poets, and even emperors, who came to wander in the fine gardens, mingle with the attractive people, and sample the excellent food for which the city was famous. By the relative standards of modern China, this reputation still holds true, for Suzhou is still a favourite destination for vacationing Chinese, especially honeymooners.

Suzhou is a city of gardens and canals. Linked to the Grand Canal before it veers around Lake Tai to Hangzhou, the entire city is intersected by an elaborate network of canals. Much as in Venice, which is Suzhou's sister city, the canals are constantly plied by a colourful assortment of old boats sculling from place to place. Suzhou is located in a rich, well irrigated agricultural basin, and fresh produce enters the city by sampan and tow-boat rather than the human drawn, two-wheeled carts common in other cities. The canals and related waterside activities form some of the most charming and original Chinese scenes in the country. Visitors should spend at least a day simply walking and driving along the canals in and around the city.

Suzhou's gardens are as famous as its canals, and many of them date from the Sung dynasty. Wealthy officials used to sponsor the construction of elaborate gardens in the city, which consequently were expanded and further developed by connoisseurs in succeeding centuries. A traditional Chinese garden consists of far more than flowers, trees, and bushes. It is an entire landscape in miniature, a self-contained little world with "mountains" of cleverly arranged rocks, "rivers" and "lakes" formed by linked pools of water, winding and hidden paths which make long strolls possible within a small area, miniature pagodas and pavilions in which

to rest along the way. The architecture, sculpture, and calligraphy one finds in these pleasant retreats are as beautiful as the horticulture, and together they form harmonious, highly aesthetic settings. The Liu Garden, Garden of Harmony, and Garden of the Master of Nets are among the favourite gardens of Suzhou.

Outside of the city, commanding a full view of Suzhou, Lake Tai, and the surrounding countryside, is Tiger Hill, where the King of Wu is said to have been buried. The famous monastery and pagoda atop Tiger Hill were completed in 961 AD and are fine examples of classical Chinese temple architecture. There are old gardens and a tea-house within the complex as well. With the loosening of religious restrictions, the monks are slowly returning to the great temples and monasteries of China, and 40 of them now reside in the one on Tiger Hill.

Suzhou is the least drab of Chinese cities. The traditionally styled Chinese houses which face the narrow sycamore lined streets are very well maintained, and the city looks the same as it has for centuries. Fortunately, the canal complex makes "modernisation" of the city impossible. The residents of Suzhou have the custom of white-washing their houses regularly, eliminating the dull grey hue dominant in other Chinese cities. The many interlacing canals add water to the city scenery and reflect the light of the sun on white washed houses. Rounded "moon-bridges" designed to permit loaded boats to pass underneath are everywhere to be seen. The narrow streets and lanes, over which small latticed windows and verandas protrude, recall a time when sedan-chairs were the only traffic to contend with.

"Suzhou produces beautiful women" is an adage which has been spoken in China since the city first appeared. It explains one reason for Suzhou's immense popularity among the leisure classes of old China. Some say it's the food, some claim it's the water, still others insist it's the climate: Whatever the reason, it is a fact

that the women of Suzhou have finer skin, more delicate features, and are generally of a more comely cast than elsewhere in China. This physical advantage, combined with the lilting, teasing tones of "Soo-Bai," the local Suzhou vernacular, and the dreamy settings of the city itself, made the women of Suzhou highly appealing. While today, sensuality and the deliberate cultivation of feminine beauty are discouraged in China, one can easily see than Suzhou still has all the potential elements for becoming an exquisite pleasure-centre, should conditions ever permit it.

No Chinese city could attain a reputation as a haven of beauty and pleasure unless the food were as good as the women and scenery were beautiful. So famous are

A network of large and small canals characterises Suzhou as the "Venice of the East."

Suzhou, founded in the sixth century on the old Grand Canal, is famous for its silks, gardens and beautiful women. An ancient Chinese proverb states that in heaven there is paradise, on earth Suzhou and Hangzhou. The architecture of Suzhou is quite appealing, with its white stucco houses and streets lined with sycamore trees.

Hangzhou's physical beauty attracts tens of thousands of visitors each year to enjoy its tranquil West Lake, beautiful gardens, reflecting pools, lavish temples and cheery lakeside teahouses. Hangzhou is famous for a special kind of tea (above) called Dragon Well Tea, its freshwater West Lake carp, and a curious local vegetable, chuncai.

the seasonal specialities of Suzhou that even today bus-loads of Chinese gourmets from Shanghai drive up for the day to sample the crab, the fresh-water eel, the Mandarin fish, and other local dishes. There is a restaurant in Suzhou that has been in operation continuously for close to 300 years. The great Qing emperor Qianlong visited it during one of his pleasure excursions to the south. So impressed was he with the food that he called for brush and ink and wrote a couplet in his fine calligraphy in which he named the restaurant the "Pine Crane." Few establishments in Chinese history have been so honoured. It still bears the name today and still serves the same succulent dishes at the same address. Highly recommended delicacies are Sautéed Fresh-Water Eel, Mandarin Squirrel Fish, Shredded Crab Meat, Fragrant Crispy Duck, and Fried Prawns.

The Chinese like to sum up their common knowledge and experiences with terse sayings, and naturally they have one to describe the role of Suzhou, Hangzhou, and the surrounding region in their national life: "Above there is Heaven, below there is Suzhou and Hangzhou." Since time immemorial, poets and scholars have likened this area to a Heaven on Earth, and indeed the sensual life-style and pleasures we read about in Chinese history and literature seem to fully justify this reputation. It's possible that Suzhou may regain its full-blown flair and sensual life-style some day in the distant future, but in the meantime, on a far less extravagant scale, Suzhou still remains one of the most charming and attractive spots in China.

Hangzhou (Hangchow) — "District of Hang"

Three hours by train southwest from Shanghai you will find the other half of Heaven, Hangzhou. The contemporary capital of Zhejiang province, Hangzhou also has a history of several millenia. For 150 years it served as the imperial capital of the Southern Song, after it was driven from the north by the Qin Tartars.

Hangzhou enjoyed an even greater reputation than Suzhou as a pleasure city. In addition, it was considered the cultural centre of "Jiangnan," the fertile, temperate region "South of the Yangtze." Magistrates longed for posts in Hangzhou, and two who received them — the famous poets Bai Juyi (Tang) and Su Dongbo (Song) — both praised its beauties in verse and improved its scenery with major landscaping projects.

Hangzhou is built around West Lake, which has been famous for its scenic beauty ever since the Tang dynasty. Originally a shallow bay branching from the nearby Chienjiang River, it became a lake when accumulated silt and man-made embankments cut it from the river. Since the Tang dynasty, it has been landscaped, beautified, and dotted with artificial islands and causeways by succeeding generations of devoted city magistrates and provincial governors. The lake has a circumference of 15 km. and is bordered on three sides with gentle hills, where many famous temples, pagodas, and springs are to be found. The banks of the lake, islands, and causeways are planted with trees and bushes that bloom in all four seasons. West Lake and its islands abound with scenic spots with such poetic names as "Three Pools Reflecting the Moon," "Autumn Moon on the Calm Lake," "Orioles Singing in the Willows," and others. The government keeps a guest-house on West Lake where visiting heads of state are inevitably invited to relax and enjoy themselves after gruelling talks in Beijing. President Richard Nixon stayed there during his official visit in 1973.

Much of old Hangzhou was razed to the ground during the turbulent Taiping rebellion in the mid-19th century, which explains why so little pre-Qing architecture remains there. The Ling Yin Temple, originally established in the fourth century, was rebuilt after the Taiping insurrection and today remains one of the most impressive temples still extant in China. It boasts a beautiful gilded Buddha 25 metres high, set in a huge three-storey temple hall.

The grounds are riddled with caves and hidden pathways, along which images of Buddha have been hewn from living rock by generations of disciples. In addition to being a popular tourist attraction, the Ling Yin Temple also attracts the faithful. Since freedom of religion was restored a few years ago, some segments of the Chinese population are gingerly beginning to worship again, and in the Ling Yin Temple you'll see people making obeisance, praying, and offering incense beneath the tranquil gaze of ornate Buddhist idols.

Hangzhou shares Suzhou's reputation for beautiful women. Indeed the entire Lake Tai region has always been famous for the beauty of its landscapes and its people. Today, most women in China dress in baggy pants and simple, loose-fitting shirts, wear no make-up whatsoever, tie their hair in long braids, and act most reserved in public. Other than basic facial features, it is difficult to discern both the obvious and subtle signs of feminine

beauty with which we are familiar in the West. However, Marco Polo, who visited Hangzhou in the 14th century, when the place was in full bloom, has left us this description of its feminine charms:

> The ladies are highly proficient and accomplished in the use of endearments and caresses, with words suited and adapted to every sort of person, so that foreigners who have once enjoyed them remain utterly beside themselves and so captivated by their sweetness and charm that, when they return home, they say they have been in "Kinsai," that is to say in the City of Heaven, and can scarcely wait for the time that they may go back there.

Marco Polo lingered 17 years in China, and no doubt the pleasures of the "City of Heaven" was one of the main reasons.

Today, Hangzhou is far more subdued than it was when Marco Polo visited. Gone are the courtesans and entertainers, the poets and pleasure-seekers. But the tranquil ambiance and beautiful settings are still there, and they are still capable of

evoking the same feelings of serenity and heavenly peace which visitors have described through the centuries.

While the erotic arts are currently forbidden, the culinary arts for which Hangzhou has been equally famous through the ages are still very much a trademark of the city. Everywhere in modern China it seems that good food is the one luxury in which people indulge freely and frequently. At the Hangzhou Wine House, Executive Chef and General Manager Dong Dong-cun, who has worked there continuously for over 40 years, supervises a team of highly skilled chefs and charming, attractive waitresses. The VIP dining room on the top floor is one of the most pleasant in China, and both the food and service are unrivalled.

Another famous restaurant, the Lou-Wai-Lou, is located on the banks of West Lake and has been operating at the same location under the same name since it first opened for business during the Song

dynasty 800 years ago. Both of these restaurants feature fresh-water fish from West Lake. The most famous dish is "West Lake Vinegar Fish," an unforgettable taste treat made with West Lake's "qing yu," a special variety of carp.

The only thing missing in modern-day Hangzhou is night-life. This is the case in all Chinese cities, but it seems more glaringly absent in Hangzhou. With its lovely lake-side settings, temperate climate, humorous and attractive populace, exquisite cuisine, and colourful history, Hangzhou's silence at night is deafening. Hopefully the "City of Heaven" will open its Pearly Gates of pleasure again some day and host modern-day Marco Polo's in a style befitting its history.

Xi'an (Sian) — "Western Peace"

The ancient city of Xi'an is located up in the northwest corner of China proper. It is the capital of Shaanxi province. The city lies amidst the cradle of Chinese civilisation, where Chinese culture, society, and institutions first took definitive shape. It was the fabulous capital of the great Tang dynasty (618-906 AD), when it was called Changan ("Everlasting Peace"). At that time, Changan was the largest and by far the most civilised city in the world.

Xi'an retains the flavour and feeling of old China. The downtown area is often dusty, grey, and dismal during inclement weather, but the lay-out of the streets and the architectural styles are very reminiscent of an ancient Chinese city as you might expect it to look. The old city wall, moat, and gates have been preserved and give the best impression of what Chinese cities were like before the modern age. The Tang dynasty was China's "Golden Age" of culture, and in Xi'an there remain many fine examples of Tang architecture, bronze, and other cultural achievements.

Within the old city limits are numerous historical monuments dating from the Tang dynasty. Among these are the Drum Tower, the Bell Tower, an ancient Chinese Moslem mosque, several pagodas, city-gates, and numerous old mansions. One of the most pleasant sights, however, is located 25 km. outside the city: the Hua Ching Pools, an ancient hot-springs resort, what clearly evokes the ambiance of old China. This is where the "Precious Concubine" Yang Kui-fei, favourite of the Tang emperor Ming-Huang, used to go for her beauty baths. The sunken tub she used is still there, and there are a dozen private pavilions with spacious sunken tubs for use by visitors. Paths and pavilions are built into the hills around the resort, and most of the architecture dates from the Tang. The farmers who live nearby use the warm mineral water to grow vegetables in the freezing cold of winter. Consequently Xi'an has abundant supplies of fresh vegetables all year round.

Xi'an is one of China's most important archaeological sites. Recent excavations near the tomb of China's founding emperor Qinshihuangdi (third century BC) have revealed a treasure trove of well preserved artifacts from that era. Among them are 6,400 life-size clay figures of soldiers and horses, guardians of the emperor in the other world. The facial features of these figures are highly individual. They also reflect the ethnic traits and costumes of the north-western Qin tribes (source of the word "China"), who first conquered and unified China in 221 BC. The entire excavation site has been enclosed under a roof and has recently been opened to tourists. It is well worth visiting, for the clay figurines, apart from their historical and aesthetic interest, give one the best impression of the militant, war-like aspect of the Chinese character. The Shaanxi Provincial Museum, located in Xi'an, contains many additional artifacts from the Qin, Han, Tang, and other eras.

The people of Xi'an are as hospitable and courteous as they are in Beijing. Ironically, for such a remote city, they seem far less surprised by the sight of foreigners than elsewhere. The reason for this is that Xi'an lies near the borders between China proper (Han China) and several minority regions such as Gansu and Xinjiang. Moslems, Tartars, fairhaired barbarians from Siberia, and other foreigners have been visiting and living in Xi'an for two millenia. In Xi'an, the people are more curious about the details of life in Western countries and less impressed with "outlandish" appearances, to which they have become well accustomed. There's an excellent language school in Xi'an, and English is now much in vogue. English-speaking residents of Xi'an are quite unabashed about accosting lone foreign tourists to practice their English and glean from them a few details about life in the West.

In Guan Xian, near Chengdu, are fine examples of traditional agricultural waterworks. Chengdu itself (above) is one of China's oldest cities.

The food is surprisingly good in Xi'an, although it does not lie in an area traditionally noted for *haute cuisine*. There are several excellent restaurants, among them the "May First Restaurant" and the "East Asia Restaurant." Being in the north, you can sample some wheat staples, such as steamed buns, dumplings, and various pan-cakes, instead of the usual rice. Among the best dishes are Fragrant Crispy Chicken, Braised Duck, Braised Yellow-Fish, and assorted cold-plates and snacks "Xi'an-style." By all means try the fresh-fermented glutinous rice wine called "Chou-jiu," a milky, slightly sweet beverage; it is absolutely delicious and available only in Xi'an.

Though not one of China's most glamorous cities, Xi'an offers the visitor a true taste of old China and a fine historical perspective. It is probably more interesting to China buffs who already have a background in Chinese history than to the average visitor. Xi'an's great attractions are the ancient and authentic atmosphere, architecture, and artifacts which are so well preserved there.

Chengdu (Chengtu) — "Capital City"

Chengdu is one of China's oldest cities. It predates considerably the founding of a unified Chinese empire in 221 BC, at which time it was the long-standing capital of the ancient Chinese Kingdom of Shu. Today, it is capital of China's most populous province, Sichuan.

The city is old in appearance as well as history. The squat houses with miniature verandas hanging over the portals, corniced walls and roofs, ornate doorways, and other typical features of urban architecture in ancient China still line most of the streets. Bearded old men sit in bamboo chairs by the doorways, smoking the long, sometimes beautifully carved and cast pipes indigenous to the region. In many neighbourhoods, water is still rationed out to residents from a public pump, where women can be seen lining up with wooden buckets slung from bamboo poles. Vegetable and meat stalls sprawl

Chengdu, the capital of China's most populous province, was once considered to be one of the most beautiful towns in China. Many picturesque sections of the old city remain though its landscape is dominated by new construction. The new industrial districts are spreading outside the old city walls.

into the streets, and human-drawn carts are relied on for transporting goods more than anywhere else in China. The scenes could come from any century.

Despite the rustic simplicity and aged appearance of Chengdu, it is one of China's most dynamic, vital cities. The people of Sichuan have always been known for their feisty spirit, independence, and artistic talents. Many of China's greatest poets and statesmen came from here, and today several key figures in China's top government hierarchy, including Deng Xiaoping, hail from the province of Sichuan. In every respect, Sichuan has always been innovative and energetic. Chengdu's greatest pride is the irrigation works located 40 km. outside the city. The Dujiangyan was constructed 2,500 years ago, harnessing the fierce flowing flood waters of the Min River by forcing it to flow along several man-made "mini-rivers," which irrigate a vast agricultural area. This irrigation system is still in use today.

The drive between Chengdu and Dujiangyan offers timeless views of Chinese agricultual life. Endless fields of well tended rice paddies and vegetable patches stretch to both horizons. Brigades of farmers in straw hats using archaic hand tools and draught animals work the fields. Guan-xian (Kuansian), the little town where Dujiangyan is located, is a colourful and charming old place,where life hasn't changed much for many centuries. The rest-house there serves excellent food, and the town itself distils the very essence of Sichuanese local colour.

Sichuan food is as spicy as the people are feisty. Currently much in vogue in the West, the cuisine features liberal use of red chillis, fresh garlic, and ginger root. In a manner typical of the down-to-earth Sichuanese character, the chefs here dispense with fancy appearances and concentrate their efforts on flavour and freshness. Sichuanese dishes do not have the picture-perfect gloss of other famous Chinese cuisines, but they rival the best in taste. Duck Smoked in Camphor and Tea, "Ma-

Pwo" Bean Curd, Fragrant Egg-Plant, Spicy Shredded Pork, and Chilli-Sauce Fish are a few of the local specialties. The Chengdu Restaurant, a huge four-storey structure where the VIP dining room is furnished with antique Chinese hardwood furniture, is the best bet in town for banquets.

Like Xi'an, Chengdu is interesting for its ancient air of Chinese authenticity. Beyond that, the people of Chengdu are the most engaging aspect of the city. Their spunky spirit and aggressiveness are unusual among Chinese, who generally tend to be more reserved and placid. Should the Chinese authorities ever relax their grip on entertainment and individual freedoms, Chengdu would probably soon become one of the livliest "hot-spots" on the Chinese tourist trail.

Guangzhou (Canton) — "Broad District"

Down in the tropical southeast corner, far from the heart of China, is Guangzhou, capital of Guangdong province and the gateway through which most foreigners enter and exit China. Historically, Chinese from other regions have disliked this part of their country because of the unbearable heat and humidity and the extravagant, unconventional customs of the people. No doubt this is why foreigners have been confined to this port of entry for close to 200 years. It is literally China's "back door."

Ever since China and the West embarked on their wary exchange of goods and ideas, Guangzhou has been the main point of contact. It has remained open to foreigners even when the rest of China has been sealed off, and today the semi-annual Guangzhou Trade Fair still draws foreign businessmen to that city in droves.

With all this foreign contact for two centuries one would imagine Guangzhou to be a hybrid of East and West like Hong Kong, or a facsimile of a Western city like Shanghai. Strangely enough, however, Guangzhou remains one of the most quintessentially Chinese cities in the country, stubbornly clinging to traditional customs that have long since fallen by the wayside

in the rest of China. The Cantonese still celebrate such traditional festivals as the Dragon Boat Festival, Mid-Autumn Moon Festival, Lunar New Year, and many others with colourful pomp and ceremony, while in the rest of China "socialist-realism" often dampens the spirit of celebration.

Guangzhou has a history of over 2,000 years, and there are many interesting historical sites scattered throughout the city. It is a city of beautiful gardens and broad boulevards shaded by arcades. The Pearl River and Sha Mian Island are points of interest for Western visitors. A boat ride on the Pearl offers charming views of many facets of traditional Chinese river-life. Sha Mian Island, formerly a

Guangzhou is one of the three centres of foreign trade in China, and is the major city in the South.
Because modern Chinese architecture ignores regional design elements, a view of one city (Guangzhou, following pages) *looks much like any other.*

foreign concession closed to Chinese, is almost like a period movie-set with its authentic old colonial atmosphere and excellent examples of 19th century European architecture. Today, the luxurious villas and offices that once were the exclusive domain of English and French colonialists have been converted to hospitals and schools for the Chinese proletariat. A new hotel is currently being built on the island, invested by Hong Kong Chinese interests.

Guangzhou is China's most modern city. It has close financial and business connections with Hong Kong, the city which also provides China with its greatest quota of Westernised Chinese tourists. Fleets of brand-new Japanese taxis ply the streets instead of the old "Shanghai" models used everywhere else. The modern problem of pollution is also more evident in Guangzhou. A slight change in wind may well bring a black cloud of sooty smoke from a nearby factory floating over your dining table, as you sit on a terrace overlooking the Pearl River. One suspects that if black marketeering, gambling, prostitution, secret societies and other social evils still exist anywhere in China, it might well be in Guangzhou, for here people seem to be less awed by the imperatives of "building socialism." A slight edge of irritability and impatience is beginning to form among residents of Guangzhou, a

modern urban trait which we take for granted in the West but which contrasts sharply with the rest of China.

The Cantonese, small and wiry compared with other Chinese, have an ambiguous reputation in China. On the one hand, like the Shanghainese, they are highly respected for their keen business sense, stubborn determination, and persistent practicality. Guangzhou was also a hot-bed of revolutionary activity in the early decades of this century: both Sun Yat-sen and Chiang Kai-shek began their drives for power here, and it was also an early centre of Communist activity. The Cantonese are respected as people not to be dealt with lightly.

On the other hand, they often seem to be the butt of Chinese cultural jokes. The Cantonese dialect is notorious for the odd, animal-like sounds it produces. It is often said that when a Cantonese couple snuggle up and speak of love, it sounds like a vehement, nasty quarrel to the non-Cantonese bystander. "Bird chatter" is what the Mandarin-speaking officials from Beijing used to call it. The Cantonese are also very cliquish and well-organised, and even today family ties remain important. Chinese from other provinces often feel isolated in Guangzhou.

Another common remark heard in China is that "if it has four legs, the Cantonese will eat it." This comment seems in

fact to be true, though it reflects more the culinary prejudices of other Chinese than a Cantonese fault, for the Cantonese prepare these beasts for the table with the exquisite style of China's unrivalled king of cuisines.

Which brings us to the main attraction of Guangzhou — food and restaurants. The Chinese have another ancient aphorism which describes the ideal course of life: "To be born in Suzhou, to eat in Guangzhou, and to die in Liuzhou." The first wish refers to the natural beauty and perfect complexions of those lucky enough to be born in Suzhou. The third wish stems from the fact that coffins made with the local woods of Liuzhou (a town in Guangxi near Guilin) preserve the bodies of the deceased from decay for many decades, highly desirable in Confucian society. And the second wish refers to the undisputed primacy of Cantonese cuisine in Chinese culture.

What makes Cantonese food so special is the incredible variety of ingredients and presentations and the highly complex, sophisticated methods of preparation. What passes for Cantonese food in the West does not even qualify as a pale imitation of the real thing. Neither the ingredients, nor the tender loving care, nor the time and patience required to prepare genuine Cantonese dishes are available in the West.

Equally impressive in Guangzhou are

the restaurants themselves, which are the most beautiful in China. The North Garden and the South Garden Restaurants are two of the loveliest in the world. Set in elaborate gardens of flowers, rocks, lotus ponds, and bamboo groves, these sprawling restaurants are well preserved examples of traditional Chinese architecture and luxury. Foreigners who wish to sample some exotic four-legged creatures may visit the Wild Flavour Fragrance Restaurant, a spacious, four-storey structure where monkey, civet cat, dog, fox, and other beasts less familiar to Western eyes await their fate. The Datong Restaurant, located atop a building along Guangzhou's Bund, has a series of terrace dining rooms which offer marvellous views of the Pearl River. The Guangzhou Wine House is a multi-storied maze of dining rooms and private terraces which look over a central courtyard. The entire restaurant reverberates with the sounds of hundreds of diners laughing, chatting, toasting, and wielding their chopsticks over steaming platters of succulent food. All Chinese love to eat, but the Cantonese are food fanatics. One of the best ways to enjoy your stay in this city and also absorb authentic Cantonese local colour is to eat all your meals in the many fine restaurants located throughout the city.

For most travellers, Guangzhou is both the first and last stop on their visit to China. As a first stop, it appears interesting and very "Chinese." As a last stop, however, after having covered half a dozen other Chinese cities, Guangzhou is often disappointing and depressing, The heat and humidity are oppressive most of the year. The people seem, more curt than courteous, more tolerant than friendly. Guangzhou lacks the innocent charm of inland China. This perhaps will always be true because Guangzhou has been relegated, whether it likes it or not, to continue its traditional role as the main point of entry and exit for foreigners, whether on business or pleasure. This role may somewhat account for the cliquish and aloof attitude of the inhabitants, who, in order to preserve their own identity and ideas, tend to close ranks against both visiting "outlanders" and meddling Chinese from the north.

Although the cities of China house only one fifth of the country's population and thus do not represent the economic or social mainstreams, they do form clear windows through which we may view the mix of old and new cultural cross-currents at work in modern China. The cities are, as they always have been in the past, the cultural centres of China. They attract the best products, the finest talents, and the greatest efforts of the vast population in the hinterlands.

The cities are the flowers of the Chinese provinces. Each one exudes the unique colour and essential flavour, the regional pride and predilections, and the native personality of the surrounding people and geography. Since culture — not politics or economics — is still the essential key to understanding Chinese civilisation both old and new, a visit to the major cities of China is a quick and effective way to get a feel for both the greatness of China's past achievements and the boldness of its current efforts.

Some hisorians claim that a town has existed on this spot on the Pearl River, opposite since 214 BC, Guangzhou first developed substantially as a shipping and trading centre during the Song dynasty, and welcomed its first foreigners in 1514 when the Portugese established an embassy. Left: Greenery and billboards are a feature of present day Guangzhou.

Guangzhou city proper has expanded well beyond its ancient city walls. Treed boulevards (above) distinguish the newer parts of the city from the older sections. Opposite: With sails unfurled, junks ply the waters off the coast of Shanghai. Institute. During a violent clash with Chiang Kai-shek's forces that year, more than 5,000 in Guangzhou workers lost their lives.

Until a few years ago, Guangzhou was the primary foreign trade centre of the country, hosting the Chinese Export Commodities Fair (now the Guangzhou Foreign Trade Fair) each spring and autumn.

ZHAO ZIYANG

"Tough guy" and "man on the move" are both likely epithets for former Sichuan province communist party boss Premier Zhao Ziyang — widely tipped as successor to the ageing Deng Xiaoping, the architect of post-Mao China.

Zhao — thought to be in his early or middle sixties — has had a career spanning the two poles of Chinese politics: At-Attempting to make Mao's agricultural policy work — and being purged for several years for his pains; and taking over political control of Sichuan, one of China's biggest and potentially richest provinces, and a place in which his mentor Deng takes a particular interest because he was born there.

In common with many high party officials, Zhao's past is obscure, though he is reputed to have been born into a rich land-owning family — which could account for the suavity and authority of his manners.

He surfaced as a young commissar in the Fourth Field Army of the late (and reviled) Marshal Lin Biao, during Lin's conquest of Central China at the end of the civil war in 1949. During the 1950s, he worked under Deng's old friend and fellow bridge-player, Tao Zhu.

Tao — who died in obscurity and disgrace after his purge in 1967 — held sway over the central-south provinces of Hunan and Guangdong for a decade and a half,

and Zhao was evidently working closely with him for most of that period. The young cadre gained experience in the ruthless land reform of the early 1960s — when many landlords were given drumhead trials and shot — and this marked a lifelong interest in agriculture. He was also entrusted with important tasks linked to the convening of China's new rubber-stamp parliament, the National People's Congress, in 1954. He also began publishing propaganda articles in the Beijing media.

Early in 1967 — as the Cultural Revolution swept across the length and breadth of China, sowing chaos and strife wherever it passed — Zhao was made a target of Guangdong province's vociferous and vindictive Red Guards. But he was luckier than many: After four years spent in obscure exile somewhere, he surfaced again as a senior administrator in the wild and windswept steppes of Chinese-ruled Inner Mongolia.

For the southerner Zhao, life in Mongolia must have seemed hard and unpromising — on top of tense security situation caused by th day-to-day anxiety about a Soviet invasion from the pro-Moscow Mongolian People's Republic just across the border. He probably had to hold down his gorge and learn to eat mutton — a dish most people from South China detest. But his eyes were on higher things.

In 1973, the indomitable Deng was rehabilitated in Beijing, and it was not long before he saw to it that Zhao was re-appointed to the Party Central Committee and sent back to Guangzhou in the key post of Party First Secretary. Hand-in-hand with this job went the post of chief commissar for the Guangzhou Military Region — one of the largest and most powerful in the country.

Hosting a tour of top British newspaper editors and publishers in 1975, Zhao gave a tough and humourless impression. His speech of welcome referred just sufficiently to the current left-wing campaigns to show his understanding for the need for a show of national unity; but his nose wrinkled visibly as he chanted the Maoist litany of the day.

A few months later, Deng had Zhao transferred to Sichuan as First Secretary. Mao died in 1976. Deng — again disgraced shortly before the Great Helmsman's demise — made a triumphant comeback in the following year, and his protégé's future was assured from then on.

In 1979 Zhao was appointed an alternate member of the all-powerful Politburo in Beijing, and in the following year Deng promoted him to full membership — an unprecedented rapid rise through the hierarchy of less strong-willed Party officials. He succeeded Party Chairman Hua Guofeng in the same year.

The Tourist Trail

Carol Wright

China's history is studded with contrasting periods of xenophobia and warm cordiality towards the foreigner and indeed it would be surprising if the yin-yang duality so central to the Chinese character did not manifest itself in public and national life, even to the point of influencing the development of hard and soft line foreign policies.

During the enlightened Ming dynasty (1368-1644), emperors encouraged contacts and trade with other nations. Great sea voyages were undertaken such as those led by the eunuch Cheng Ho which took the Imperial fleets to as far as what is now Tanzania in east Africa. A gifted and determined Jesuit, Matteo Ricci, was welcomed by the Emperor and contributed to the development of Chinese science and technology. But mandarin officials were both suspicious of this strange interloper and envious of his entree with "The Son of Heaven." They ventured that the Jesuit's health could be damaged by a lengthy sojourn in Beijing — even in those days not the most agreeable place to reside — and suggested that he be sent to tranquil, and very distant, Jiangxi where people were known to attain great age. The mandarins were not concerned about the stranger's health but with the influence that this first Jesuit envoy to China could have upon the illustrious master of the Middle Kingdom. The Emperor spurned the mandarins' advice and kept Ricci in Beijing where he lived until his death in 1610, seeking converts, helping to introduce Western technology and scientific thought and assisting with the reform of the Chinese calender.

It was Ricci who remarked, from his first hand knowledge, that the Chinese "look upon all foreigners as illiterate and barbarians and refer to them in just these terms."

The dynasty which succeeded the Ming, the Manchus (1644-1911), were not Han Chinese but descendants of the northern Tartars. Nevertheless they inherited the widespread belief that China was the earth's geographic core, the Middle Kingdom, which existed in a sea of rough, ill-mannered barbarians who could disturb the serenity — and security — of what was in fact an upstart dynasty. Writing from Guangzhou in the 18th Century, one Manchu mandarin commented on what he called the red-haired or western foreigners: "Their natures are dark, dangerous and inscrutable." He added for good measure that these westerners were a "fierce, violent lot." So worried were the Manchus about contamination by this seaborne horde that they literally withdrew Chinese from outlying islands and penned the barbarians in Guangzhou. There they became known in the Cantonese dialect as *gwai lo* — foreign devils. The origin of this label would appear to be the Dutch (the first northern Europeans in the China trade) whom the Chinese saw as red-haired. The term *gwai lo* likens the foreigners to demons who, in China, are traditionally painted with red and blue hair.

In a way the fears of both the Ming mandarins and the Manchu rulers were borne out. Ricci, though he himself made few actual converts, did help plant the seed of Christianity in China which is now being allowed to flourish again under the watchful eye of Dengian pragmatists who seek all help and support — even from the small, 700,000-strong Christian community — for modernisation. And the *gwai lo* of the late Manchu era of course brought in the drug which undermined Chinese society and contributed to the shocking, tragic opium wars which led to the grotesque end of Imperial China.

From this period the term *gwai lo* lingers and those lucky and prescient enough to spend a vacation in China will — should their ear be finely enough tuned — catch the phrase flickering through the curious crowds in the southern areas where Cantonese is spoken. Also inherited from this and earlier periods is the deep seated suspicion of foreigners and the influence that they might exercise on Chinese society. All evidence indicates that despite their embrace of Western technology and economic methods, the Chinese communists are just as xenophobic as their Manchu predecessors. But these feelings are being put aside as China seeks to tap what could be a great, unexploited resource — the world's jaded tourists.

There have of course been many visitors to China since the Revolution of 1949; Russians toured in the 1950s, and, in the 1960s and 70s, pilgrimages were organised for ideologically pure barbarians, those earnest fellow-travellers of Maoism whose tours were an exhausting, mind-numbing succession of visits to factories, communes and schools. As one Beijing official wryly remarked in 1980, the Maoists did not fully understand the economic potential of tourism, they allowed it only out of friendship.

But now, as if by revelation, the Dengians have seen tourism's possibilities and are set to realise the country's great potential. Today everyone is welcome, as long as they are not white South Africans or Israelis, have the money to pay the steep prices and are willing to travel in a group. The "foreign devils" are being transformed into "foreign friends" because China needs hard currency for modernisation.

The country, seat of the world's longest continuous civilisation, has, of course, a great deal to offer. There are breathtaking landscapes, wild gorges, seething cities, mountains, museums, palaces and pagodas. There is Chinese cuisine, wonders such as the 2,500-year-old Great Wall and the minority peoples in all their rich diversity. Foreigners have not been slow to respond to China's invitation. The first Western cruise liner docked there in 1977 and by 1980, a dozen airlines were flying regularly into Beijing while the Chinese flag carrier, CAAC, had its first jumbo jets and itself served about a dozen routes.

Chinese officals forecast that the hotel problems will soon be solved thanks to a massive hotel building programme which got underway in the 1980s. Eight new hotels are promised for Beijing including a 126 storey, Western-style hostelry with 1,500 rooms, an indoor swimming pool, health club and computerised management. Guangzhou, the country's southern gateway, is to get five new hotels in the 1980s and others are to be constructed at Shanghai and Nanjing and elsewhere.

The body responsible for overseeing tourism, the China International Travel Service is a venerable outfit, first started back in 1954.

The beauty of ancient China can be found practically everywhere.

Preceding pages: *The Drum Tower, Xi'an, a finely restored hall in the imperial style.*

Top, this page: *A temple in Guan Xi'an, Sichuan province.*

Bottom, this page: *The Great Mosque, in Xi'an, said to be the largest of 14 mosques in the city. The buildings date from the end of the fourteenth century and have been restored several times.*

Opposite: *The Great Mosque, Xi'an.*

But its system was virtually destoyed when its cadres were packed off to labour in the countryside during the Cultural Revolution of the 1960s. The Maoist hard liners of those days saw tourism for pleasure and dalliance at beauty spots as an aberration if it was not counter-revolutionary. The travel service has now been restored and China's tourist officials are eager to learn the ropes of mass jumbo tourism. Delegations are dispatched abroad to painstakingly pick the brains of experts on the needs, tastes and foibles of the new-found foreign friends.(In Shanghai an institute has been set up to offer a two-year course on tourism) Cooks, waitresses, room personnel and the indispensable interpreters are being drilled.

Officials say that state funds will be spent on developing 40 major tourist centers and plan to offer more than what can be exhausting "travel-and-look" holidays; they say that China will eventually provide facilities for leisure sports such as yachting, skating, skiing and even hunting. Perhaps the Chinese will be able to enjoy these too. Already in the 1980s, under the new liberal dispensations, a tiny fraction of the people were begining to take Western-style holidays, spending their seven-day annual leave away from home. Most of these ethnic tourists were students or honeymooners, who now have special hotel rooms set aside for them. Chinese couples who travel however have to remember to pack their marriage certificate otherwise they risk being refused a double room by the still puritanical hotel reception staff.

The development of this internal tourism has emphasised one of the more unfortunate aspects of visiting China — what can be best described as the rip-off. In its rush to acquire foreign exchange, China has adopted a two-tier price system under which visitors can pay up to five times more for travel and tourist services than Chinese sightseers. Officals tend to justify these very high prices by saying that the foreign visitors have extra services and privileges, for example air-conditioned buses. But the sternly regimented system often leaves the tourist with no choice: foreigners are not allowed to purchase second class rail tickets for example. Regulations preventing travel more than 15 miles beyond Beijing without special authorisation means that Western visitors are practically forced to take expensive group coach tours around the capital's region.

Early in 1980, Beijing introduced currency certificates which are issued to foreigners against foreign currency for payment of essential goods and services. These certificates have been created partly to eliminate a black market in foreign currency — especially the Hong Kong dollar — which started to flourish in the late 1970s. Foreign currency could be used to purchase consumer durables and other luxury goods in special shops.

Such curbside dealing in Western currencies was an indication that, once again, the barbarians or *gwai lo* were up to their old tricks and proving to be a pernicious influence. China's dilemma today is how to get its people to absorb what is deemed as good in Western society and reject which is deemed as bad. Even in the world's most tightly controlled nation, this screening of what the West has to offer is proving extremely difficult.

It is apparent that increasing exposure to Western life-styles is hastening the erosion of socialist values among a number of Chinese, especially the young. Tourism may be essential for the country's economy but it increases this hazardous exposure to the West.

Tourists in China are subjected to constant and intense scrutiny by the millions among whom they travel — and sometimes at odd, intimate moments. Officers had to warn young soldiers guarding a guest house in a resort city not to play "peeping toms" with Western visitors who, the soldiers were informed, engaged in amorous practices during the balmy spring evenings. The implication of that tale is clear: sight of Western couples tenderly embracing could weaken the moral fibre of

Every first-time visitor to Beijing plans at least one morning for a stroll through the Forbidden City. The inscription on the gate (opposite) *is its name,* Shunzhen Men, *or the Gate of Obedience and Purity, written in Chinese and Manchu script:* Above, *films on sale in a hotel lobby shop.*

Top, this page: *A sculpted marble mounted on cauldron shaped stone base of Ding Ling, the main tomb of the 13 Ming Tombs.*

Bottom, this page: *A marble figure of Sun Yat-sen, a Chinese revolutionary hero, in the mausoleum in Nanjing.*

Opposite: *A garden in Wuxi.*

the clean-living Communist recruits.

The influx of affluent foreigners with
their fashionable Western clothes, expensive leather shoes, sunglasses, digital
watches and their dazzling collection of
tourist impedimenta — movie and still
cameras and tape recorders — is in a way
helpful to the current pragmatic leadership.
It helps to get the message across: if the
Chinese want to be rich and have all the
material possessions taken for granted by
these pampered tourists, then they had better start working harder. But the tourists,
with their obvious wealth, must also
prompt the Chinese — especially the
young — to ask if perhaps Western
methods and the capitalist system are not
as distasteful and evil as we have always
been told.

Already the Chinese maintain that
exposure to the Western life-style through
foreign films is primarily responsible for
the rise in juvenile delinquency which, by
1980, had become a major concern.
Western influence was blamed for the
spread of sexy dancing in public parks, the
vogue in pop music and rock'n roll and the
wierd clothing that was glimpsed in the
parks at Shanghai. One outraged reader of
that city's *Wenhui Bao* newspaper
protested about young girls having
photographs taken of themselves with
cigarettes in their mouths.

Take the case of Chang Wenming and
Li Guosheng. They, we learned in June,
1980, committed Bejing's first bank rob-
bery in 30 years and all because they had
suffered from the spiritual pollution caused
by listening to decadent music on tape
recorders. As they had no money with
which to purchase this gadget or cassettes,
they went out and robbed a Beijing bank
of about US$700 and spent it on a recorder,
food and new clothes. "The spread of
this decadent music has a corrupting effect
on the life and morals of the masses, and
especially the young," wrote the *Beijing
Daily*.

Tourists therefore seem, like the
bucaneering China Traders of the 19th
Century, to be taking their own brand of

opium into China. It is that dreaded drug called "Western Influence" and the *Beijing Daily's* complaint. awakens echoes of the moral address that Commissioner Lin Tse-Hsu wrote to Queen Victoria about the opium trade more than a century ago: "Formerly smokers were few in number, but of late the contagion has spread, and its flowing poison is daily increasing."

When travel agents talk of places that are "different" or exciting they usually mean undeveloped, uncomfortable and more than a little primitive. China is certainly "different", but not in the primitive sense. It is still something of an almost magical mystery tour. Agents Thomas Cook say on one hand in their China departure dossier "it is difficult to glamourise China". But they also call it the "travel experience of this century".

Although visitors pay high and constantly rising prices, they certainly don't yet get a plush tour. The Chinese, inscrutably, do not let tour operators know more than the names of towns listed on the tour programme. Hotels and sightseeing details are often a mystery until a group is met on arrival by the local guide with a wide smile and halting English.

There is no individual travel unless as a VIP. The ordinary China tourist must be a groupie and be strictly punctual. The Chinese are irked by tardiness. As a group, tourists eat, tour, even sleep together on trains and ships. The tour days are long, beginning at 8:30 AM and often going on into the late evening with arranged entertainments. Meals are swift, and speed and efficiency with chopsticks can mean an extra hour to shop, flop, sip tea, or wander unrestrained about the town.

The Chinese issue what they call "visa invitations", and though these are on the increase, the tourist is still largely regarded as a guest of the Chinese people. This leads to misunderstanding when visitors think that because they have paid to come to China they are free to do what they themselves decide. The Chinese are puzzled and sometimes hurt if tourists resist being taken to yet another factory and prefer just

to sit and write postcards or stroll in a park. But then again, the Chinese are also extremely adaptable. Heavy industry, particularly the petrochemical plant in Beijing, is being featured less and less on tourist programmes. Factories, if they are included, tend to be of the consumer goods variety producing anything from carpets to ceramics and all have their gift shop. The Chinese are an inherently commercial race; a trait overcoming ideology in dealing with tourists. Souvenir shops are now springing up at every major site from the Temple of Heaven and Ming tombs to the few working monasteries open to foreigners. Though tourism is not yet regarded as being of great commercial national importance, its earning power is already impressing the Chinese. Their natural hospitality is being stiffened by sales sense. Hotels no longer include beer and soft drinks in the all-in price; deviations from the set breakfast menus, such as an extra yoghurt in Beijing, are immediately charged.

With China's low wage structures — about US\$40-US\$114 a month for an apprentice worker — tourist wealth must be tempting. But so far, courteousness has overcome covetousness. Honesty, to date, prevails; a fistful of money always brings correct change and a receipt; a discarded plastic bag or laddered tights are returned to the guest who tried to get rid of them. One girl's disposable paper panties were carefully ironed and sent on a thousand miles to her next hotel. There is no tipping, but guides like to be given books and magazines. In airports like Guangzhou's White Cloud and other public places used by foreigners, there are Lost and Found cupboards. "Take what is yours," the notices say rather invitingly.

In time, more than the current 10,000 non-Chinese visitors a year will know more about China's tourist trail; but for now, hotels in particular, are criticised as of low standard, most of them over 20 years old and many located far from city centres. But it's not so much a question of what has not been done, but what has been

Local people are reminded of the importance of foreign visitors by billboards saying that foreign trade promotes friendship. Very few Chinese ever get to see a foreigner and when they do, they tend to stare at him boldly. From time to time, local governments mount campaigns urging people not to stare at foreigners or to follow them around.

Visitors have an increasing number of activities from which to choose, including having their pictures taken in fancy opera headdresses (here, in Hefei), or enjoying finely prepared Southern cuisine in restaurants set amid ponds and lush vegetation like the Beiyuan Restaurant (opposite) in Guangzhou.

achieved in tourism in the relative short time since the Chinese government set up a tourist system. When the tourism authorities in Beijing can take over control of hotels, for instance, from local authorities and coordinate tours, accommodation will be less of a muddle. The Chinese are not blind to their shortcomings: As my Shanghai guide said: "I hope you will understand our difficulties and put up with existing conditions." Who can fail to respond sympathetically to a guileless request like that?

The Chinese may be camera-shy with visitors but are certainly not hesitant about scrutinising the foreigner. They wait outside hotel doors, surround tour buses, hold babies up for a child's eye view of what must seem to be outrageously exotic clothes, jewellery and hair-styles. Blondes and painted toenails can stop the teeming bicycle traffic at peak travel time. Legs are fascinating, but only foreign ones are ever seen in skirts, though little pre-teen Chinese girls wear attractive cotton skirts and coloured tops. At Beijing's zoo, the crowd watching the baby panda born by artifical insemination turned as a man to watch my tour group watch the pandas; the same sort of massed fascination occurs in theatres.

This curiosity is by no means covetous — not yet, anyway. No-one begs or tries to buy one's clothes. The visitor is given pride of place and rushed to the front of any queue. The "foreigners only" floors in department stores and Friendship Stores give visitors a chance to shop in peace for consumer goods, antiques and traditional arts and handicrafts. Prices and exchange rates are fixed nationally. Visitors are free to go to any shop and find prices marked clearly on the counters. And, whether shopping for a paper twist of crysanthemum tea, a baby back satchel, packet of Panda cigars, a poster of a tiger on the prowl, or cheap "Mao" cotton worker's cap, there's as much reward in contact with the people as there is in mulling over the "mutton fat" of white jade. Though free to wander about, with no

danger of hostility or Western-style mugging, the visitor is nonetheless segregated. He or she has separate hotels, different rooms in restaurants, separate transport, special waiting rooms in airports — and is shepherded everywhere by guides and interpretors.

Every detail of Chinese life is a source of intense fascination. It is a country where an old woman at her moon-shaped gate, the man at the factory bench, the child in his revolutionary red Pioneer scarf is as intriguing as the Forbidden City's golden roofs. Many tourists click through an incredible amount of precious colour film (hardly available locally and not of Western quality) on their first few days just snapping kids, old folk and animals.

The traditional entry point is from Hong Kong to Guangzhou (Canton). Though hovercraft are now running daily up the Pearl River and there are air links in the summer season, the most interesting way is by train. Starting a tour at Guangzhou, not the most appealing of Chinese cities, and ending in Beijing is the most comprehensive way of seeing China for the first time. After the Hong Kong emigration checkpoint at the border at Lo Wu, there is a sign that states simply "To China". Beyond is a walk across a covered railway bridge spanning a muddy river, and the first of the Chinese customs officers with their immaculate white suits and closely cropped black hair. Overstuffed armchairs with anti-macassars cushion the lengthy document checks in the PRC terminal. Long corridors to the station have little anterooms for VIPs and massive halls for the tour group with more deep chairs, tables with beautifully embroidered cloth and massive "friendship" murals and the first trickle of what will become a river of tea — green tea in the south, black in the north — wherever the tourists move. And the first culture shocks: hole-in-the-ground toilets with waist-high screens. The coffee drinker will pay heavily and have to virtually plead for a cup from reluctant hotels.

Trains in China are huge, efficient and

undoubtedly the best vehicle from which to China-watch. Many still have steam-engines. Stalwart visitors can bully their guides into travelling "hard class" over-night; it's usually cooler in the six-berth compartments with clean sheets, pillow, towel-cover and blanket. Hostesses con-tinually clean the trains and there are Asian lavatories at the end of each carriage. "Soft class" overnight means car-peted corridors and sealed-off four-berth compartments. The food is excellent, with beers and wines available.

The Guangzhou train is a delight of lace curtains, Maugham-era ceiling fans, potted plants on little cloth-covered tables. The reserved seats are twosome sofas that twist around to face the window for the passing panoramas of water buffalo, rice fields, black smudged villages with curled tile roofs, bamboo stands, processions of ducks and men crouched under rattan collie hats. The hostess serves tea in large mugs with lids that are the China-style cups everywhere except in restaurants; you can even see them in official portraits of Mao and Chou En-lai. Martial music blares over the loudspeaker, interspersed with poems and propaganda read by the hostesses. Any foreigner prepared to broadcast his own national or folk songs is welcome to do so. The Chinese love poems and songs.

It's advisable to avoid Guangzhou just after the spring or autumn trade fairs when everything from ships to soft toys are on sale. Then, 30,000 foreigners pack the city, the Hong Kong papers fill with sen-sationalised stories of theft and graft, inflated prices and fights for hotel rooms. After these trade-fests, the hotel staff are exhausted and some of their famed patience and inscrutability becomes plain irritability. The city's leading hotel is the 2000-bed Dong Feng (East Wind) adja-cent to the Exhibition Hall. For women, hotels are a good place for a hairdo costing about US$2.00, for a shampoo and set cheaper still, and more amusing are the local salons, where assistants are likely to be eager for information about Western dyeing techniques, and the cost of a perm is about US$1.20.

The Guangzhou Hotel was the former Trade Fair venue overlooking Pearl Square, and another vast block where many groups stay is the Bai Yun (White Cloud), named for the mountain behind it. This stark 34-floor high-rise block costs about US$15.00 a night for a single room. It is not comfortable, the plumbing is dilapidated, hot water is a rare luxury and there are no rugs on the stone floor. The antique fans don't deter flying insects and other bugs either. The "convention" writ-ten in English and hanging by the floor service desk is, however, friendly in its naïvety: "All guests are welcomed here and are led to their rooms first. Taking care of

Most visitors travel through Guangzhou, and may enjoy the city's limited number of tourist activities. On the other hand, one may choose to forego the sights of the city and spend his or her days going from one restaurant to another, sampling the city's culinary offerings.

This page: *Children play on the grounds of the Guangzhou Museum.*

Opposite: *The Sun Yat-sen Memorial Hall, used for meetings and performances.*

old and young person in various ways. Keeping our attitude towards the guests politely and not roughly. Standing up to reply to questions and explain in detail The public health is always guaranteed. Warmly seeing the guests off while they leave. We prove this convention be resolutely observed." In the lobby, more notices promise that suites are on every floor and on the 28th floor there is a goldfish pond in the seven suites. "Lifts of high, middle and low speed" are also described; the slowest ones always seem to be in operation.

Meals, as in all Chinese hotels, are served to tour groups all at once to each table. Lunch and dinner usually comprise about six dishes of basic, but well prepared Chinese combinations with soup and always a big bowl of rice. Outside Guangzhou, getting a piece of fruit for

dessert is almost impossible and tourists usually buy their own supply in the markets. Chopsticks are laid ready on the tables, but knives and forks are supplied on request to the uninitiated. Meals are at strictly set times: breakfast at 7:30 AM, lunch at noons and dinner at 6 PM on the dot. Bigger hotels have after-meal coffee and snack services in the lobby areas. All main meals are Chinese, unless Western food is ordered the previous day — usually a menu confined to stews and casseroles. Breakfast is Western unless Chinese is specified in advance — omelettes, fried or hard boiled eggs with doorstep toast, butter, preserves and tea. Butter and milk are in short supply and not usually consumed anyway by Chinese. Yoghurt is available in Beijing. Beer is just over 50 cents a large bottle and is very good, having been originally developed by

German brewers. Meals are included in the tour price, but groups often arrange to go out at night to taste the best of the surviving Chinese restaurants. It's advisable to book 24 hours ahead for large numbers. A per-head cost is about US$19.00, including red wine that tastes like thin port, beer, mineral water and *Mao t'ai*, a powerful rice-based clear liqueur.

Guangzhou is known for its garden restaurants and a charming spot is the Bei Yuan (North Garden) which has little bridges curving across carp pools and leading to the dining rooms, which are furnished with dark carved ebony screens and marble-seated chairs. The food is excellent, from the cold duck in seven colours, mushroom and pigeon soup, baked goose, prawn *dim sum* balls crisp with sesame seeds, steamed perch and "Cantonese four treasures". The restaurant is crowded day and night, though tourists naturally have their own banquet rooms away from the local diners.

Guangzhou has not a lot to offer for sightseeing. It is a place of hospitals, schools, factories, communes and a sparsely stocked museum. The city sprawls over 50 square kilometres and has a population of three million. The Pearl River divides it into the industrial Honai district and Hopeh with its shopping, restaurants and hotels. The river itself is 1,200 miles long and the third largest in China. The best view of the city is from the fourth floor of the red-timbered Zhenhai tower above the 30,000 seat sports stadium and the blue tiles of the Sun Yat-sen Memorial Hall. The tower is also the city museum, but has little to offer outside revolutionary mementos and has no English translators of the inscriptions and notes on each exhibit.

Beijing Road is the shopping centre. You can also find the Friendship Store next to the Bai Yun Hotel and Guangzhou's answer to Piccadilly Circus in Haizhu (Pearl) Square with its central plinth and red and white slogan that says: "Study seriously Marx and Lenin and Maoist thought". The Cultural Park is a kind of Chinese Tivoli Gardens with a huge stage for evening dance performances, men playing Chinese chess under the banyan trees, everyone sucking water-ices and the Cantonese teenagers roller-skating in near-darkness to the "Blue Danube" played raucously over loudspeakers — a tune also heard in the less likely setting of Beijing's Temple of Heaven.

Guangzhou has its memorials to its martyrs but, as everywhere in China, history began only in 1949 with the Communist revolution. One may hear a lot about the Great Leap Forward, but little detail of more historic events and figures. Old buildings and temples may have survived but the guides are more often than not puzzled at the visitor's interest; and the buildings are like museum-pieces, devoid of human feeling. A few English-language guidebooks are now being published but typical of the sort of un-information they contain is this quote from the booklet on Beijing's Forbidden City: "Every hall and every brick in the Forbidden City is the creation of the labouring people. Under the social conditions of those days, the construction of these magnificent buildings of such proportions speaks volumes for the great wisdom and creative ability of the labouring people in ancient China."

A glimpse of Guangzhou's pre-revolutionary past is on Sha Mian, an island where banyan and palm hang warm and humid over red brick paths that meander between fine old Victorian verandahed buildings, now workers' apartments, administration blocks and schools — the relics of the British and French merchant communities of the last century. The town strolls here. Lovers entwine at night in the darkness beneath the gables of old opium godowns. By day, the elderly perform their *Tai Qi* callisthenics along the island waterfront while children clamber over the cannon that defended the foreign "merchant princes" in the Opium Wars.

Guangzhou is subtropical, and very humid compared with Beijing, a city in which summers are dry and dusty, even a dessert dish is called 'Beijing Dust' and the famous Beijing ducks are dried in the fierce winds. An oasis of calm, and a chance for cool contemplation, is Guangzhou's Orchid or Lan Pu Gardens — not many orchids but quiet, all the same, beyond the Moongate entrance bordered by ferns at Yuexiu Park in the city centre. There are pretty paths meandering among bamboo and palm groves, little lakes framed with stone lanterns and pavilions; an ideal spot for postcard writing. You will write many. The Chinese sell them in packs of twelve and every hotel has an efficient post office offering lovely designs ranging from galloping horses to Revolutionary motifs. A charming tea pavilion lies in the heart of the Lan Pu Gardens on a small lake teeming with greedy carp.

If you are passionate about gibbons and pandas, Guangzhou's 33 hectare zoo is claimed to be the best in Asia. Another pleasant and relaxing attraction is White Cloud mountain, feature of a 70 square kilometre mountain range north-east of the city with stunning views of lakes and pine forests.

A commune is usually a feature on a tourist itinerary. When in Hangzhou, the visitor may be taken out of the city to one of the nearby tea-growing communes (opposite).

In places important to communist history, one museums of politically significant institutes such as the one above in Guangzhou.

Most visitors also find themselves on a half-day tour to Foshan, an old pottery-making city about 16 km. southwest of Guangzhou. The route is bumpy, bouncing along rutted roads past communes and rice paddies. The tour bus, like every other vehicle, is checked by armed guards at the city limits. No one leaves a city without a check. The guides will take advantage of the dull scenery to improve their English. Tourism is recruiting new guides by the hundreds, and not all foreign language standards are high. The guides learn on the job and many haven't previously visited the major tourist spots. I found myself struggling with prepositions and analysing an obtuse passage from "Lark Rise to Candleford"; trying to describe the life of 19th century farm labourers in Oxfordshire as we rattled through the oriental sun and water buffalo along the way. "Jane Eyre" and "Limelight" were the only foreign films on show in Guangzhou's cinemas, but Olivier's "Hamlet" had recently been shown on TV, dubbed in Mandarin.

Foshan is one of China's oldest cities with a 1300-year history. An arts and han-dicrafts centre, its offerings are paper-cutting, silk lion-head masks, opera masks and lanterns. At nearby Shiwan, porcelain production reveals the infinite patience of girls putting decorative pin-head pieces of clay on little hand-carved statues. Foshan's cultural masterpiece is the Temple of the Ancestors, an 11th century Taoist temple featuring elaborate roofs lined with porcelain figures — hundreds of them — and antique stone and wood carv-ings. One set of figures is 1.3 metres high and 30 metres long. The courtyard overlooks a large pool full of turtles and carp, and one temple is now a museum of exquisite porcelain and other historical relics from Han dynasty tombs in the area.

It says much for Guangzhou's charms that a half-day visit to a country commune is usually considered the highlight of the entire stay. The commune is the main form of production and social organisation in the rural areas. No longer do families all

Top: *Inside a temple in Foshan.*
Opposite: *Pottery figures from Foshan. Most arts and crafts factories have a sales room attached where visitors may purchase the factory's products.*

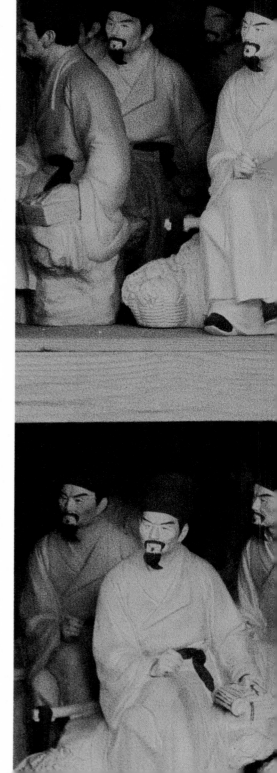

eat together in commune canteens, but the co-operative emphasis is still strong. The Ren Ho commune near Guangzhou is accustomed to tourists and gets about ten visits a month in the high season. It is a rich rice-producing commune and therefore a rural showplace. The visit starts with a briefing over tea by the commune leaders followed by questions and answers. It's sometimes like a long press conference. Visitors are free to ask details about wages, working conditions and social welfare. The commune school is visited, and in building reminiscent of a "High Noon" movie set, 10-year-olds copy Keats in the most pains-takingly beautiful English script. The hospital is next, with its pharmacy — patients waving cheerily from their beds — and then the medicinal herb garden, before a visit to a private house for more tea and talk of wages and work. Afterwards, there's an excellent lunch of commune produce — the commune director actually helping us all to rice on our particular visit.

Guangzhou's White Cloud Airport is, like the other major air terminals in China, blessedly empty, huge, with red and gold slogans declaring: "We serve the people". The foreigner, who rarely handles or even sees, his luggage from city to city, hotel to hotel (China is fussy, by the way, about overweight bags on internal flights), is led to a special departure lounge to await the flight in cane chairs, close to the inevitable Lost and Found cupboard, and tea service area. CAAC, the national airline serves 80 cities with Ilyushin and Trident jets. Tridents are used on the Guangzhou/Hangzhou route. Martial music blasts from speakers as visitors board. Inflight service is austere but hospitable — a bag of sweets and gum, a sweet orange drink, a souvenir notebook and an ice-cream.

Arriving at Hangzhou the guide says the city is famous for silk, scissors, green tea, and freshwater fish from its lakes. The welcome is an understatement, for this is a most beautiful area, the sort of scenery that Western tea caddy designs and paintings have portrayed as China. The man-made West Lake lies serene as an image on a scroll; little causeways and bridges snake across it, encircling azalea gardens and pavilions. In the background mists soften the gentle rise of mountains. The leading lakeside hotel is The Hangzhou, built around the former villa of a rich pre-Revolutionary silk merchant; a solid pre-war building, reminiscent of spas at Sochi on the Black Sea. The corridors are immense, the dining room has a stage and dance floor, there is a good shop for Hangzhou silk, tea and scissors. Rooms are high-ceilinged, looking out on tall pickets of pointed cypress. The furniture is worn, however, and there are no wardrobes — but plenty of big fluffy towels, hot water and soap. The tariff is about US$15 a night.

Little scenic paths wind up into the hills behind the hotel, ideal for walking and enjoying the panorama of the lake. Silk factories — where the most popular line, a series of woven portraits of Mao and Joseph Stalin, cost only a few cents — and a remarkable exhibition of basket-work are the highlights of the city tour. In the evening, a concert at the City Hall, which has 1978 seats and was built, no surprise, in 1978, is the main cultural attraction. It lasts three and a half hours and features non-stop arias from "The Volga Boatman", a ballad to Chou En-lai and excerpts ranging from "Madam Butterfly" to "Home on the Range" in English. It is both an uplifting and bottom-numbing experience.

But the lake and surrounding countryside are Hangzhou's biggest attraction. Serenity is absolute on an afternoon on the lake, sipping cool drinks, as the tour launch chugs past villas in old recreation spots with names like "Listening to Orioles Among the Willows" and "Autumn Moon on the Calm Lake", and then proves it's all more real than simple poetry by cruising out to a formal island of pavilions and places to view the moon, lily ponds and promenades. Alongside the lake are botanical gardens, superbly kept, as all public gardens are in China. There is the 13-storey Pagoda of the Six Harmonies, first built a thousand years ago and 60 metres high, from the top of which can be viewed one of the five largest rivers in China, the Chang Jiang, once famous for its floods. Elsewhere on the lake, the temple of Ling Yin features a massive reclining Buddha 90 metres long and a fairy island of brightly coloured mythological figures thrown together like a Bruegel view of Hell. Nearby is a legendary spring and grove of unusual square-stemmed bamboo. There are also some fascinating caves around the lake, including the famed Yenxia Cave which features life-like stone sculptures.

The Pagoda of Six Harmonies in Hangzhou (opposite) *dates from the year 970. It's almost 60 metres (200 feet) high, with seven levels and a staircase inside, and 13 levels outside. It's on the south side of West Lake.*

The lake is a picturesque and romantic spot, surrounded by monasteries, pagodas, towers and temples tucked in among the weeping willows and peach trees.

Tea is the universal beverage of the Chinese. All hotel rooms offer big flasks of water, packs of tea and mugs. At night in Hangzhou, visitors can stroll the lakeside under Chinese willows, peach and cassia trees to tea-house pavilions set out over the water. There are sweet sandy-textured biscuits to nibble with the earthy green and black teas. Dragon Well is one of China's most superlative green teas and can cost US$10 a pound in Beijing. It is said to bring a sparkle to the eyes, calm the senses and soothe the kidneys. There's a tea commune near Hangzhou where visitors can watch girls plucking the young leaves, which are graded in the qualities — the best of the crop actually rolled by hand in hot metal pans to curl the leaves.

From Hangzhou to Shanghai it is three hours by train. Shanghai Station has a magnificent Foreigners' Exit Hall with tea tables set between huge flowering azalea bushes and a stately grandfather clock. Shanghai is big-city China, her biggest city, with 10 million inhabitants and 10,000 factories. It is China's manufac-

turing capital, her chief producer and consumer of industrial goods, and it runs round the clock, 24 hours a day, pulsating with activity. It is still almost as cosmopolitan as it was in pre-Revolutionary times, with its international air links with Japan and Hong Kong and fleets of foreign ships hauling up the river past the Yangtze Delta gateway to the big, lively docks.

The Chinese may have no private cars and rely on the pedal-power of millions of bicycles, but Shanghai makes up for the lack of traffic with its own version of urban noise. Lorries and river boats hoot unceasingly amid a raucous cacophony of jangling bike bells. The Heping (Peace) Hotel is not exactly famous for its tranquility, situated as it is right in the middle of the din. It was formerly The Palace, built in 1928. Rooms are the usual 40 years behind international hotel design with deep square armchairs, old-fashioned upright telephones, silk shaded lamps on heavy Victorian room desks, which feature bottles of ink and nibbed pens. More

Some of China's cultural heritage is well preserved. Little systematic work has been done and finances are rarely available for research or restoration. During the Cultural Revolution, millions of dollars' worth of irreplaceable paintings, porcelains and other artworks were destroyed. Recently, when evidence of damage to the Imperial Palace by pollutants was discovered, an official group was formed to develop a way of maintaining the structure for posterity. Above, *detail of roof in the Yu Yuan Garden, and* right, *the Jade Buddha temple, both in Shanghai.*

sophisticated touches are a shower cap and luggage stickers (without much of a "stick"). The tariff is competitive, though — about US$18 a night.

Unlike Beijing and Guangzhou, Shanghai has retained a definite street-life; one can while away sleepless hours going out to noodle houses and eating *boazi* or stuffed bread snacks or stroll along at 6 AM to watch the citizens gather in the waterfront public gardens to do their *Tai Qi* exercises. A more professional calisthenics display can be seen at the permanent Acrobatic Theatre, where pandas and monkeys pedal bicycles and literally ape the flying trapese artists' dramatic stunts.

Shopping in Shanghai is the most satisfying in China. The city now has advertising hoardings urging the purchase of radios or "Lucky Cola". The lengthy Nanjing Road has no less than 400 shops on each side and some are open 24 hours a day. A leading tourist mecca is the Number One Department Store (they are graded down to number 15 in their size and variety of goods). Number One has 36,000 types of merchandise and a staff of 2,000. It is hardly Harrods, looks like a dilapidated Selfridges inside and has the inevitable top floor "foreigners only" array of jade, ivory and porcelain.

Shanghai's Friendship Store, tucked furtively in the corner of a small park near the waterfront has the best souvenir selection, and a separate antique section on Nanjing Road. Antiques are not cheap in China and only those marked with a red seal are allowed to be exported. Keep receipts to show customs officers when you leave. The Friendship Stores, open 9 AM to 9 PM, have currency exchange counters and mailing facilities. They sell a wide variety of crafts and manufactured goods including acupuncture outfits, ginseng, fur coats, silk pyjamas, cashmere sweaters, radios and TV sets. Those who fear their duty-free goodies will run out before the tour ends can stock up — for foreign currency — with imported Scotch (cheaper than in the UK) gin, vodka and other spirits and American cigarettes.

This once-international trading city still reflects its old foreign influence in the architecture of its buildings. The Bund could be part of Birmingham; European churches are now warehouses; mock Tudor frontages peep out of oriental facades. But the racecourse has been turned into a cultural park and the guides are keen to show off new workers' housing complexes rising slab-like round the city. It's unusual in most of modern China to step from a narrow street into the courtyard of a working temple and be welcomed with low sweeping bows by a black-robed monk. The Temple of the Jade Buddha has such a welcome — but the monk is only a carving — also flower-painted ceilings, a 500-year-old bronze Buddha and many other pre-Revolutionary cultural relics.

The Yu Yuan Garden reached, approached by way of a maze of market shops, is 400 years old, small but quaint with its sculptured dragons, artificial mountains, carp pools and tea-houses. The Garden of Leisurely Happiness is anything but that, with the surrounding jostle of Chinese coming off shift-work from the naval dockyards or leisurely taking photos with the big old-fashioned cameras that have survived years of austerity. The Long Hua Bonsai Park is more of a place for garden enthusiasts with one of the best collections of dwarf trees in China.

Nanjing, all my life, has been synonymous with white cherry blossom on navy-blue china that my seafaring father brought home before World War II. Nanjing today still produces these colours and designs on stately vases and ginger pots — its traditional craftsmanship now combined with modern technology. The city is proud of all its technological achievements. For example, the 4000 metre river bridge over the Yangtze, one of the three largest river bridges in all of China, is a double-decker affair with a railway running beneath the traffic carriageway. It was designed by the Russians during the old Sino-Soviet detente and completed by the Chinese in the 1960s. To the visitor it's interesting, but after being taken there a number of times, including once at night to see it illuminated, it's just another bridge.

Still, Nanjing has preserved a lot of its past, which is something rare in China outside Beijing. Tombs are a speciality. There is the Ming tomb complete with avenue of carved exotic animals similar to ones near Beijing. The Emperor Tai Zu, founder of the Ming dynasty, who died in 1398, and his Empress Ziao Xi who died in 1382, are buried at the southern base of the Purple Mountain. Two Tang tombs have been excavated at Niu Shoushan (Bull's Head Hill). More contemporary is the Dr. Sun Yat-sen mausoleum on the southern slope of the second Purple Mountain peak, a huge memorial covering 130 hectares. This edifice took three years to build and was completed in 1929. The Republican revolutionary's remains are confined in a room 24 metres above the ground. The site is magnificent, with 392 Suzhou granite steps to the tomb lined with carved stone lions and a beautiful park featuring trees presented by foreign nations.

Among other attractions there is the Jiangsu Provincial Museum, featuring a jade warrior's armoured suit linked with silver which was found in 1970 in a Han tomb, and the Museum of the Heavenly Kingdom of Great Peace, once the palace of the leader of the Taipings, a quasi-Christian rebel movement of the mid-19th century. The medicinal properties of plants and the improvement of rice strains are studied at the Sun Yat-sen botanical garden. Another popular Nanjing garden is The Terrace of Raining Flowers, whose delightful name comes from a legend in which a monk preached there and was so convincing that the gods showered the hill with flowers. The site includes a monument commemorating patriots executed by anti-Communist forces during the revolution.

Nanjing has a forest-in-the-city feel about it, surrounded as it is by the undulating Purple Mountain, which local folklore sees as a dragon curling round the city. A good view of the Yangtze River and environs can be obtained from the Purple Gold Hill Observatory, one of the finest in China, founded in 1934. To the north-east of the city is Lake Xuan Yu, another idyllic spot with five islands linked by dykes. The area was once forbidden, and was turned over to the public as a park in 1911. The Nanjing Hotel, one of the city's two biggest hotels, is a large four-storey edifice hidden in gardens behind big gates on the outskirts of the city.

Nanjing, formerly the Kuomintang capital, has many sights for the visitor; the Sun Yat-sen Mausoleum (opposite), *the famous bridge over the Yangtze River* (top) *and the Linggusi Park* (above).

Chinese tour guides often point proudly to nondescript buildings, monuments, dams and bridges. Many a traveller has wondered why he or she is standing at the top of a reservoir or walking through a rundown factory. The Chinese have been understandably proud of these small symbols of achievement under communist rule, and the visitor may come to appreciate this. Somewhat unfortunately, as the Chinese learn more about the West, through the media and tourism, some become embarrassed about them and refuse to accept them as accomplishments. This page: *Nanjing, Yangzte river and bridge and Mao memorial,* opposite and left. Above, *Ornamented gateway to Sun Yat Sen Memorial.*

The imperial throne opposite, *stands in splendour surrounded by precious cloisonne incense burners. This hall, the Palace of Heavenly Purity, in the Forbidden City, was once used as an audience chamber to welcome foreign emissaries.*
In today's China, many of the foreign emissaries are businessmen who come to display their countries' industrial and technological wares at this Beijing Exhibition Centre.

Beijing, with its spacious avenues, thin trickle of cars and vast flood of bicycles, and rice plains sprawling for miles around it, is something of a disappointment after the urban bustle of Shanghai. But monuments, palaces, courts and the relics of its magnificent cultural past make it the inevitable climax of any China tour. Your view of the city can be coloured right from the start by whichever hotel you're allocated. Peijing has a chronic shortage of hotel rooms, but although tours are based on double-room sharing, it is possible to pay extra and get a single room in some establishments. Some hotels, however, are sneaky about check-out times, which are not clearly posted. The ideal hotel is The Beijing, which is said to be China's finest. Its three massive blocks date from 1915, and are worth visiting for their lobby and banqueting hall pillars which echo the architecture of the pavilions in the Forbid-den City. There's a central 1950's "Russian period" block, and a modern 1974 section with 1800 beds. There's also air-conditioning, good bathrooms and furnishings, individual telephone (local calls are free and one can ask anywhere to make a call), electronic window drapes, radio and colour TV. For the foreigner, there's not much TV apart from English lessons and an occasional Hong Kong-made film with its views of Westernised Chinese life. Tariff at the Beijing is about US$34 a night.

The Beijing is on Changan Avenue, the main central artery of the city, and within a half hour's walk of the Forbidden City. It corners Wangfujing, the main shopping thoroughfare. Also on Changan Street, nearer Democracy Wall, is the Minzu Fandian (Nationalities) Hotel with 900 beds and a tariff of about US$22 a night. The Xinqiao, mainly for businessmen, is a block away from the Beijing and is where foreign companies now keep permanent suites. The hotel no one wants to be assigned to is the Friendship Hotel, a vast, guarded, and barrack-like place built by the Russians in the 1950's. However, it has a dinner-disco club, forbidden to locals. Its other main drawback is its location — 37 km. from the city centre in the north-western suburbs.

Because Beijing has so many important cultural sights, factory tours and "tea briefings" are mercifully limited here. The tourist is a little less regimented; he or she can walk unescorted to the Forbidden City, shop and take taxis in a way either not possible or not worthwhile elsewhere. Taxis called by the hotel will cost a little over one dollar for a tip across the city centre, with no tips and correct change and a receipt always given. But a good tip is to get the address written in Chinese characters before leaving. The city has a 37 km. subway, for which you pay as you board the trains; and on buses you pay as you get off.

The Forbidden City was the home of the emperors from 1421-1924 — 100 hectares of architectural grandeur set inside a four km. wall. The regal enclave is a series of now empty places and gold-tiled pavilions approached via five beautiful white marble bridges and the gate of "Supreme Harmony". Some of the architectural features are a good pointer to old imperial status: the more dragons on the roof edge, the more important the building. It requires a lot of time to study and contemplate the imperial relics and treasures — like a 440 kg gold pagoda, studded with precious stones, in which an emperor's fallen hair was kept. Outside the palace ground, the magnificent Temple of Heaven, covering over three million square metres, is so resplendent that the familiar single blue-tiled tower seen in most tourist pictures can hardly do justice to it. The temple and its courts fan out over many terraces of marble; there are two "echo walls" which combine geometry and acoustics to transmit any sound that is made right along their surface.

But the Summer Palace is the most appealing of the three great sights. Set at the side of Kunming Lake, where hundreds of Pekinese take their relaxation each weekend in row-boats, a maze of no less than three thousand cultural and ornamental structures are linked by garden courts and a 700-metre covered promenade along the lakeside. The pavilions and halls, all part of what is actually a vast museum of Chinese art and architecture, scramble up and over the steep Hill of Longevity. Having taken in the Seventeen Arch Bridge, Marble Boat, Hall of Benevolence and Longevity, Garden of Virtuous Harmony, Hall of Jade Billows, the Pavilion of Propriety of Weeding and Arbor of Strolling in a Picture, to mention but a few, visitors welcome a change to relax over the excellent food served in the restaurant pavilions north-east of the Marble Boat, listening to orioles; and for once, getting the courses one by one with a change to fully appreciate their different flavours.

Beijing's most famous attraction, the Great Wall, was the only man-made struc-

On the Avenue of the Animals, approaching the Ming Tombs, stone animals, warriors and officials line both sides of the road.
   This page: The entrance to one of the country's distinguished seats of higher learning, Beijing University.

The majesty of the Great Wall must truly be seen to be appreciated. The mood at the Great Wall changes depending on the time of day, the time of year and the kind of weather — definitely worth a special outing every time one goes to Beijing.

ture recognisable to the Apollo-moon-shot astronauts. It fairly dominates Beijing sightseeing, and has been packaged into a day-tour with the Ming tombs, with a special train which takes 700 or so tourists up to Badaling. From here, a 20-minute walk or sluggish mini-bus service takes them on to a section of the 2,300-year-old, 4,500-km-long wall. An hour is allowed in which to clamber up either the "easy" side, where visiting statesmen ranging from Richard Nixon to Margaret Thatcher have usually been photographed, or the harder, steeper side with worn stones for an arduous ascent rewarded with racing blood-pressure and sweeping vistas of the dragon-like edifice slithering along the tops of green-clad ridges into the distant mountains. Not surprisingly, helicopter trips and camel rides are among the new tourist facilities planned for The Wall.

A box lunch is offered, along with a well-earned rest, on the train and then the buses that take tourists down to the five km ceremonial avenue leading to the Ming tombs — the roadway flanked each side with 24 carved stone animals and 12 human statues; and the elephants, by the way, are ideal places to have your photo taken. Only one of two tombs, the Ting Ling, excavated and restored out of a total of 34 in the valley is actually open to visitors. This has small museums of relics and photo exhibitions showing how the hidden entrance was found. Away from the hot dust of a summer afternoon, this underground tomb is pleasantly cool with thick marble doors leading to corridors with carved marble altars and ceremonial chairs for imperial ancestor worship. The tomb's main chamber has replicas of the big plain full-bellied wooden coffins of an emperor and two empresses.

Beijing is also China's political capital, and one of the first places most tourists are taken to is the Tienanmen Gate and Square — the largest square in the world, with its vast pavements marked out for military reviews. The Congress Building, or Great Hall of the People, is on one side, the Museum of Chinese History on

Top: *A stone stele marks the entrance to one of the Ming Tombs.*
Opposite: *An underground chamber in Ding Ling, the tomb excavated in 1958.*

To approach the Ming Tombs by road is to capture a sense of former dynastic times when an elaborate funeral procession made its way through the white marble arches that mark the start of the Sacred Way. Half a mile further is the Great Red Gate, through which only the emperor's body was allowed to pass. Visible on the other side of the gate is a huge stele, behind which begins the Avenue of the Animals.

another. In the centre is the sacred Chairman Mao Memorial Hall. Recently reopened to public view on three mornings a week, the shrine welcomes foreigners, who are edged into the long, slowly moving queue of workers and their children to file past the crystal casket in which Mao's embalmed remains are draped in a red flag.

For shoppers, Luilichang in the old city is the main area for antique hunting, and the inevitable Friendship Store is in the foreign ghetto down Changan Avenue, where all the embassy staff and foreign business representatives live. For some good "nature" walks in the city, the footsteps of the emperors may be followed and strolls taken on Coal Hill, reopened in 1977, at the rear entrance of the Forbidden City, with good views of Beijing from the top. Beihai, also reopened in 1977, is a little like a miniature version of the Summer Palace, with pavilions and painted covered paths and a boating lake. There are rows of fish tanks here which feature beautifully coloured oriental fish. The Western Hills, an hour's drive north, is a popular canvas of autumn colours.

In the evenings, Beijing opera is requested by most visitors. Opera is not what a Westerner would call most performances, which may take place in huge working men's clubs and include superb acrobatic dancing and mime, and gorgeous costumes, which compensate for periods of what visitors would regard simply as high-pitched wailing. Recently traditional operas banned by the Gang of Four have been revived with love and infidelity replacing a lot of the revolutionary propaganda themes. The Chinese seem to use the theatre as a chance to catch up on gossip and meet friends, so your guide can give you a running commentary without hisses and protests and it is not essential to clap at the end. Clapping, though not so much a part of etiquette that it once was, is reserved for greetings, political toasts and ending the interminable briefing sessions at the factories.

There'll be a lot of these sessions on your China tour, for Chinese tourism has been established primarily to show off the country, its problems and its achievements to the West — to gain Western sympathy, admiration and support for its modernisation programmes. But a lot more than backyard factories and ceramics plants is being offered in return — the remnants of the antique past of the world's largest living civilisation, for one thing. And it's a sight that's been shut off to Western eyes for over 30 years — only a flicker of an eye by Chinese historical reckoning, but a wide, almost unbridgable gulf in the speed of time today.

The Temple of Heaven (opposite) *and the* Summer Palace (preceding pages) *have been painstakingly restored by craftsmen of long experience. The rich detail and elaborate design of the painting of these pictures and beams can be appreciated by even the most uninformed visitor.*

Some historians view the Summer Palace and especially this monstrous Stone Boat (this page) *as a fitting monument to the Empress Dowager's extravagent rule and to the decline of the Qing dynasty.*

A visitor can easily spend days wandering through the maze of courtyards at the Forbidden City. No matter where one stands, one will always have a captivating view of the imposing tiled roofs that shimmer like gold in the sun. In front of many of the gates, palaces and pavilions stand bronze tortoises, cranes or lions or, as here in front of the Yang Xing Gate, enormous gilt pots, all impressive in their size and craftsmanship.

Some visitors may prefer the bold, rich style of the Summer Palace, as in this Pavilion of Buddha's Fragrant Incense (opposite) high on a hill overlooking the man-made Kunming Lake.

Located in the heart of Beijing, the Forbidden City covers an area of one square kilometer (250 acres). It's surrounded by a wide moat and protected by 10 metre (35-foot-high) wall. The complex, including six main palaces and dozens of smaller buildings, contains more than 9,000 rooms.

Three flights of marble steps (opposite) lead up to the terrace of the Hall of Supreme Harmony. The steps flank a central carved marble ramp, over which the emperor was traditionally carried.

The basic plan of the Forbidden City survives as it was first built in the fifteenth century when more than 200,000 labourers worked for 13 years, hauling stone from nearby quarries, and fashioning beams and columns from trees of the Sichuan and Yunnan forests.

As succeeding emperors gained their positions, the original buildings were redecorated and relocated. The current buildings date mostly from the eighteenth century.

The tortoise is a Chinese symbol of immortality. Here it sits on the terrace in front of the Palace of Heavenly Purity, which was originally the emperor's bedroom.

The side buildings of the Forbidden City were once libraries, shops and private apartments. Then, the palace was a self-contained city, holding just about everything and everyone the ruling family might need. When the emperor ventured forth among the people, he was usually on his way to some ceremony or other, perhaps at the Temple of Heaven, or one of the other ceremonial sites such as the Altar of the Sun or Altar of the Moon.

ZHOU PEIYUAN

China's most famous scientist, Zhou Peiyuan, was born in 1902 and received a good education from his wealthy family, who occupied properties in the balmy lake-district of Jiangsu province. After graduating in physics from Beijing's Qinghua University, he travelled to the United States in 1925, taking a Ph.D. at California Institute of Technology three years later. (He also studied at the University of Chicago.) He returned to China to take up a professorship at Qinghua, and during World War II taught at the provisional university set up by supporters of Chiang Kai-shek in Kunming. In 1943 he returned to the United States and researched methods of aerial torpedo warfare for the U.S. Government.

Zhou went back to China shortly before the Communist victory in 1949, and after a period of indoctrination during which he confessed to having once been hostile to Communism, he was appointed to important academic posts and allowed to continue his own research. He was made a vice-president of Beijing University, helped found key scientific bodies and served on the government's Planning Commission. In the 1950s he travelled in the Soviet Union, Britain, Poland, Italy, Canada and Switzerland as a member of Chinese delegations, topping these tours off with visits to India and Japan in 1961. In 1957 he attended the first "Pugwash Conference" aimed at establishing non-political ties between scientists of East and West. In the early sixties he visited Albania, Rumania and New Zealand.

Zhou willingly associated himself with the Communist Party's international propaganda effort, coming out against nuclear weapons in the 1950s and playing a role in the then-fashionable international Peace Movement. He was not slow to attack his less politically astute colleagues in the "anti-Rightist" campaign in 1957.

Aged 64 when the Cultural Revolution broke out, Zhou was lucky to be let off fairly lightly by the Red Guards, though he dropped from public view for about five years. His gift for political opportunism apparently helped him survive the purges of people with "bourgeois" outlooks and with too many contacts in the West and the Soviet Bloc.

From 1972 on, Zhou became a familiar figure among Western embassies in Beijing, attending receptions and hosting visits to Beijing University. He was active in the new programme of scientific exchanges between China and the outside world which accompanied the recognition of the People's Republic by the United States and most of its allies. His "Indian summer" career took him to such posts as Vice-Chairman of the Scientific and Technical Association of China, and eventually the presidency of Beijing University.

Further testimony to Prof. Zhou's political acumen was his survival of the anti-intellectual movement which Mme. Mao and her supporters masterminded in the universities in 1974-76. Many of his senior colleagues were not so fortunate, and had to undergo the humiliation of being denounced in student wall-posters both at Beijing University and at Qinghua (Tsinghua), his alma mater. But he never became so hand-in-glove with the left-radical faction around Mao that he had to suffer for it after the old Chairman's death. On the contrary, he was given honorary posts in the National People's Congress and seemed destined to end his days in peace and enjoying the respect if not admiration of his colleagues.

Few prominent men have ridden the currents of China's political scene so adroitly — which makes it ironically appropriate that his main academic work has been in the study of turbulence.

The Sporting Challenge

Bert Okuley

Only 30 years have elapsed since the five-star red flag representing the successful conclusion of Mao Tse-tung's revolution began fluttering over Tien An Men Square in Beijing, symbolising the birth of modern China.

One does not have to be totally acquainted with Chinese history to realise that physical culture and sports were all but unknown in the previous 5,000 years of the Celestial Kingdom's existence as a semi-feudal, semi-colonial country of extreme wealth and poverty.

In the early part of this century, the sporting life was the private domain of the privileged few, well-to-do colonialists afflicted with the deadly monotony of what, to them, was life in heathendom.

The mighty River Yangtze became the sportsman's elysium, and along its noble banks, from the sea for hundreds of miles into the interior, game abounded for the bemused foreigner. Houseboats or light draught yachts became floating shooting boxes, their occupants repairing to a good fire in the saloon after a hunt. In that particular era wildfowl of every description — swan, geese, mallard, teal and duck — literally covered the waters of the Yangtze for miles at a stretch. Along its banks in certain localities could be found tigers, leopards, horned deer and wild boar. But nonetheless exclusively European, and the national motto for the Chinese themselves might just as well have been "semper idem."

Its history of revolution and the approach of the Second World War aside, the standard of sport in China was so backward that a nation which even then had some 500 million people could manage to qualify but a single athlete for the 11th Olympic Games in 1936. It thus was only after the establishment of the People's Republic on October 1, 1949 that sports became a major facet of the socialist cause in China. In 1952 Chairman Mao declared that there should be undertaken a campaign to "promote physical culture and sports and build up the people's health." The All-China Sports Federation was founded and Mao formulated a policy whose primary characteristic was the motto "Health First."

"Whenever feasible," the Chairman said later, "physical culture and sports of all kinds should be encouraged, such as physical exercises, ball games, running, mountain climbing, swimming and traditional (Tai Qi Chuan) exercises." Those leading sedentary lives such as government office workers found themselves walking, swimming, mountain-climbing or doing setting-up exercises to music broadcast over Radio Beijing. Institutes of physical culture were formed in such centres as Beijing, Tianjin, Wuhan, Shenyang, Xi'an, Chengdu, Shanghai and Guangzhou for training sports teachers and coaches. The largest is the Beijing Institute of Physical Culture, with 600,000 square metres of campus and facilities to accommodate some 2,000 students. They learn gymnastics, participate in track and field and weightlifting, basketball, football and, of course, swimming. (China's most celebrated swim was made on July 16, 1966, at the outset of the Cultural Revolution, when Chairman Mao — then aged 72 — swam about 15 kilometres in the Yangtze at Wuhan. The event drew banner headlines inside China as well as full international reportage. In subsequent years tens of millions of swimmers took to rivers, lakes and sea on the occasion of the anniversary of Mao's river crossing. Even special stamps were issued to commemorate the event.)

Prior to 1949 only one outdoor stadium existed in Beijing, the Xiannongtan Stadium whose capacity was subsequently enlarged from 16,000 to 30,000 seats. In 1954 the Beijing Indoor Stadium which accommodates 6,000 spectators was completed, and in 1959 The Beijing Workers Stadium which seats 100,000 was built. According to statistics of the All-China Sports Federation, there exists today in the People's Republic some 26,000 stadia, gymnasiums, swimming pools and shooting ranges of various sizes. Factories across the country turn out equipment to meet the needs of the masses in sports activities with as much attention being paid to the needs of those participating in winter sports. Ice skating is a popular pastime in the winter months in different parts of the country.

Many mountains in China's northern and northwestern regions are permanently blanketed with snow and the plainlands and plateaux in these areas are under a white mantle for several months of the year. Herdsmen in Xinjiang and Inner Mongolia use skis made of hide to pursue Mongolian gazelles, foxes and wolves. So when the first skiing competition was held in Jilin in 1951 it attracted wide interest. Only 70 skiers took part and there were no trained judges but skiers from neighbouring Heilongjiang and Inner Mongolia were soon going to Jilin to ski competitively. In 1957 the Winter Sports Association of China (formed in 1953) organised the first national skiing championships. But these events came to an abrupt halt in 1966 when the Cultural Revolution began and did not resume until eight years later. Standard ski slopes will soon be built at Jilin and Heilongjiang so that international events can be staged with athletes from other countries taking part.

Throughout China people have taken to sport with a great deal of enthusiasm. Those outstanding ones did so with a dedication and a fervour that only truly great sportsmen and sportswomen are capable of — straining themselves against the limitations of their own bodies and enduring considerable hardship and pain so they could go those steps beyond which, in time, enables them to smash records. Unlike their counterparts in the West they applied political philosophy to their training methods.

An article in *China Reconstructs* (April, 1971) written by high jumper Ni Zhigin, who jumped 2.29 metres in November, 1970 to break the existing world record is enlightening. In it he tells how he shed his personal ambition and replaced it with a desire to win glory for Chairman Mao Tse-tung and his socialist motherland. Discussing his approach to leaping higher Ni says: "The world record for men's high jump has been called an unsurpassable limit. To break this limit requires a stubborn will and extraordinarily rigorous work. But more importantly one must guide oneself with Chairman Mao's philosophical thinking, explore the laws of high jump and blaze a trail of one's own."

China does not have a long sports tradition, unless one puts such activities as tai qi chuan (opposite), *Chinese shadow boxing,* in that category. In 1936, only one Chinese athlete qualified for the Olympic Games.

The western notions of athletics and physical fitness are barely as old as the communist revolution. In 1952, once the communist party was firmly in place in Beijing, Chairman Mao first urged the nation-wide development of physical culture and sports, and emphasized the need to build up the people's health.

"In training I tried applying three fundamental viewpoints of materialist dialectics: First, the accumulation of quantitative change leads to a qualitative leap; second, grasp the principal contradiction and concentrate a superior force to solve it and third, constantly create the new on the basis of destroying the old. Applying them to the high jump, I summed them up as rigorous training, working for perfection and breaking the old.

"In 1969, I greatly increased the amount of exercises for my winter training. Such rigorous training upset the balance of my bodily functions. My back ached, my legs were sore, my blood pressure rose, I felt dizzy and had stomach pains. Give up or keep it up? If I gave up, I would not be able to improve my performance. If I kept it up, I would be able to tap the maximum potential of my body, temper my will and lay the spiritual and physical foundation for improving my performance. From my own practice I knew that the loss of balance of my organic functions was only temporary. I would gain new balance if I kept up the training. In keeping up I applied another of Chairman Mao's observations: 'Frequently a favourable situation recurs and the initiative is regained as a result of holding out a little longer.' So for every training session I deliberately set targets for holding out a little longer. By doing this again and again, I gradually increased the amount of my exercises. Many small successes led to a big success — quantitative changes led to a qualitative leap. Finally I reached the level I aimed for."

"Chairman Mao says 'There are many contradictions in the process of development of a complex thing, and one of them is necessarily the principal contradiction whose existence and development determine or influence the existence and development of the other contradictions.' I applied this to the high jump. There are three elements in the high jump: the run, the jump and clearing the bar. The most important of these is the jump. I analyzed the jump and found that leg strength is not only vital to the jump but helps the run and the clearing of the bar. So I concentrated in building up the legs and kept up the exercises all of the year round, gradually increasing the amount. When I had mastered the jump, I found that sometimes after jumping five or six centimetres higher than the bar, I still did not clear it. So I concentrated on my clearing action thus finding and solving the principal contradictions one by one."

"A decade of experience had taught me that I could not break a world record unless I broke away from conventions and dogmas. Bourgeois authorities have laid down some rules: Relax before competition, rest after competition; in order to be in top form, do not take part in successive competitions within a short time. All this sounds scientific and rational. Actually it is not. I had followed these rules closely and wasted time and lost opportunities to set good records. So I began working in the spirit of Chairman Mao's teaching to seize the day, seize the hour and give full play to our style of fighting — courage in battle, no fear of sacrifice, no fear of fatigue and continuous fighting (that is, fighting successive battles in a short time without rest)."

"In four months from the end of June to early November (1970), I took part in more than 20 competitions and exhibitions. I never stopped training between competitions. I was in excellent form throughout, my willpower rose. My records improved steadily. In the four months, I cleared 2.23 metres once, 2.24 metres five times, 2.26 once and 2.29 twice."

Interviews with other sportsmen and sportswomen reveal similar approaches, determination and dedication. Woman pentathlete star Ye Peisu, took her inspiration from the late Premier Chou Enlai who urged Chinese athletes to remain humble in victory, never lose heart and to apply themselves to hard training.

Results of testing by her coach in 1975 when she was 16 years of age showed an imbalance in the development of her physical and motor skills. While lacking coordination and suppleness, she possessed tremendous explosive power and quick reflexes. With these points in mind he put her through a basic conditioning programme. She lifted a total weight of 5,000 kilogrammes every day to increase her strength; climbed long flights of stairs with two 1.5 kilogramme sandbags strapped to her ankles to improve her spring; practised fartlek (fast and slow running) on the track to build up her endurance and speed; and went through numerous repetitions of throwing movements to achieve better coordination between her legs, waist and arms, especially in the shot put, her weakest event. As a means of sharpening her competitive spirit she often trained with male decathletes.

Mao's policy was clearly stated: Whenever feasible, physical culture and sports of all kinds should be encouraged. Even the elderly were included, and tai qi chuan *gained increasing popularity as simply good exercise for that age group.*

During the next four years Ye's pentathlon marks grew at the astounding rate of 300 points a year. At the China National Track and Field meeting in 1977 her overall total was 3,905, only two points behind the winner. In April, 1978 she created a new national record of 4,019. At the Eighth Asian Games held in December that year in Bangkok, she achieved a runaway victory in the pentathlon scoring 4,133 points, coming first in the 100 metre hurdles, the high jump and the long jump, second in the shot putt and fourth in the 800 metres. In the high jump she cleared the bar to draw level with Japan's Tamami Yagi.

The prospect of reaching world rankings is spurring Ye Peisu onto greater efforts and she is enthusiastically stepping up her training, according to sports writers.

Training in sport begins early in China. Children upwards of three years of age are taught to swim and those in kindergarten and primary school train for competitive events. Those that show any real promise are given every possible encouragement and are enrolled in special part time sports schools where they are given the benefit of good coaching and training facilities.

Training methods are being left less and less to chance. Scientists have been busy since 1958 doing research work aimed at improving the standard of athletic performances. There are now some 120 technical personnel working at the National Research Institute of Sports Science in Beijing engaged in departments given over to training in athletics, swimming and gymnastics; training in ball games; sports medicine; physiology of exercise; mass sports; information services; developing instruments for sports science and audio visual services. Most of the work is done during competition and training. Speaking about the institute's work, staff member Xiong Douyin said "During the Third National Games in 1975, in cooperation with the Beijing Physical Culture Institute, we made a general survey of the performance and morphology of some 5,000 athletes together with a control group of

600. An analytical study of the 500,000 figures computerised out of an original 200,000 gave us a better understanding of the effects of different sports and events on the physical dimensions of the human body and provided us with valuable data for selecting and training athletes.

"In 1975, our institute conducted ECG (brainwave) tests on climbers just returned from Mount Qomolangma (Everest), the world's highest peak. Based on the effects of low oxygen a regimen was recommended for their recuperation.

"During the Fourth National Games held in Beijing in September, 1979 our research efforts intensified. In the high jump finals, a newly made seismic instrument was introduced to record the action of the take-off leg on the ground when different jumping styles were used to clear different heights starting from two metres for men and 1.75 metres for women. Hundreds of swimmers and track and field athletes were given tests, among other things in PWC 170, cardiography, consumption of oxygen under load and level of lactic acid after work, in order to find out the relationship between the capability of work and the cardio-respiratory functions. Myodynamic and myoelectric measurements were taken of 60 weightlifters' seven muscle groups. Technical films were made in track and field, gymnastics, weightlifting and diving events, while basketball, football, volleyball and badminton games were videotaped. All this has proved useful for improving training methods and athletic performances," the scientist said.

The prevention and treatment of sports injuries is a major task of the institute. Medical staff go regularly to training centres and competition sites to collect material for a systematic study of common sports injuries. They recently studied hundreds of cases of cracked and dislocated vertebrae and worked out effective ways of treatment. Acupuncture and traditional massage are used to treat injuries.. Hydraulic massage machines have been recently developed and these have been

tested on a number of sportsmen and dancers and found effective in overcoming fatigue, promoting sleep and preventing and curing the stiffening, convulsion and pulling of muscles as well as the accumulation of fluid in joints.

For many years the fact that the government of Taiwan, known as the Republic of China, was recognised as the official government of China, kept the people of the biggest nation on earth from being represented in the international community. This applied as much to sport as it did to United Nations membership. Interestingly it was through sport that China began its emergence on the world stage. The first barriers were broken down by a team of ping pong players from the United States and these paved the way for the international community's belated recognition of the Beijing Government as the legitimate rulers of China.

China entered the international sports world for the first time when it joined the Asian Games Federation in 1974 in time for the Tehran games, held the same year. The People's Republic, which had previously chosen exclusion from the world sports body, was to carry out startling successes, particularly in table tennis and badminton, at Tehran. Chinese girls walked off with three jumping and throwing medals and were able to take silver and bronze medals in a number of events. The Chinese won team titles in badminton and observers were impressed by their proficiency in gymnastics.

The Chinese performance was overshadowed at the Asiad by Japan, the region's sports superpower, which took 75 gold medals at Tehran in an awesome display of athletic prowess.

Over the years which followed, those which culminated in the Eighth Asian Games in Bangkok in December of 1978, Chinese athletes continued to make deep inroads into Japanese sports supremacy.

Two months prior to the Bangkok games, the International Amateur Athletic Association of the People's Republic became the sole representative of China. A

Sports schools that could identify potential athletes while still youngsters and train them for competitive games, were opened in the 1950s.

few weeks later, meeting in Strasbourg, France, the International Gymnastic Federation took similar action. It brought to 18 the number of international sports organisations which have recognised the People's Republic. Its sporting contacts now extend to about 130 countries and regions.

Many children in China learn to swim at a very early age. The talented ones are routinely selected for extra training in special programmes. While China's swimmers are not yet highly developed, its springboard divers are considered to be world class.

(It was at this particular time that Li Meng-hua, who also heads China's Athletic Association, made the first official overtures to athletes from Taiwan to compete in events on the mainland. The official New China News Agency quoted him, "I would like to point out that all national sports organisations of China always have Taiwan sportsmen and women at heart . . . We ensure sportsmen and women now living in Taiwan freedom to come and go when they come to participate in competitions").

China's "Great Era" in the international sports arena dawned at the Eighth Asiad in Bangkok's National Stadium complex. The Chinese sent a nearly 400-strong delegation to the games, joining some 3,000 athletes from 25 countries in 12 days of intense competition held under the slogan "Ever Onward." The events produced 66 new Asian Games records, including track and field, swimming, shooting and weightlifting — some of them approaching world marks. China participated in 15 of the 19 events (remaining on the sidelines for boxing, field hockey, bowling and yachting) and the team's overall performance produced results far superior to those achieved in Tehran.

Japan, because of its overwhelming dominance in swimming and diving events, once again took the overall team championship, but Beijing's representatives made extremely strong showings in all events except badminton and tennis.

The Chinese went home with 56 gold, 60 silver and 51 bronze medals (an increase over 1974 of 23 gold, 15 silver and 24 bronze medals) and moved from third to second place in the final standings. In track and field, shooting, weightlifting and swimming, Chinese athletes broke 24 and equalled two Asian Games records; they also smashed 34 of their own national records.

Gymnastic events were almost exclusively monopolised by China, which also swept table tennis events by taking all seven golds at stake along with three silver

and two bronze medals. Entering archery competitions for the first time, the Chinese posed serious threats to dominant powers Japan and Indonesia.

Chinese divers took all of the gold and silver medals for both the men's and women's springboard diving, and a number of foreign coaches believed they were approaching top world level in technical execution. Of the 14 gold medals at stake for gymnastics, the Chinese won 10 — including one for the men's and another for the women's all-round competition.

In track and field, Chinese competitors took 12 golds, 9 silver and 13 bronze medals, surpassing their Japanese counterparts for the first time in any major international competition. Chinese girls established Asian Games records in the high jump, pentathlon, shot put and javelin throw. Competing in six weightlifting categories, Beijing's representatives took second place in the standings (behind Lebanon) with six golds, nine silvers and five bronze medals.

Chinese marksmen shattered 11 Games records and five national standards in winning the shooting competition. In winning the men's free pistol event, Su Chih-po with 560 points broke a Games record which had belonged to Japan for 16 years.

At an average age of only 21, Chinese fencers won four gold and four silvers in eight events and replaced 1974 winners Japan at the top of the standings. The President of the Federation Internationale d'Escrime, Pierre Ferri, said the Chinese fleurettes were fast approaching world levels.

A youthful Chinese water polo team won all six matches they played, overwhelming Japan (11-1) in the title-clincher. Both the men's and women's volleyball teams were somewhat disappointing at Bangkok, finishing behind South Korea and Japan respectively. The Beijing footballers meanwhile were never in contention and were far below world level.

Not suprisingly, China is placing special emphasis on improving the standard of its

swimmers. Of the 29 gold medals at stake in Bangkok, 25 went to Japan and none to China. British Olympic Champion, David Wilkie, who set a world 200-metre breaststroke record in 1976 in Montreal, visited China in mid-1979 for a series of clinics and training sessions for the country's leading swimmers and coaches. He was accompanied on the trip by Hans Fassnacht, an Olympic silver medallist from West Germany. Both expressed amazement at the individual height of some of the Chinese swimmers, many of them more than six feet while in the 13 to 18 age level. "And they seem to have every book there is on swimming," Fassnacht said. "They could tell me some things about myself that I had forgotton. I never even had time to read. The Chinese wanted to know everything about training methods, schedules, diet, nutrition . . . everything."

Chinese swimmers were reported to have set four national records at a meeting in Beijing to commemorate the 13th anniversary of Chairman Mao's celebrated swim. The New China (Xinhua) News Agency said that Lieng Wei-fen, 17, recorded a national mark of one minute 14.5 seconds in the women's 100-metre breaststroke, Yu Ping had set a new time of 18 minutes 13.5 seconds in the women's 1,500-metre freestyle, army swimmer Wang Li-jung set a mark of nine minutes 41.9 seconds in the women's 800-metre freestyle, and Huang Wei-dong set a record of 16 minutes 54.9 seconds in the men's 1,500-metre freestyle.

For some time Chinese swimming coaches have been touring European centres and elsewhere to improve their training methods and their efforts are paying off.

At its 1979 meeting in Montevideo, Uruguay, the International Olympic Committee made an epochal decision: to recognise the Chinese Olympic Committee in Beijing while at the same time retaining Taiwan as a member. The ruling meant that for the first time since 1952 in Helsinki, athletes from the People's

Republic were made eligible for the Olympics. The 81st IOC session held that:

"In the Olympic spirit and in accordance with the Olympic Charter, the IOC resolves: 1. To recognise the Chinese Olympic Committee located in Beijing. 2. To maintain recognition of the Chinese Olympic Committees located in Taipei. All matters pertaining to names, anthems, flags and constitutions will be the subject of studies and agreements."

In October 1979, at a three-day meeting of the IOC Executive Board in Nagoya, Japan, momentous decisions were reached — all of them in Beijing's favour. The IOC decreed that Taiwan's Olympic committee drop its traditional name and adopt a new anthem, flag and emblem if it were to participate in future Olympic Games. Under the decision, the Republic of China (Taiwan) Olympic Committee was henceforth to be known as the Chinese Taipei Olympic Committee, its flag, anthem and emblem to be replaced with substitutes approved by the IOC board. The Taiwanese also were required to revise their constitution. The ruling enabled China to become an IOC member under the new name of the Chinese Olympic Committee, paving the way for its participation in both the Lake Placid, New York, and the controversial Moscow Olympics. The IOC decision was final and irrevocable, said Lord Killanin, the organisation's president, who expressed the hope that Beijing and Taipei would "put sports first and take part in the Moscow and Lake Placid games." He went on to say that while "whatever we do will be criticised, we want to be free from political situations."

Taiwanese representatives were conspicuous by their absence from the announcement ceremony, but Beijing delegates shook hands all around and then went off to a dinner given by the city of Nagoya, which is to host the 1988 Olympics. They also issued a statement which said, "There is but one China in the world, that is, the People's Republic of China: Taiwan is part of China. The decision (in Nagoya) will certainly enjoy the support of

The level of tennis is understandably low. Tennis requires expensive equipment (which few can afford) and land (a scarce resource in the cities) even for the beginning tennis player. In October 1980, China hosted an international invitational tennis meet in Guangzhou. It surprised no one that all of China's players were knocked out of competition in the early rounds. Right: Children admiring their colleague's gymnastic skill.

most IOC members who are upholding the Olympic ideals."

It was a bitter pill to swallow for the Taiwanese, who just prior to the Nagoya meeting had extended VIP treatment to Lord Killanin when the IOC chief made a fact-finding visit to Taipei. He was received by President Chiang Chiang-kuo, Premier Y.S. Sun and other ranking ministers. And, as part of its IOC presentation, Taiwan dispatched its two most famous athletes to Japan — Chi Cheng, once the world's fastest woman runner, and C.K. Yang, an Olympic medal winner in the decathlon. Also included was C.S. Shen, a physics professor known for his advocacy of a "peaceful competition" policy, which basically calls for Taiwan and China to compete with each other peacefully while setting the unification of China as a long-range objective.

Within a matter of days, at an executive committee meeting in Zurich, the International Football Federation (FIFA) took its cue from the IOC and accepted China as a "provisional" member, tossing Beijing's hat into the ring when the qualifying groups for the 1982 World Cup soccer were compiled. Without public argument, Taiwan also remained a member of FIFA, and would take part in the World Cup under the name of the "Chinese Football Association of Taipei."

The World Cup without doubt is the world's most famous single sporting tournament and the thorny issue of "two Chinas" apparently was cleared with ease by FIFA following the difficult IOC decision-making.

China, by its own admission and evidence displayed on pitches around the world has a long way to go in soccer before reaching world class level. At the same time, the Chinese have the raw talent and the application needed for football success. As in many other countries, football is the most popular sport in China and huge crowds turn out for the matches.

An official of the English Football Association, after a series of exhibition matches in China, said, "They are among the best self-taught players I have ever seen and it will not be long before they become a power in the game. They are not as physical as we English, but are skillful and full of running."

The Chinese face an even longer road ahead in basketball, although the national team has had wide exposure — solely because of the presence in its rank of one Mu Tieju, a 2.2 metre-150 kg. centre whose appearance on the court causes opponents to gawk like spectators at a circus sideshow. "Mr Mu," as he has come to be known, is however, a plodding performer most usually utilised in passing to his

smaller teammates.

When the Washington Bullets, former champions of America's National Basketball Association (NBA), toured China in 1979, their players stood in awe of Mu. Said Elvin Hayes, one of the NBA's top all-time scorers, "He is the biggest man I ever played against. Wilt Chamberlain was big, but Mu is BIG."

The Americans, however, were making no comments about Mu's ability on the court, and instead singled out Guo Yunglin, a young guard from Liaoning who scored 27 points against them in one match in Beijing, as a player who could probably make his way in the top U.S. professional basketball league. The Bullets meanwhile delighted Chinese fans (and coaches who came from all parts of the country to study) with dazzling displays of skill, twisting in midair like kites above the Forbidden City to sink long shots and "dunking" shots at the basket itself with robot efficiency.

China staged a spectacular "dress rehearsal" for the 1980 Moscow Olympics when it held its Fourth National Games in Beijing, an event which very nearly coincided with the Nagoya and Zurich meetings. Earlier National Games were held in 1959, 1965 and 1975 and the 1979 festival was timed to close on the eve of the 30th birthday of the People's Republic. It brought together some 9,000 competitors from 31 provinces along with city teams.

Mao Tse-tung's successor, Chairman Hua Guofeng, set the tone for the proceedings by declaring: "The promotion of sports concerns the health of a nation as a whole. It has a bearing on the country's outlook." In the past, the Chairman observed, China had been a "sick man" in the sports arena — but no longer. "With a developed national economy and improved living standards, extensive participation in sports, improved health, and better family planning, the whole nation will prosper," Chairman Hua said on the eve of the National Games. "Sport is now a big undertaking capable of bringing the masses good health."

(In 1978, the Chairman had placed in China's Constitution the stipulation that the country's educational policy "must enable everyone who receives an education to develop morally, intellectually and physically," that "the State pays special attention to the healthy development of young people and children" and that "the State encourages and assists the creative endeavours of citizens engaged in . . . sports and cultural work.")

The National Games, if measured strictly in colour, quite possibly outstripped the Olympics themselves. The main venue was the 80,000-seat Workers' Stadium, laid out with a new synthetic track and electronic and laser-measuring equipment from Japan. Twenty-thousand standees thronged the stadium for the opening ceremony, also attended by China's top leadership, led by Chairman Hua and Vice-premier Deng Xiaoping.

A torch which had touched the hands of 100,000 young Chinese was lighted. It had left Shanghai on July 1 and the tens of thousands of runners traced the route of the Communists' Long March of 1934-35. Athletes from each province of China paraded about the stadium (with rousing applause for a contingent of former

Taiwan citizens), and soldiers, sailors and air force cadets goose-stepped in close precision (bringing even more applause) while shouting nationalist slogans.

In the background, thousands of school-age youngsters in the stands held aloft coloured cards which formed pictures, from scenes of the Great Wall to individual portraits of top leaders to flowers on which frogs hopped as the cards moved.

A staggering finale to the pageantry had 2,000 doves swooping over the stadium. Simultaneously, acrobats sailed on wires from the top of the stadium to the ground like oriental Peter Pans and hundreds of coloured balloons soared aloft. The background cards flashed an enormous "2000" — the year by which China hopes to be modernised. Present among the overwhelmed spectators were Denmark's Queen Margethe and Prince Henrik and (possibly of more importance) IOC committee members from Japan, Norway, Uruguay and India and sporting delegations from Romania, Sweden, Japan, Ecuador and France.

The 32 events on the programme for the six-day event included most of those contested in Moscow as well as others considered more Chinese in nature: sword

To bring a nation of a billion people to reasonable physical condition is a formidable task. One programme which is being carried out in many places is to encourage pre-school and pre-work organised morning exercises. Instructions and music are broadcast over loudspeakers (opposite) to stores, offices, factories and schools each morning.

In China, sports play a political role as well. In 1971, the decades-long enmity between the People's Republic and the United States was broken when a ping-pong team toured America.

China has been kept out of the Olympic Games because of politics. In 1979, when Taiwan was no longer recognised by the International Olympic Committee as a separate nation state, China was allowed to join the IOC and to participate fully in all future Olympic activities.

Left: *Taiqichuan exercises on a city street.*
Above: *An impromptu table tennis match in Tianjin.*

play, gliding, motor-cycling, model plane flying and chess.

By the time the games had drawn to a close (again with 80,000 to 100,000 spectators on hand) the Chinese, by their reckoning, had improved eight world and eight Asian records and 102 national records over the 16 days of competition. The eight world standards improved (and three equalled) were in rifle and pistol shooting, under-20 weightlifting and model airplane flying. The eight Asian records and national marks were in athletics, swimming, weightlifting and other events. (Earlier foreign tourneys produced 1979 world records in rifle shooting, cycling and archery).

The party Central Committee and the State Council pronounced the games a "big success" and a spokesman for the leadership, declared that "sport is a big undertaking, good for the people and helping make the country stronger and more prosperous while inspiring the national spirit." He predicted that China's sports movement would continue to progress "and reach even higher standards."

Chairman Hua himself presented medals to the athletes who had set major records as foreign dignitaries, including personages from international sporting circles and diplomatic envoys to China, looked on with warm applause.

The games were afforded massive coverage by the Chinese media, and one dispatch distributed by the official Xinhua News Agency reported that the oldest (chess) competitor, Lin Mian, 58, was a native of Taipei, where he learned the game under the tutelage of the Japanese Master Hashimoto. Lin Mian is now editor of a monthly magazine in Shanghai.

Wu Lanying, a cinema usher from Henan Province, surpassed the world record in women's skeet shooting by hitting 194 flying objects out of a possible 200. A four-member pistol shooting team totalled 2,307 points to better by four points a world record established by a Soviet team in 1974.

For the first time in China, an ice

hockey tournament was included on the programme of the National Games, being played on an artifical rink at Beijing's indoor stadium. Football, basketball and other ball games were played in a dozen sports centres.

While many new national records were established in swimming and track and field events at the Beijing games, the Chinese remained well below world standards, with the exception of diving. An observer, the American Olympic diving coach Dr. Sammy Lee, is of the opinion Chinese divers rank among the world's best. According to Dr. Lee, they need only additional seasoning in international meets to adjust to the pressure of Olympic-type competition. He noted that a Chinese woman diver, Chen Xiaoxia, had taken a gold medal a few months earlier in the 10-metre event at the University Games in Mexico City.

Another world class Chinese athlete is triple jumper Zou Zhenzian, a physical education student at Beijing University. He holds the Asian record of 17.02 metres. A third major hopeful is Shen Maomao, who holds the Asian record of 86.81 metres in the javelin. In women's track and field, Zhang Huifen broke an Asian mark during the National Games by winning the 400 metres hurdles in 59.79 seconds. It was the first time in Asia the one-minute barrier had been broken.

Chinese weightlifters competing in the National Games also broke all three world records in the flyweight division for lifters under 20 years. Wu Shude lifted 108 kg in the snatch to better his own record combined total of 235 kg for the snatch and jerk to top the record of 232.5 kg set by Anton Kodjabashev of Bulgaria. The third record was made by Zhang Yaoxin, who lifted 130.5 kg in the jerk event to beat Kodhabashev's previous standard of 130 kg.

In archery (women's 50 metres) Guo Meizhen, from the Xinjiang Uygur autonomous region, and onetime national champion Song Suxian both equalled the single-round national record of 318 points. This is just two points short of the current

China prepared vigorously for its return to the Olympic stage. The Fourth National Games held in Beijing in September 1979 were practically a dress rehearsal for Moscow. But when China joined the boycott of the Moscow Olympics, the world had to wait until 1984 for China's Olympic debut.
Opposite: A Peking girl practices ballet exercises.
Above: Children are encouraged at an early age to study some forms of traditional sports.

world record.

The early China traders introduced tennis to the country in the 1840s, but it has remained to this day a "rich man's" sport and there are only about 3,000 people in the entire country who even know how to play the game. Courts are few and far between, admits national tennis coach Lu Zheng-yi, and tennis basically is limited to only the 12 largest cities in the country.

The high cost of equipment is a factor in restricting tennis to a select few, the most promising of whom are admitted to special government subsidised schools. These academies, attended after regular classes and during holiday time, provide the players with coaching staff. Students enrolled in the tennis programme are selected by the Tennis Association of the People's Republic based on their achievements in provincial and national tournament play.

Top Chinese junior tennis players made a 1979 tour of American East Coast cities, including New York, and impressed their hosts at all points. June Ferestein, 16, the top-ranked junior player in New England, defeated the 20-year-old Chinese national champion Wang Ping, and afterward remarked: "I was really surprised at how good she was after hearing that the

Chinese didn't have many tennis facilities or players over there. I'd say they are just a few years away from being able to compete with our junior teams as well as our collegiate teams."

The Chinese players received instruction at a tennis camp operated by the Australian professional John Newcombe and, as a finale to the tour, attended the US open championships in New York.

"Our country now of course has the programme of four modernisations," said Wei Ji-tong, who headed the Chinese delegation to the World University Games. "We consider sports to be part of our modernisation, and competing on an international level helps us in our move to modernisation."

As to when China might have an impact on the Olympics, Wei was hopeful of "some measure of success" in Moscow, and he talked of a sports master plan: "Just like the other parts of our society, we have a five-year plan, a 10-year plan, and even a 20-year plan for sports. So far, I believe we are on schedule."

"We are very good in shooting, weightlifting, table tennis and volleyball," he said. "And archery, skiing and skating are popular in the north of our country. Swimming, diving and water polo are very

popular in the south. There was a long delay in our sports development, and our coaches have to catch up on techniques. Our new sports leadership has been developing in a big way, and rapidly."

After a long period of decline, the sleeping giant that is China has begun shaking off the effects of a long slumber, and sports have been progressing at a rapid rate.

With traditional ethnic minority activities like Mongolian wrestling (preceding pages) *and horsemanship popular among the country's minority people, there is a wealth of talent waiting to be discovered in the more remote areas of the land.*

"We have friends all over the world" is a familiar slogan in China and a fitting one as China introduces itself to yet another event of international status.

JOANNA YOUNG
(YONG JIAOJIAO)

Joanna Young (that is not her real name) was born into a family of big Shanghai capitalists in 1952. Her father was the owner of one of China's biggest rubber factories, and he had grown rich on the profits of the civil war. At the time of his daughter's birth, he was still managing his factory under the general supervision of the Communist Party, and receiving a healthy income from it. The war in Korea boosted his output to hitherto undreamed-of levels. The policy of the Communists at this time was to encourage and reward "patriotic capitalists" who stayed behind to continue their business after 1949 — instead of selling up lock, stock and barrel, and fleeing to British-ruled Hongkong with whatever valuables they could carry.

Joanna was 14 when the Cultural Revolution was initiated, and she and her parents watched in dumb amazement as bands of young students and workers roamed the streets, throwing furniture and antiques out of apartment windows, and parading people around the streets to proclaim the end of "bourgeois" privilege.

Joanna's father, always astute, donated his Daimler car to the State and renounced his monthly royalties check from the rubber factory.

The Red Guards soon picked on him,

however, and arrived one afternoon armed with sticks and "Little Red Books". They almost tore the apartment to pieces looking for "decadent" books and valuables — but missed a jewelry cache in the wall.

About 20 Red Guards announced that they were taking the house over as their headquarters. They beat up Joanna's father and mother, but left her relatively unscathed, apart from cutting her hair roughly and making her scrub floors. They raided the store-room with its imported canned foods, spices and wines, and lived like kings as long as the supplies lasted. The family had to sleep in their clothes, always apprehensive of the moment when some half-drunk Red Guard would throw open the bedroom door and beat them up in the dark. Her father died after two months of this treatment, and her mother succumbed shortly afterwards.

The Red Guards then moved out, and several workers' families were moved into the house, which was split up into tiny apartments. Joanna and an elderly aunt occupied two rooms, with a grand piano in one of them. The aunt taught her to play the piano and to speak English. She rarely went out, and did not attend school, but spent her leisure hours practising Chinese cooking.

After Mao's death, the Party reversed its policy on former "capitalists" and their

children, and announced that all property and money confiscated from them in the Cultural Revolution would be returned. Unable to elicit a response from the Party authorities in Shanghai, Joanna travelled to Beijing and located a senior official whom her father had known slightly. She demanded that her inheritance be returned to her, and he agreed in principle, but told her she might have to wait quite a while before the Shanghai authorities could get round to dealing with it.

Meanwhile Joanna recived an invitation from a distant cousin in Hongkong to pay him a visit. She was issued with an exit visa in a mere matter of weeks — doubtless because she was making a nuisance of herself and embarrassing officialdom. She arrived in Hongkong in 1978 and took up a job in her relative's export-import business.

She is totally scornful of the Party and all its works, but still thinks nostalgically of Shanghai. She finds the people of Hongkong rude and greedy, and cannot speak their dialect. She will try to emigrate to the United States at the first opportunity, unless she receives a marriage proposal from a wealthy man. But she is already in her late twenties, and still has not decided what she really wants to do with her life.

The Culinary Mystery

Kenneth Lo

The Chinese civilisation, the oldest in existence, has given the Western world a number of important inventions — printing, lock-gates, the stern-post rudder, gunpowder, to name a few. But its greatest legacy, and one that is again proving to be both a mystery and fascination in the West as China's *rapprochement* progresses, is the vast treasure-house of its native food — the celebrated Chinese cuisine. Not only is its technique and content both mystifying and remarkable, the sheer range of Chinese dishes is astonishing.

When one looks at the cuisines of the world quite dispassionately, and compares those of all the different countries, how is it that the Chinese cuisine has developed such character of its own — a character which has made it so different from cooking in the West?

Being such a vast entity in itself — a huge continent — it is easy enough to understand that it would have developed a culinary tradition of its own because of its distinctive historical and geographical heritage. But how did it come about that a good Chinese dinner would consist of at least six to seven dishes, with a range of accompanying side-dishes, sauces and condiments, while in the West the same meals would comprise no more than one soup, one main course and a dessert — perhaps with a starter added? How is it that the majority of the cuisines of the world often consist of no more than a score of dishes, or even a couple of hundred, while in China the number of established recipes and dishes runs into the many thousands?

There are probably as many dishes which are commonly prepared, cooked and served in China as there are words or characters in the Chinese language — and while there would be around 3,000 basic characters in common use, a scholar would know three to four times that many. It is not that an average Chinese housewife would actually cook several thousand dishes, but she knows that there is a vast pool, or reservoir, of recipes which exists and can be tapped if need be. This pool of dishes is like student's dictionary, and the making up of a Chinese menu the writing of a composition. It is somewhat flabergasting to think that, even in a small composition of a dozen or a score of words, a "football pool" situation is created whereby, through varying permutations, the number of possible combinations which can be created can run into millions. This is one of the unique aspects of Chinese food. Having trained as a physicist in my early Beijing days, this numerative aspect of the Chinese cuisine has always filled me with wonderment.

For the answer to the mystery of how this vast culinary reservoir was formed, you have to take into account Chinese history, China's peculiar needs and quandaries, Chinese philosophy, folk-medicine and even the celebrative aspect of China's powerful dynastic rulers. For in no other country in the world is food such an integral part of the complete way of life.

The reason for the tremendous variety of ingredients in the Chinese cuisine is first and foremost a reflection of China's most basic and essential problem — overpopulation. With huge areas of land unsuitable for food production, and with many hundreds of millions of mouths to feed, the key to the survival of China and its civilisation has traditionally been a constant, unending search for new and edible foodstuffs. Ingredients, both animal and vegetable, have been brought into the Chinese diet that would curl the hair or even disgust the Westerner — dogs, civet cats, sea-slugs, cockroaches, snakes, so many in fact that there's more than just an element of truth in the old Chinese saying: "If its back faces heaven, you can eat it." Within this huge range of foods, there are an equally incredible number of uses that each food is put to; for in the basic economics of Chinese life — limited food and unlimited mouths to feed — literally nothing goes to waste. That's why things like chicken's liver and feet are a popular, almost everyday food, while in the West they are generally thrown away. Fish heads are part and parcel of other popular, if mundane, Chinese recipes, while fish lips are something of a delicacy.

Some unusual or even exotic ingredients have found their way into the Chinese diet for health reasons — herbs, meats and vegetables selected and put to culinary use because of evidence, or simply a belief, that they promote special physical or mental well-being. The Chinese passion for food is not based purely upon survival or subsistence or even taste, but involves a whole philosophy in which certain foods are seen to deal with certain sicknesses, physical or emotional, promote virtue and have a role to play in the calender of events and changes in individual and public life. As one noted Western observer of the Chinese cuisine has commented: "Heaven loves the man who eats well. At each meal a Chinese adds to his virtue, strengthening resistance to the ills of body and mind, curing ailments or, possibly, rendering himself capable of better work."

The refinement of all this variety — the vast compendium of Chinese recipes and dishes — owes much of its inspiration to one particular point in Chinese history when the threat of famine was far from the average person's door and there was, in fact, an over-abundance of food. It was during the illustrious Song dynasty (960-1279 AD) that Chinese food really became a cuisine.

The population of China at that time was only a tenth of what it is now — around 100 million. The infrastructure of a vast food industry had begun to establish itself throughout the country; food production became commercialised and markets sprang up everywhere to pass production on to the consumer and allow demand for various foods and food-fads to flow back to the farmer. In the Yangtze region and south, rice production was given an enormous boost by the introduction of new strains from what was then Champa (Vietnam) which were disease resistant, capable of growth in the drier highlands and prolific enough to allow double-cropping.

China never had it so good. And the Song dynasty celebrated this material and spiritual abundance. It was an age of art, literature, refinement and wealth; and this was reflected in the development of the cuisine — as skilled and specialist chefs and that celebrated mainstay of Chinese food,

the Chinese restaurant, emerged to cater for refined, aristocratic culinary tastes. The aristocrat established the tradition of the connoisseur; the restaurants triggered off a continuing preoccupation with food and its ingredients that has flourished right up to the present day.

China's grand imperial tradition, and its many centuries of absolute one-man rule, was another key source of culinary variety and experimentation. Food became not only an integral part of the Chinese way of life but a celebration and even a definition of the various levels of political power in the vast pyramid of Chinese society — on top of which there sat the most powerful figure of all, the emperor. Tribute was paid to him in the tremendous food resources and virtual armies of kitchen workers, chefs and caterers — as many as 4,000 — that were on hand simply to feed the emperor and his court. Palace chefs continually invented new dishes to whet the often jaded imperial appetite. Imperial fancies and whims were allowed full reign, too — one of the most famous cases being that of a Tang dynasty ruler who established a "pony express" system simply to race supplies of fresh lychees from the western mountains of China for his favourite concubine.

Many centuries later, the notorious Empress Dowager — China's last all-powerful imperial ruler — is said to have had a dream about food one night. The next day her dream turned up on the palace menu — buns stuffed with shredded pork. Another Qing dynasty ruler staunchly resisted the many delicacies that his chefs dreamed up every day and preferred to feed on simpler meals and tidbits served up by consorts in his private quarters. To save face, and to preserve tradition, palace caterers turned a blind eye to his eccentricity and, each day, falsely recorded that the ruler had eaten all that they had placed before him.

Food was not only a mark of power, it also defined the various tiers of authority in the pyramid below the emperor; it virtually put all the mandarins and court of-ficials into their places. At vast and sumptuous palace banquets, different dishes were served to different levels of the bureaucracy. Each level was also allocated different foodstuffs, different amounts of food and cooking fuel, even different

The looks on these Nanjing youngsters, as they wait for their snacks from this street vendor is a telling reminder of the importance of food to the Chinese. And it matters little that one's table may be a slab of concrete or that maybe all one can afford for lunch is a large bowlful of rice cooked in a rich meat stock.

sauces and condiments — the allocations becoming smaller and more austere the lower that each diner was slotted in the power structure.

Aside from triggering greater variety in the cuisine and making it one of the main supporting pillars of Chinese society, this imperial tradition also provided a gathering place for all the regional dishes and cooking techniques of China, drawing recipes and chefs to the court from all parts of the country, making Beijing to China what Paris is to France — its political *and* culinary capital. Thus, the huge compendium of the Chinese cuisine was compiled and presented to posterity — an institution that has flourished over the centuries and survived wars, civil wars, famines and revolution as more a national treasure than simply a cuisine.

So important is food as a pillar of sustenance, enjoyment, intellect, art and philosophy in Chinese society that it was one national treasure largely left unviolated by the greatest revolution of all, the communist triumph of 1949, and the

destructive rampage of the Cultural Revolution's Red Guards. It's true that, after the communist takeover, China was in no position to continue supporting a rich, élitist cuisine; the new society inherited the aftermath of massive social disruption and famine of the collapsing Qing dynasty and succeeding civil calamities, and basic survival became the culinary order of the day. The vast majority of the Chinese people existed on famine diets while national efforts were made to bring agriculture and food production up to levels that would simply keep as many people as possible above the starvation level. Gourmet eating was officially forbidden, and was no longer possible anyway — there just wasn't enough food to support connoisseur tastes. Banquets became something of a face-saving echo of the opulent, decadent past, confined mainly to state affairs in honour of visiting heads of state and other dignitaries.

But while the style and content of the cuisine were tamped down to suit a common austerity — a wide social levelling

process in which the peasantry and former bourgeoisie now shared the same strictly rationed diet — no real attempt was made to tamper with its very foundations, or tradition. The essence of the Chinese cuisine simply lay dormant, awaiting better times. Nor were China's restaurants threatened by the communists, despite a campaign by the Red Guards to condemn and discard them as a hangover of the bourgeois past. The best eating places in Beijing, Guangzhou, Shanghai, Hangzhou and other culinary centres switched, like the cuisine itself, to a more low-key, austere fare and waited for the climate to change. In fact, new restaurants came into being under Mao Tse-tung's revolutionary rule: a lavish Summer Palace entertainment complex that had been built for the infamous Empress Dowager was turned into a "people's restaurant" and re-named Tingliguan (Oriole) Gardens.

Perhaps the biggest threat to the Chinese cuisine came in the mid 1960s when the Red Guards began playing kitchen politics in the major restaurants,

replacing skilled chefs — many of them trained in pre-revolutionary times — with "grass-root" cooks from the more politically favoured peasantry. But the Red Guards, and the Great Cultural Revolution that spawned them, were regarded as a political blunder, and dismissed from power, long before they could commit anything like a real culinary disaster.

When the political climate did change, with the demise of the so-called "Gang of Four", the rise to power of Deng Xiaoping and the remarkable shift away from pure, isolated socialism to moderate, open-door "revolutionary capitalism," the cuisine was ready to claim its rightful place again as an integral part of Chinese society. Leading chefs were brought back from "retirement" and restored to their restaurant kitchens — and among the sudden real signs of *rapprochement* and freer contact with the West, the trade, industry and cultural delegations that began popping up in the major cities of the West, were groups of China's foremost chefs sent to culinary capitals like Hong Kong and Paris to demonstrate their skills at cultural-exchange banquets and promote Chinese food.

China's best restaurants blossomed again, in Beijing, Shanghai and Guangzhou — first, to cater for a relatively massive influx of foreign tourists, then, amid the more relaxed, softly consumer-oriented policies introduced under Deng Xiaoping's leadership, to accommodate urban Chinese who were hungry for a touch of lavishness, colour and excitement after 30 years of drab, selfless revolutionary rule. In a perverse sense, the austerity of Maoism had enriched China's post-revolutionary culinary life: For obvious economic reasons, no new restaurants had been built in Maoist times and the leading establishments that had survived the civil war and communist takeover simply languished, untouched in the backwaters of Chinese society, so that those that are flourishing today are, in fact, well preserved specimens of the beauty, fine taste and even opulence that existed in

the "decadent" days before the revolution. This surviving grandeur, something of a shock even today amid the general material impoverishment of Chinese society, is now being promoted as a tourist drawcard at top restaurants like Teng Yu Lin (Scholar's Sitting Room for Listening to Raindrops), Banxi and Nanyuan in Guangzhou, the majestic Fangshan (Dining Room of the Monarchs), Beijing Duck Restaurant and Tingliguan (Oriole) Gardens in Beijing and others in Shanghai and Hangzhou. Something of the old splendour of the cuisine itself is now re-emerging, too. Japanese tour groups now visit the Tingliguan Gardens restaurant for special gourmet binges lasting three days or more, and the restaurant also features ordinary fish banquets made up of 50 courses.

Outside China, especially in the capitals of America and Europe, *rapprochement* and the open-door policy have promoted a new surge of popular interest in the Chinese cuisine, and, since Richard Nixon's historic visit to Beijing in 1972, one guaranteed money-making product of Western publishing, for example, has been the Chinese cookbook, offering anything from exotic pre-revolutionary recipes for the gourmet to simple and quickly prepared adaptations of *dim sum* as a new taste in hors d'oeuvres. Westerners are keenly re-examining the Chinese cuisine, fascinated by its variety, its mystique, its philosophy, its health-giving elements and its obvious tenacity and indestructibility in the face of momentous social change.

The most essential element under scrutiny is the basic *difference* between Chinese cuisine and its cooking technique and those of the West. For example, when I was writing an encyclopaedia of Chinese cooking some six years ago, I had to compile and describe the number of established heating methods employed in Chinese cooking. In the West, we all know that there cannot be many more than, say, half a dozen basic methods of heating — boiling, roasting, grilling (or barbecuing), deep-frying, steaming, double-boiling, etc.

Relatively few Chinese over the years have known the tastes and textures of classical banquet fare. Bear's paw and camel's hump are not commonly served, even at state dinners at the Great Hall of the People in Beijing. Instead, the food in restaurants and homes tends to be simply prepared using the best available ingredients, and remains true to its regional origins (opposite: Shanghai; above: Beijing).

There is little more satisfying than a large bowl of freshly steamed rice topped with a rich-tasting piece of pork or fish and a few seasonal vegetables (above, in Nanjing) *or a plateful of plump steamed dumplings filled with meat and spice mixtures, especially when those dumplings have been cooked in an oversized bamboo steamer over a charcoal fire on the street in Chengdu (opposite).*

In my encyclopaedia, I presented no less than 40 Chinese variations — a testament to the extent to which the Chinese chefs have refined "heat control" and acceleration and de-acceleration in the use of heat. Timing in heating is all-important in Chinese cooking, with probably as many as 50 different methods of heat timing in common use. This is where Chinese cooking is probably far more refined than its major Western rival, the French cuisine.

The key to the refinement of Chinese cooking lies in its past and, in its most simplistic terms, can be explained by the fact that the Chinese developed sophisticated cooking techniques long before anyone else. As long as 4,000 or 5,000 years ago, while the rest of the world was cooking by simply barbecuing animal carcasses or burying them in heated pits, the Chinese were probably already cooking food in bronze pots, with water or fat. As evidence of this, we have a wide range of elaborately fashioned bronze cauldrons, called *ting*, which are now on display in almost every major museum of the West. Most of these date from the Qin and Zhou dynasties (1,500 to 221 BC), and by this time had reached a level of artistry in their design and construction which suggests that they must have originally been developed many hundreds or perhaps a couple of thousand years before. My feeling is that it was the early use of these *ting* cauldrons as cooking pots that caused Chinese cooking to depart from the basic Western cooking practice of roasting and grilling — for it seems that slow cooking in casseroles or pot-roasting has been only a relatively recent development in Western kitchens, a belated adoption of a cooking technique that has been popular in China since time immemorial.

When meats are cooked in large chunks, or even as whole carcasses, in large cauldrons, they obviously take a long time to heat up and to cool down, and it was during this process that the early Chinese cooks began to indulge in the refinements of technique that put the Chinese cuisine on an early path of its own. Cooks began

long-cooking and lengthy simmering, culinary practices that have since made them inclined to stew ("red-cooking") or boil ("white-cooking") for much greater lengths of time than is customary in the Western kitchen. In the West, the usual stewing time is probably about one to one and a half hours, and boiling about half an hour to one hour, while in the Chinese kitchen it's normal for the cooking process to proceed over a very low heat for two to three times that long before an acceptable tenderness is reached. Meats which are cooked for such a long time attain a degree of tenderness, as well as succulence, which one seldom encounters in Western cooking. And, after such lengthy treatment, many parts of animal or poultry carcasses, such as tendons, offal, skin, chicken's feet, duck's webs etc, become edible and possible to treat as "delicacies" which would otherwise be ignored. It's perhaps because of the fact that the West has no real tradition in long-cooking that these parts are regarded as inedible and are discarded — woefully, in view of the waste of what are, in fact, good nutritious foods.

Another side-effect or by-product of cauldron-cooked meats was that quantities of fat were bound to accumulate, and in a world in which cooking oils were not naturally available, these fats were soon preserved and separated from one another. From the earliest days, the Chinese cooks came to appreciate the difference in the flavours or different animal fats and how they could be used to cook different foods, especially vegetables. This refinement is still one of the essential ingredients of Chinese cooking today. For instance, in Chinese fish or vegetables dishes it is common practice for the chef to pour a ladleful of boiling fat along the length of a fish or over the vegetables in the pan in order to give them a "gloss" before serving. This seems to add to the richness and smoothness of texture of the food and therefore its succulence, which improves the total effect of the dish.

Another culinary practice which distinguishes the flavouring of Chinese food

Every city once had hundreds of street vendors selling foods of all descriptions, from savoury buns and dumplings to sweet cakes, watermelon seeds, and almond tea. A parade of vendors, some with a complete kitchen slung from shoulder poles, would walk the streets and hutongs shouting their wares. The Cultural Revolution ended what remained of this tradition.

Today, the sight of an old-style street vendor is unusual, as the local governments control nearly all selling of foods, from eggs (above, in Shanghai) to snacks (opposite, in Hefei).

烧饼
一两粮票
四分一只

from Western counterparts is the use of salted and fermented soya beans and their numerous derivatives. The most common of these is, of course, soya sauce, and its use also dates back to the earliest times. In the history and literature of the last period of the Zhou dynasty (722-481 BC) and the time of the Warring Kingdoms (481-221 BC) there are numerous references to the *jiang yuan*, or "soya garden." These gardens were normally walled enclosures in which huge open-mouthed earthen jars filled with brine and soya beans were left to mature in the sun. And this is how much of the best soya sauce is still produced in China today. So vital is soya sauce to the flavouring of the Chinese cuisine that some 50 to 60 per cent of the vast compendium of Chinese dishes would just not taste the same without it. It is also another long-established Chinese culinary feature that's nowadays being belatedly adopted by the West — providing not only an appealing

earthy-salty-savouriness with food but also an important source of protein.

But while seasoned and marinated dishes are among the best treasures of the Chinese cuisine, its most exquisite aspect is, by far, the subtle, often surprising, combination of plain-cooked meats and seafoods with piquant sauces and condiments — the two ingredients actually coming together at the table. This practice dates back to the very dawn of Chinese history when sacrificial foods were regularly prepared and offered to the ancestors and the large pantheon of gods, goddesses and guardian spirits in Chinese religious life. Tradition decreed that all such dishes had to be cooked and presented "pure" and unadulterated by flavourers or spices. These unseasoned dishes gradually made their way into the mainstream of Chinese cooking as "white-cooked" or long-simmered meats, but a compromise was made in favour of taste

by providing a range of condiments and dips at the dining table for the diners themselves to apply. One of the most simple, yet sensually stunning examples of this combination still reigning at the table today is white-cooked chicken with ginger. A whole chicken is boiled for 10 to 15 minutes in water with four or five large slices of ginger, then allowed to cool and chopped into bite-sized portions. Although the ginger counteracts the gamey "chicken taste" of the meat and adds a hint of flavour to it, the result is still quite bland — until it's combined with the three different dips that are usually served with it: garlic paste with sesame oil and soya sauce, a slightly spicy condiment; chopped ginger with aromatic vinegar; and chopped scallions with soya sauce. All at once, what started out as a simple boiled chicken becomes something of a taste sensation.

Yet another unique feature of the Chinese cuisine, the round-bottomed all-purpose cooking pan called the *wok*, is believed to have come into being as a result of improved weapons technology. At the time of the Qin dynasty, some 2,000 years ago, China was a collection of independent feudal kingdoms. The first Qin emperor, Qinshihuangdi, did to these kingdoms what Bismark did for Germany in the 19th century — he strong-armed them into one unified empire. Then he built the Great Wall on China's northern borders to protect the fledgling state from barbarian incursions.

But Qinshihuangdi introduced an element into Chinese society which was to influence it long after the Great Wall had begun crumbling into disrepair — his armies were the first to be equipped with newly-developed iron-tipped lances, replacing the bronze that was in universal use up to that time. Not only did the iron make his troops virtually invincible in battle, it introduced a whole new technology to the craftsmen of China, who were soon refining the metal and beating it into thin sheets for a number of different uses. They were soon turning out thin-bottomed

cooking pans — the early prototype of the *wok*.

Since their predecessors, the bronze *ting*, were round-bottomed, these new pans were made the same way — probably simply a continuation of tradition. But as such, their shape was not only ideal for tossing or mixing foods but also for sitting on wood or charcoal fires and, later, a small open-mouthed terra cotta charcoal brazier which emerged as the standard and virtually universal Chinese "stove." Nowadays, the shape of the *wok*, unchanged over the centuries, allows it to sit comfortably on a gas ring, too — as many Western cooks are finding.

During the Han dynasty, which followed the First Empire and lasted from 206 BC to 220 AD, two important culinary developments occurred which expanded the variety of the cuisine and introduced a crucial new cooking technique. First, it was during this period that the Chinese, or the northern Chinese at least, learned to grind wheat and other cereals into flour. Wheat, millet and other grains were already staple foods in the northern areas,

Chinese food is usually classified into four regional cuisines: northern, or Beijing, style; Shanghainese or, more properly, the region of Jiangsu-Zhejiang which includes Suzhou and Hangzhou; southern, or Cantonese, most familiar to foreigners; and the spicy hot cooking of Sichuan and Hunan provinces.

In Sichuan (left), rows of dried red chili peppers hang in the street and in almost every kitchen. It is said that these peppers help to soak up the moisture in the climate (Sichuan is very hot and humid in the summer). Indeed, so the story is told, in Sichuan even Buddhist monks were once permitted to eat these fiery-hot peppers. Instead of getting aroused by eating them, they kept cool and dry!

The Sichuanese are also adept at salting and pickling many of their vegetables. One exotic product of this skill is preserved zha cai, for which there is no suitable English translation, so it's unimaginatively called Sichuan Preserved Vegetable. Slices of zha cai in a light broth makes a delicate gourmet soup.

Following pages: *A display of pocket-sized illustrated magazines in a book rack.*

but up until that time they had simply been cooked in cauldrons with the meat to form a mushy stew or porridge. With the advent of milling, more refined staples were now introduced into the diet in the form of noodles, cakes, steamed breads and dumplings and pasta (the pasta itself later leading to considerable controversy over whether it was the Chinese or Italians who invented it first). In the somewhat chaotic and swashbuckling atmosphere of the early Han dynasty, many flour millers became wealthy and powerful, the first of the Chinese millionaires, forming a formidable technological élite that included iron smelters, salt merchants and cattle breeders. The names and activities of some three-score of these earliest magnates are recorded in the annals of the Han period. They make absorbing reading!

But an even more important innovation that came about at this time was the practice of "stir-fry" cooking in the still relatively new *wok*. Stir frying meant that food could now be cut into small bite-sized pieces — a culinary blessing considering that chopsticks were well established by then — and the cooking itself could be speeded up, taking only a few minutes compared with the hours that were required to boil and stew in the *ting* cauldrons. The preparation of food for stir-frying soon became something of an art: in one of the many early references to it in Chinese literature, a writer describes fish being cut into such thin and delicate slices for the *wok* that it was like "snowflakes" that would blow away in a gust of wind. But more important still, stir-frying meant that a vastly increased number of dishes could now be easily prepared, and an incalculable number of different foods and ingredients could be blended and mixed together. This is where one of the chief characteristics of the Chinese cuisine first evolved.

And what of those strange, unique and, to the Westerner, absolutely infernal Chinese eating implements, the chopsticks? How did it come about that the Chinese took to these instruments for

A Chinese dish may be judged by its flavour (natural taste, characteristic fragrance or aroma, strength of taste and oily-not-greasy richness) and by its texture (crispy-crunchy or soft and tender).

The food of Beijing is coarse, but full of robust flavour. The flavour was born in the kitchens of people's restaurants, some of which claim stock pots that have cooked continuously for 100 or 200 years, with resulting rich sauces of unique taste. Adventurous visitors who sit down to a meal among ordinary folk in an ordinary restaurant (above) *can know they have eaten real Beijing food.*

Northerners are wheat-eating people, and there are dozens of varieties of steamed and fried breads and noodles (opposite).

eating while the West went the way of the knife and fork? The answer to this lies in the dawning of Chinese food, probably around 2,000 BC, when the practice of boiling and stewing large hunks of meat in bronze pots first emerged. In the West, meats were more often than not roasted and barbecued, and since most meats harden with this type of cooking they required a knife, and later a fork, to remove them from the bones. In China, long-cooking in cauldrons meant that the meat became extremely tender and could be pulled or pushed off the bones while still hot with the most easily available implements around — sticks or twigs. As time went by these improvisations became standardised, then refined into chopsticks as we know them today. There's plenty of archeological evidence to show that by the time of the First Empire and early Han dynasty they were already in common use throughout China. In later centuries, a whole technology, art and mystique developed around chopsticks. First made of wood, then bamboo, they were soon fashioned out of bone, then intricately carved ivory and finally heavy silver and gold. It is said that they even played a crucial role in the many complex and dangerous intrigues that took place in the imperial courts and wealthiest households of the Ming and Qing dynasties: Since it was believed that silver chopsticks would tarnish very fast if dipped in poison, and ivory ones would fall apart, they gave a dinner guest a fairly clear picture of his social standing, whether he was still in the host's good grace or the target of conspiracy.

Thus, the Qin and Han dynasties were momentous times in the history of China. From the political and social point of view, these periods saw the destruction of feudalism and the unification of the country into a centralised state under an autocratic monarchy. Confucian principles and precepts were solidly laid down as moral guidelines for all the Chinese, even the emperors, to follow. The general structure and pattern of Chinese society became formulated and set — and was to

A visitor has to make a special effort to eat among the people. The practice even on trains (opposite), *is to discourage visitors from eating in the dining car with fellow local travellers. Instead the visitor is invited to eat after the Chinese travelling in the second and third class sections have finished, and he is seated at a table set with a freshly laundered tablecloth and offered a ''foreigners''' menu.*

In the cities, the visitor will be treated to at least one banquet in each place; other meals are taken in private rooms in the better restaurants, where the dishes have been ordered for him or her in advance.
Opposite: *A street vendor ladles noodles and broth into bowls for lunch-time visitors.*

prevail that way, virtually unchanged, for all but the next 20 centuries, right up until Dr. Sun Yat Sen's republican revolution of 1911.

In one sense, the development of the cuisine virtually came to a standstill after the Han dynasty. By then, its essential and major characteristics had already come into being — a combination of plain-cooked long-simmered and steamed "pot" dishes and those stir-fried in the *wok*; the use of soya bean products and soya sauce — and other condiments — for flavouring; the blending and mixing of small-cut foods over the fire. The basic principles of the cuisine were to remain that way for as long as imperial China reigned — again, because of the rigid, and later stultifying, traditions and codes of Confucianism. But while the rules were codified, the range of foods themselves burgeoned during successive dynasties. One principal culinary development in the centuries immediately following the Han times was a gradual expansion of the population, first into the lush Yangtze River Valley (lush, compared with the arid, austere north), and later into the abundant semi-tropical south. Many new foods were brought into the Chinese diet. Rice, which was a product of the well-watered Yangtze region, began to replace wheat, maize and millet as the staple Chinese cereal. The whole population developed a sweet tooth (though not to the extent of subsequent Western passions) when sugar came into wide culinary use, refined from cane grown in the southern provinces of Fujian and Guangdong. Many more sweets, sweet cakes, sweetmeats and crystalised fruits began to appear on the market. By the time of the opulent Song dynasty, China's teeming urban dwellers were regarded as possibly the best-fed mass of people in the world. And when Marco Polo toured China during the Yuan (Mongol) dynasty of Kublai Khan, he was immensely impressed by the sheer abundance of food, the vast and well-stocked network of markets throughout the country, the incredible restaurants, tea-houses and

taverns with their apparently abandoned feasting, wining and merry-making and their attendant sing-song girls and courtesans.

It can generally be said that, except for increased refinement, China's culinary development made a great leap forward during the early history of the civilisation, then slowed down to a crawl in the many centuries after, dominated by Confucianism which was forever gazing back to a distant and golden past — to the "Sage Kings" — for all the inspiration and codes which the Chinese were now to strive for. It is significant that when the civilisation began to crumble and fall apart, during the 19th century reign of the Empress Dowager, this tyrannical, vicious despot — "Old Buddha," as they rather generously called her — had about 4,000 palace workers on hand simply to cater for her food requirements and those of her court. This was probably only about 1,000 more than the number of cooks, caterers and servants who staffed the grand courts of the Qin and Zhou dynasties some 30 centuries before. And although new dishes and combinations of foods had evolved around Old Buddha's time, the essential cooking rules and techniques — and the whole philosophy of food — still largely followed precepts established by the *Li Chi*, or Book of Rites, which ruled the Qin and Zhou courts. And those same precepts reign even today.

The geography of Chinese food is as fascinating as its history — for both cover vast territories. In a country of such immensity — China is even bigger than the United States — where large populations have lived for many centuries in virtual quarantines because of poor or restricted transport, culinary practices and traditions are bound to develop which are characteristic to specific areas. Also, some of China's regional cuisines evolved because of the particular produce of an area, or its climate and terrain: the north and north-western areas of China border on the steppes and high grasslands of Inner Mongolia and Xinjiang, where cattle-

In early October, north of the Huaihe River, when the cabbage starts rolling into the cities — on trucks, carts, bicycles and anything else that can pull a load — there is a carnival atmosphere in the air. Cabbages are unloaded at almost every street corner; people hurry home from work to get their pick of the crop; nearly everywhere one looks, people are carrying cabbage.

Cabbage dominates most dishes during the winter, from Shanghai to Xi'an (right) and Beijing and in the far north to Shenyang and Harbin. It's put out onto window sills and when finally removed for cooking, the hearts of the cabbage are still fresh. It's pickled in dozens of variations of vinegar, salt and spices.

There's almost no regrigeration, and virtually no produce grown in hothouses. So, when the tomatoes are ripe, everyone buys them. When the aubergines are in, almost every dish has aubergines in it. And when it's time for beans, every market is overrun by them (opposite, in Xi'an).

raising is the principal pursuit; and consequently, more beef is consumed in the north than the seaboard south. Conversely, the people of Guangdong and Fujian regard lamb and mutton — another staple meat of the north — with almost the same distaste as that with which the northerners regard dog-meat, a traditional southern food. China's long eastern and southern coastlines mean that its cuisine, especially in the Shanghai and Guangzhou (Canton) areas, is rich in seafood. In east China, where the mighty Yangtze flows into the sea, there's a great abundance of rice, fish and vegetables, natural products of an immense freshwater region. In the far west, the mountainous terrain has produced a cuisine in which peppers and spices are used to counter high-country chills.

Today the Chinese cuisine has been compartmentalised into four main culinary regions, or schools — those of the North (Hebei, Shandong and Henan), East (Jiangsu and Zhejiang), Southeast, including the universally known Cantonese cuisine, and the Western or Southwestern cuisine of Sichuan and Hunan. The Northern style, sometimes loosely labelled Beijing food, very much reflects the frugal, austere character and climate of China's sometimes forbidding northern regions — the cuisine is largely wheat-based, with dumplings, wheat-flour noodles, baked and steamed breads providing the sort of staple fare that is replaced by rice in the south, and includes a great deal of mutton and lamb, pepped up with scallions, leeks, pickled cabbage and cucumbers. Yet Northern food is by no means mundane. It's a culmination, in fact, of distinctive regional dishes, palace dishes from Beijing's Forbidden City, Moslem and Mongolian dishes and Shandong dishes, which are considered to be the *haute cuisine* of Chinese cooking. Shandong chefs reigned supreme in the palace kitchens and in the best restaurants of Beijing, famous for dishes often served with delicate cream sauces or stir-fried with vegetables, crab, shrimp, chicken or meatballs. The monarch of all the northern

dishes, as much for its popularity as taste, is Beijing duck — the whole bird basted until a golden brown then served in thin flesh and crispy-skin slices with unleavened pancakes, fresh scallions and a salty-tasting plum sauce.

The cuisine of the East, an area including Shanghai and the cities of the lower Yangtze delta, owes its heritage to the region's great historical prosperity and coteries of high government officials, aristocrats, wealthy merchants and skilled chefs that formed elitist *salons* there through the golden ages of imperial China. Their culinary rivalry and experimentation made good use of the area's abundant foodstuffs, especially seafoods, and some of China's finest fish, shrimp and crab dishes come from here. The Eastern cuisine is noted for its rich tastes — a tradition that is said to have been started by imperial chefs, coming from the south, who presented "unnecessarily elaborate dishes and overly opulent banquets." Many present-day dishes are still well seasoned with garlic and pungent sesame oil, and are warming, substantial and oily — so much so that steamed breads are served instead of rice to soak up the oily juices. Shanghai itself is noted for its celebrated range of braised dishes (or red-cooked, with soya sauce, wine and sugar) which, in these present egalitarian days in China, are prepared in small, unglazed, disposable casserole dishes for workers who want a good hot and nourishing mid-day meal. Other features of the cuisine are its variety of vegetable dishes, the famed smoked meats and poultry of Nanjing, a former imperial capital, the *haute cuisine* of Hangzhou (Hangchow) which was developed by its splendid restaurants and traditionally rich and powerful aristocracy, and, in the autumn months, an annual speciality — Shanghai hairy crab, which arouses a province-wide culinary fever as fierce and heady as the durian season in Thailand and mangoes in The Philippines.

For many outsiders, the Southern, or Southeastern or Cantonese cuisine is what Chinese food is really all about — the

doyen of the four regional schools. One reason for this is simply its popularity: It was the main cuisine that spread all over the Western world in the great waves of Chinese emigration during the crumbling Qing dynasty. Another reason is that, when all is said and done, it is probably the most varied and most imaginative cuisine in all of China. Its birthplace, the sprawling, sub-tropical Guangdong province, is a virtual cornucopia of foodstuffs. Its long coastline is teeming with fish, squid, oysters, eels, shrimps,

The combinations of ingredients in Chinese cuisine developed in part from the poor storage conditions for food. For instance, wine will improve the taste of spoiled poultry or meat; pepper, seafood. Ginger (opposite, in the baskets) and scallions will suppress offensive flavours of meat and seafood. Sesame seed oil, added before cooking, will take away the fishy odours of shrimp and crab.

crabs and lobsters. Its myriad inland waterways abound with freshwater fish and crustaceans, its farms produce an abundance of chickens, ducks, pigs, geese, pigeons, a tremendous variety of vegetables and melons and other tropical fruits. Because of the climate and the variety of fruits, one feature of the Cantonese cuisine is the extent to which meat and poultry dishes are sweetened with fruit (though contrary to popular belief, it is not noted for its sweet and sour dishes). Another distinctive element is the variety of sauces used in cooking — black fermented bean sauces, for example, along with oyster sauce (usually teamed with meats) and even lobster sauce. The Cantonese also excel in steamed fish dishes and barbecued and roasted pork. Also, they often blend meat with fish, and dishes like stir-fried abalone, mushrooms and eggs are a good example of the Southern *penchant* for combining more than one ingredient on the same plate.

The Western cuisine of Sichuan and Hunan is perhaps the poor sister of the lot — but one with a slightly vicious tongue. While not as popular or as widely known as the other three culinary schools, it is nonetheless unique for its liberal use of green and red chillis, garlic, ginger and peppers to season the food. The reasons for this fiery approach to food are probably three-fold: The close proximity of the hot Burmese, Indian and Pakistani cuisines; the rigorous mountain climate and mists, calling for "warming" and disease-resistant foods; and the fact that while the area has always been known as the rice-bowl of China, and has rarely experienced famine, many other foodstuffs have been scarce, and spicy sauces have tended to compensate for meagre portions. Whatever, the vegetable, meat and poultry dishes of this region are best described as "characteristically spicy, fiery and generous in the use of oil . . . (with) more braising, deep-frying and often several cooking methods employed in creating a dish." Since, under such climatic conditions (cold and wet in winter, hot and

The government controls the production and distribution of all food except the bit that peasants are allowed to grow on their private plots and sell in the free markets. The government buys produce at a fixed price from the farm communes, and sells it at controlled price in the urban centres.

In 1979, the government, yielding to pressure from the rural areas, raised the prices at which it bought produce from the communes, but chose to keep the prices unchanged in the cities. As a result, some peasants came into the cities, bought produce at the state-run market at the lower prices, and re-sold it through the free markets — where prices are higher than the state's. In this way, they made an additional profit for themslves.

People grumble about the quality of fresh foods available in the state markets (opposite, in Beijing). They complain, for instance, that apples are bruised, wormy or too small. Or that the meat has too large a proportion of fat. Some criticize the special markets where only senior officials, the military and others with privilege can shop, and where the better foods are sold.

humid in summer) most fresh foods need to be quickly preserved, the tradition of salting, drying, smoking and pickling foods is more prevelant here than elsewhere in China. And since all such processes have the tendency to intensify the flavour of the foods, the dishes of Sichuan and Hunan are undoubtedly more stronger tasting. In the Western world, where Sichuan food has trailed behind the other major schools in popularity, these chilli-based dishes seem to have struck the American palate in particular, and several Sichuan and Hunan restaurants have sprung up in New York in recent years.

All this is obviously a loose categorisation of the Chinese cuisine as a whole, and it would take a whole book to explain the exact regional breakdowns of different dishes and techniques, how each regional school is influenced by others on its borders, how Mongolian, Moslem, Buddhist and ethnic minority tastes have added variety to the culinary compendium. But the geographical examination of Chinese food cannot be completed without mentioning its greatest latter-day triumph — the extent to which it has spread, flourished and, in some cases, conquered far outside the borders of China itself.

I have often been tempted to call the expansion and transplantation of Chinese food in foreign parts as the "Chinese gastronomic imperialism" — a phenomenon as pervasive as and perhaps more insidious than all the other imperialistic adventures of the last three centuries. Nowadays, the pseudo-Chinese restaurant sign is so familiar in so many parts of the world that I would venture to add that the sun never sets on sweet and sour pork, and rare is the place — be it London, New York, Johannesburg or Albany, Western Australia — where one cannot sit down to a dish of chow mein. In fact, there's only one area in the world where Chinese food is not regularly enjoyed — the Eastern European communist bloc where, since the abrupt and angry schism between Beijing and Moscow, all Chinese chefs seem to have packed up and gone home.

It would be audacious to suggest that there is a parallel between British imperialism of the 18th and 19th centuries and the Chinese culinary expansion of the latter years. But it is also very compelling to think that both expansions were to some extent fired and fuelled by nations that had achieved a highly refined level of technology in their respective fields: Britain was the first country to harness and promote industrial power; China had a superbly developed culinary expertise to

A scholar in the fourth century B.C. wrote about a skilled chef and how he used his cleaver: "Every blow of his hand, every heave of his shoulders, every tread of his foot, every thrust of his knee, every whshh of rent flesh, every chhk of the chopper, was in perfect rhythm".

In recent times, the food of China has suffered from the low quality of ingredients, inexperienced young cooks, and an uncritical clientele. During the Cultural Revolution, it was politically unfashionable to concern oneself with the quality and richness of food. Food was merely fuel. Many of the best chefs in Beijing, Shanghai and elsewhere were taken away from their stoves, to work as labourers, or as ordinary cooks in "masses" restaurants. Food in China has not yet recovered from that tragedy.

This page: The kitchen of the famous Songhelou (Pine and Crane) Restaurant in Suzhou.

Opposite: A roadside restaurant in Hefei.

offer. Of course, when the British were riding high as an imperial nation, and forcing trading and territorial concessions from the Chinese, they largely ignored what was to become the main weapon of Chinese "expansion." They called it "chow" — a term which, if further qualified by the epithet "Chop, chop," sounded vulgar as well as derogatory to the ears of the mandarins, or high government officials, who were accustomed to the more cultured nuances of Oxford English. But the British attitude has been gradually changing ever since they suddenly found Chinese in occupation not only in London and Manchester but Greenock and Inverness, Guildford, Plymouth, Taunton, Ramsgate, Dover and Sheerness.

Actually, Chinese "imperialism" had begun well over 2,000 years before: Chinese traders had spread throughout South-East Asia around the time of Christ, to be followed centuries later by another wave of merchants and entrepreneurs who followed the glorious maritime adventures of the Ming dynasty admiral, Cheng Ho. These immigrant Chinese trading communities injected their culture, and their cuisine, into national bloodlines in places like Malaysia, Indonesia and The Philippines, taking root so firmly that in The Philippines, for example, it's difficult today to determine where the native Filipino cuisine ends and the imported Chinese influences take over, and vice versa. In the ill-fated Qing dynasty, the point at which the Chinese civilisation collided with modern realities, and disintegrated, millions of Chinese — mainly from the south — fled the famines, brutal civil strife and general social impoverishment and migrated as labourers to America, South Africa and Australia, where they joined the fabled gold rushes; others poured down into South America, trickled through Africa, establishing themselves as merchants and traders. Millions more fled China after the downfall of Sun Yat Sen's republic and the onset of further bloody civil war, and more famine. And wherever these "overseas Chinese" went, they took their cuisine with them.

In the similarly brutal gold rush and frontier life of America and Australia, Chinese food wasn't exactly welcomed with banners and brass bands; in fact, it has taken many years for the cuisine to triumph over national prejudices and basic high-protein "red-meat" tastes and establish itself as a culinary attraction. There's a much-quoted, and much-misquoted, story of the first triumph of Chinese food in the United States. Depending upon the particular version, it seems that either a restaurant owner in San Francisco, or Chinese chow-wagon cooks engaged on the construction of the great Trans-American Railway, threw together a dish of left-over scraps, warmed it up and served it to a bunch of famished Caucasians. That dish became known as chop suey — a recipe and term that have done

untold damage to the reputation of Chinese food, and the Cantonese cuisine, ever since. If you prefer the second version, it seems that the Chinese were building the Pacific end of the railway, and Irish labourers were driving it through from the east. When both sides met in the Rocky Mountains the Chinese cooked up a dish that was as close to Irish stew as you could get — rough-chopped vegetables (onions, celery, cabbage etc) with chunks of meat, long-cooked and seasoned mainly with salt and pepper. The Irish apparently loved it, and chop suey became an American culinary legend.

Chop suey has had a great deal of insult and abuse thrown at it over the years since then. Gourmets and self-proclaimed scholars of Chinese food have condemned it as a Western bastardy, as Chinese as camembert cheese, while others have regarded it as simply a plate of leftovers, something similar to the bubble-and-squeak served up for days after the British Sunday roast. British traders and sailors on the China Coast used to call it the "bloody lot." The dish itself has become somewhat devalued over the years, too — prepared in a slap-dash manner with quick-cooked shredded meat, handfuls of bean sprouts and a sprinkling of industrially produced soya sauce. Yet it's only in recent times, with Americans — and other nationalities — drawn by the Chinese cuisine into a real understanding of its virtues, that the true dignity of chop suey has been restored. It is, in fact, a traditional Chinese dish prepared by a small fishing community on the south China coast. They call it *capcui*.

When the Chinese cuisine was introduced by immigrant "indent labourers" into Australia, it made even less impact than in the United States. The original Australian palate, attuned to a diet of red meat, strong tea or liquor and *damper*, could not really appreciate what was what in the culinary world as there existed no basis or means of comparison. It has taken nearly a century for Australians to accept and enjoy the Chinese cuisine — as carefully tailored to taste as it is in Chinese restaurants "down under" — but the culinary triumph has been even greater than that in America. It's nowadays estimated that there are 2,000 Chinese restaurants in the city of Sydney and its suburbs alone, and that the average Australian family eats Chinese food not just once, but sometimes twice or even three times, a week.

In Britain, the triumph of the Chinese cuisine really began during World War II. On the one hand, the massive buildup of American and Commonwealth servicemen in Britain — many of whom had already been introduced to Chinese food in their own countries — established new culinary demands. At the same time, because of the Japanese occupation of major ports in the Far East, Chinese merchant seamen serving under Allied flags were discharged in Liverpool — some 20,000 of them, many of whom were ship's cooks and caterers. Demand and supply met, and the Chinese cuisine won a foothold in the U.K.

Within a decade, Mao Tse-tung's communist forces had taken control of China, and thousands of Chinese were fleeing across China's southern border into the British Crown Colony of Hong Kong. This in turn led to an overspill of Chinese into Britain, which at that time had relatively lax immigration laws. This early wave of immigrants, and other which were to follow, caused an upgrading of Chinese food in Britain. Instead of restaurants simply dishing up chop suey and chow mein for the "natives," establishments now sprang up where the Chinese gathered and catered for themselves. The result was a more authentic cuisine — largely Cantonese — which the British public soon got wind of and wanted to try. In Hong Kong, growing prosperity led to better, bigger and more fashionable restaurants, and by the middle of the 1970s the colony's more authentic, or opulent, restaurant decor was beginning to influence some of the larger Chinese establishments in London, some of which were financed by Hong Kong interests.

One bastion of "barbarian" cooking that remains to be conquered is the Third World, yet the variety, health-giving properties and economy of the Chinese cuisine (unlike the French cuisine, which caters largely for the élite) are proving attractive to people in undeveloped countries whose own native cuisines are also fairly basic or primitive. In many African and South American countries, and even in the oil-rich Middle East, the Chinese cuisine is riding in on a wave of Chinese-manufactured foods — cheap but nourishing and well-prepared canned meats, vegetables, fruits and delicacies

which have spearheaded the People's Republic's export drives in recent years. Already in the West Indies there's emerged a new hybrid of Chinese and native cuisines called "Creole Chinese Food."

It remains now to see what will happen to the Chinese cuisine within China itself. Have 30 years of austere Communist rule brought about a dangerous lowering of culinary standards in China? Can the country's culinary establishment turn back to the variety and glory of the past and restore the cuisine to its traditional splendour? In this new "open door" era, there's no lack of evidence to suggest that this culinary national treasure is in fact being brought out of mothballs, dusted off and prepared for the high pedestal on which it has always belonged.

From the very beginning of the "New China," immediately after the 1949 revolution, the Maoist regime appeared to be fully conscious of the fact that Chinese food was an important part of the national heritage. Despite the need for austerity and rationing, a deliberate effort was made to keep alive and maintain the old culinary traditions, to the extent of opening up the Tingliguan (Oriole) Gardens in Beijing and establishing another restaurant, the Fangshan (Dining Room of the Monarchs) in Beihai Park — to which a number of skilled and elderly former palace chefs were invited so that their imperial skills would not be lost. This establishment was closed down during the Cultural Revolution, but has since reopened to become one of the capital's grandest venues for tourists and the more privileged Chinese workers, cadres and officials. The government is also attempting to bring about a restoration of the pre-Cultural Revolution standard of cuisine by establishing a number of cookery schools in Beijing to train new cooks and chefs.

The Chinese trend now, it seems, is to find their feet again in the culinary world and, in doing so, to revive and incorporate something of the quintessence of the golden past. This revival, with the need for new organisation, new research, new experimentation and the mass-training of new chefs, will almost certainly make Chinese food and cooking a self-conscious activity once again. And with the past to call upon, the present natural wealth of foodstuffs to use, new development and modernisation rules to follow, and new world markets waiting to be tapped, perhaps the Chinese cuisine is on the threshhold of another golden age.

Above: *A Nanjing bakery. The region from Shanghai to Nanjing has long been renowned for its sweets.*
Opposite: *The Songhelou Restaurant, Suzhou. As early as the second century, the Chinese language had more than 9,000 characters which described different foods, drinks and methods of cooking.*

LIN SHAOWEN

Lin Shaowen is a pseudonym of a Chinese dissident active in the "Beijing Spring" of 1979, when wall posters appeared in their thousands at "Democracy Wall" calling for a basic rethink of Chinese socialism and the freeing of political prisoners and redressing of grievances.

Lin was born in 1950, one year after the establishment of the People's Republic. His parents were middle-school teachers, and he assumed from childhood that he would follow the same career. In 1966 he joined the Red Guards in his middle school, protesting against the fossilised teaching methods and strict discipline imposed by the teachers. They destroyed books and blackboards, and put two of the middle-aged teachers "in the cowpen" — sleeping beneath a staircase at night, and doing menial jobs during the day.

At about the same time, Lin's parents were similarly victimised at the school where they worked, and the boy could do nothing to help them — though he was able to smuggle a little extra food and warm clothing into the school where they were being held in a cellar and brought out periodically for "struggle sessions" and beatings. Lin's father developed chronic bronchitis, and his mother lost the sight of

one eye during a beating session. Lin protested to the Red Guard leadership at their school, and was promptly seized and "investigated."

When they found whose son he was, they marched him back to his own school to be dealt with by the young rebels there. But his friends promptly beat up the escort, and sent them back with black eyes and bleeding noses. A few days later, Red Guards from Lin's parents' school attacked him and his friends with sticks, iron bars and knives. Several were badly injured.

The police intervened, and took Lin — the evident cause of the trouble — into custody. He was kept in solitary confinement for eight months, undergoing daily interrogation for several hours at a time, and spending the rest of his days writing self-criticisms and confessions — all of which were rejected as "insincere." He was fed on corn-mush, and lost 10 kg. Repeated shackling and manacling caused festering sores on his ankles and wrists, and the cold, damp cell gave him rheumatism.

Later Lin was moved into a cell with 29 other prisoners, whose daily task was to "struggle" him — screaming abuse and insults at him, stealing his food and forcing him to write more and more self-criticisms. He suffered a nervous breakdown and was

taken to the prison hospital for a period of merciful release. He was then sent to a "reform-through-labour" camp, digging irrigation ditches in a remote part of Chinese Central Asia, and remained there for five years.

After the disgrace and death of Defence Minister Lin Biao in 1971, Lin's parents — who had been set free in 1968 — petitioned for his release. After numerous meetings with Party and judicial officials, they were told he would be returning home — "as a result of the clemency of the Government." He arrived back in Beijing in June, 1973, and began studying at home under his parents' guidance. In 1978, he was accepted to the Beijing Teacher Training College.

In late 1978, Lin seized on the new freedom of "Democracy Wall" to write an account of his sufferings and to call on the authorities to reinstate his parents to their old jobs (they were still working as cleaners). He became involved with one of the dissident groups producing a political journal, and while distributing this at the Wall one Sunday afternoon in March, 1979, he was seized by uniformed police and arrested for spreading counter-revolutionary propaganda. His parents have heard nothing from him since, except to be told by the authorities that a court case is being prepared against him.

SONG QINGLING

Song Qingling (Soong Ch'ing-ling) is the
"grand old lady" of the Chinese revolution
— widow of Sun Yat-sen, sister-in-law of
Chiang Kai-shek, and a leading figurehead
in the National People's Congress.
Born in 1890, as daughter of an American-
educated Chinese Christian missionary in
Shanghai, she went to the United States to
study and attended Wesleyan College for
Women, Macon, Georgia. On returning to
China she joined the staff of Sun Yat-sen,
the Western-trained physician who had
become the focal personality of the anti-
Manchu revolution, and was made
Provisional President of the Republic of
China in 1911. He married Qingling in 1915
in Japan, after he had been chased out of
China by the usurper and director Yuan
Shikai.

Sun returned to China and acted as
President of the Republic founded after the
overthrow of Yuan, and on Sun's death in
1925 his widow continued her career in
politics. Song Qingling opposed the
Kuomintang's anti-Communist policy, and
visited the Soviet Union in the late 1920s.
During the thirties she worked to rally international support for China in its war
with Japan, and in 1941 went to work in
hospitals and nurseries in Communist-held

areas behind Japanese lines.

In recognition of her support, the Communist Party appointed her to the body
preparing the First National People's Congress, at which she was a Shanghai delegate
in 1954. In the meantime she was active in
organising women's political organisations
and child-care, and in promoting friendly
relations with the Soviet Union.

She also undertook semi-diplomatic
missions to India, Pakistan, Burma and Indonesia, and political youth work. By the
1960s, her functions had become mainly
titular, but she was one of the few veteran
revolutionaries who did not suffer persecution in the Cultural Revolution, during
which she apparently lived quietly in
Shanghai.

Song Qingling has been important to the
Party as a symbol of its continuity and
legitimacy in the succession of the Chinese
revolution. Her outspoken opposition to the
Kuomintang's anti-leftist and often brutal
policies in the 1930s and during the war
were a factor in undermining American
confidence in Chiang Kai-shek.

She was also a key figurehead of the
revived "united front" movement, through
which the Communists have sought to
obtain help and co-operation from all
sections of Chinese society and foreign
countries which are not bitterly opposed

to Beijing.

Until her death in 1981, she conducted an
active correspondence with old friends and
acquaitances in many parts of the world
and has undoubtedly done much to improve
the Communists' image among Overseas
Chinese. Hopes that she might have been
able to mediate in the Beijing-Taipei
dispute, however, proved groundless,
perhaps because her relations with her
younger sister, Mme Chiang, were distant
for decades.

Her funeral was a major event in 1981.
Beijing officials went so far as to invite a
Taiwan delegation, but, predictably enough,
the invitation was snubbed.

Index

A

Acupuncture 94, 331
Advertising 139, 141
  agencies 136
  See also Billboards
Aerospace installations 107
Afghanistan 147
Agriculture 108-116, 177
  during Cultural Revolution 54
  history of 108, 183
  incentives in 115-116
  land area available for manpower
  manpower in 115
  mechanisation in 115, 116
  modernisation aims for 108-111
  on communes 115-116
  outlook 111-116
  private lots 116
  problems faced 108
  specialisation of 111
  under Mao 111
  waterworks for 261
  See also Four Modernisations
Air Force, China's 103
All-China Sports Federation 325
Ancestor worship 43
Animal species in China 147
Animism and magic 43-45, 147
Antimony deposits 126, 177
Archery 339-343
Architecture
  modern 227
  traditional 227, 276
  See also Cities, and individual cities
Armed forces 79-80
  conditions for 79
  privileges of 79
  travel for 79
  see also Peoples' Liberation Army
Armour 99-103
  non-nuclear 99-103, 108
  nuclear 99-103, 107,108
  See also Nuclear Power
Arts and Crafts 51, 53, 54, 56, 59, 63,
  66, 121
  education in 56, 58
  effect of Cultural Revolution on 294
Asian Games, China's performance
  in 331-332
Asian Games Federation 331
Auspices 45
Austronesians 183, 193
"Authority Street" case 83
Autonomous Regions, Perfectures and
  Countries 215, 218
Avenue of Animals 307, 313

B

Bai people 201
Banks 135
  deposits in 135
Baoshan Steel Works 116-120
Barefoot doctor 126
Basketball 335-336
Beauty parlours 79
Beijing 227, 240-250, 284, 306-317
  architecture of 233, 240, 243, 245,
  310-317
  food and restaurants of 246-250, 358
  history of 240-245, 306, 307
  inhabitants of 246
  Institute of Physical Culture 325
  nightlife in 317
  population of 147
  shopping in 317
  sites near 245-246, 307-310
  tours in 306-307
  University 128, 307
Beijing Daily 282
Beijing Evening News 127
Beijing Review 83
Bicycles 79, 139, 222
Big Five 99
Billboards 30, 103, 116, 141, 283
Birth control pill 99
Birth rate, 1979 139
Black marketeering 84, 135, 279
Bo Hai Sea 151, 164, 173
Boxer Rebellion 10, 237
Bo Zhuyi, poetry of 48, 174
Buddhism 45, 47, 48, 51, 53, 93

C

Canals
  construction of 154
  Grand 154, 177, 257
  Ling 154, 156
  Red Flag 154
Cao Yu 26
Celestial Kingdom 325
Censorship 12,16
Central Committee 80
  on inflation 135
Centralisation 12
Chairman Mao Memorial Hall 317
Chairman of the Party 80
Changan, See X'ian
Changhe River 154
Chemical industry 161
Chengdu 262-265
  architecture of 34, 262-265
  food of 265
  history of 262
  inhabitants of 265
  waterworks near 261
Chengshan Cape 147
Chen Jingrun 225
Chen Yonggui, biographical sketch 179
'Cheongsam' 84
Chiang Kai-shek 13, 99, 116, 270, 375
Chientang River 164
CAAC 273
China and the West 9, 12
  see also Foreigners and Foreign
  Tourism
China International Travel Service 273-
  279
China, physical dimensions 147
China Reconstructs 325
China's Sorrow, See Huang He
China Traders 282
Chinese Academy of Sciences 126
Chinese bureaucracy 12
  disruption of ideological
  campaigns 21
  opposition to Mao's policies 19
  rivalry in 20
Chinese civilisation, early 183-193, 227,
  240, 273
Chinese Communist Party 9, 12, 22, 71,
  80, 99, 108, 111
  history of 17, 27
  internal differences in 22
  split into factions 19
Chinese culture 41-55
  tolerance level of 193
See also Minorities
Chinese currency, See Renminbi
Chinese customs 201
  protection of 48
Chinese Export Commodities Fair
  See Guangzhou Foreign Trade Fair
Chinese language 41
  local dialects 141, 233
Chinese medicine 331
  herbs in 347
Chinese New Year
  celebrations in China 55
  pictures 56
Chinese philosophy 41, 43, 48
  post-revolutionary 53
Chinese politics
  Western analysis of 15
Chinese religious beliefs 41-53
  folk 45
  reactions against 43
  See also Buddhism, Taoism etc.
Chinese socio-political system 43, 48, 54
  post-Mao 89
  self regulation in 51
Chinling Mountains 151
Chop-sticks, origins of 258-261, 360
Chou En-Lai 13, 19, 20-21, 76, 108
  mourning death of 34
  portraits of 27
Chousan Archipelago 164
Christianity 48, 61
  initial entry of 273
  purging of 48
Cities 227-269, 284-317
  food and restaurants in 233
  foreign tourism in 237-240
  hygiene in 227
  leisure life in 233-237
  mechanisation in 227
  nightlife in 237
  pace in 227
  pollution in 227-232
  problems in 117
  provinciality of 232-233
  transport in 227
  See also individual cities
Civil War 9
Classes in China
  armed forces 79-80
  intellectual/educated 76-79
  party and government hierarchy 80-
  84
  peasant 71-73
  pre-revolutionary/educated 51
  relatives of Overseas Chinese 84-89
  returned Overseas Chinese 84-89
  urban industrial 73-76
"Clean" industry 168
Climate 108, 147, 151, 153, 156, 163
Coal industry 121, 173
  deposits 177
  investment in 121
  problems faced in 121
  production in 121
Collective enterprises in the '80s 135
Communes, tourist visits to 289, 290-
293
Communist Revolution in China 41, 51,
  53
  accomplishments of 108
  differences from the Soviet case 116
Communist rule, features of 12
Confucianism
abolition of 53
  and Yin-Yang 50
  attitude to foreign religion 47-48
  concept of State 43
  doctrines of 41, 47-48, 51
  standards of behaviour 50, 51
Confucius 41, 53
Conscription 79
Constitution of the Peoples' Republic of
  China 218
Consumer durables industry 135
Consumer revolution 135
  availability of Consumer durables 15,
  90, 92, 135
Cooking, See Food
Copper deposits 126, 177
Cotton 111, 164
  areas 164, production 164
  See also Crops and Livestock, and
  Textiles
Creation of the Universe 147
Crime, effect of tourism on 282
Criticism, intolerance of 25, 80
  invitation to 25, 80-83
  Mao on 25, 83
Crops and Livestock 164-173
  See also Textiles, and individual crops
Crotale air-defence system 107
Cult of heroes 55
Cultural Revolution, See Great Proletarian
  ...
Culture and Propaganda Department 71

D

Dai people 163, 191, 215, 224
Dalai Lama 93
Daqing (Taching Oilfield) 121
Dazhai Commune 111
Dazhai Production Brigade 179
Defence budget 108
"Democracy Movement" 25
"Democracy Wall" 25, 306
Demonstrations, See Strikes and ...
Deng Xiaoping 16, 17, 19, 20, 21, 76,
  83, 99
  army connexions of 80
  on food 351
  on light versus heavy industry 120
  on mineral policy 126
  on modernisation 99, 130-132
  on opening China 63
  on population control 139
  on technological training 76, 126,
  130-132
  on tourism 273
  opposition to Mao 19
  pictures of 29
  programme of pragmatism 23-25
  rehabilitation of 21
Deserts 156, 161
  Gobi 160, 161, 166
  stopping the spread of 161
  Tyngeri 161
Devaluation 121
Ding Ling 25
Discipline in Chinese society 51
Dissidents 374
Disunity 9
Djilas, Miroslav 71
Dragon dance 56
Dragon Well Tea 258
Dust storms 166

E

Earthquake alert service 126
Economic policy, in th '80s 9, 132
    under Mao 132
    under Deng 130-132
Education 19, 128-130
    effect of Cultural Revolution on 54, 73, 128, 132
    higher 89
    in Economics 130
    in English 132
    outside the classroom 130
    overseas 130, 132
    part-time 128
    role in modernisation 128
    television channels for 128-130
    under Mao 128
    See also Schools, and Universities
Egalitarianism 25, 71, 84, 89
Electronics industry, 122
    expansion of 122
Elites
    "Authority Street" case 83
    food as symbol of 349
    intellectual/educational 130
    post-Mao treatment of 89
    press coverage of 83
    problems in abolition of 83-84
    See also Classes in China
Empress Dowager 317, 361
    dream about food 349
"Emulation campaigns" 13, 55
Energy 121-122
    coal 121
    conversion efficiency 122
    crises in 122
    oil 121
    water powered 122
European colonialists 12
Exports 121
    coal 121
    light industry products 121
    oil 121
    textiles 121
Ewenki people 201-204

F

Family 43, 51
    as living institution 54, 55, 139
Farm machinery 108
    See also Tractors, Chinese
Fertiliser
    chemical 111, 116
Filial piety 43, 50, 62-63, 139
    downfall of 54
Fish farming 164
    at Suzhou 168
    breeding methods 164
Fishing, sea 164, 168
    biggest grounds 164
Flash cards 34
Flood control 151
Food
    as mark of position 349-350
    Confucian rules for 360-361
    cooking techniques for 351-361, 365
    Eastern 365
    effect of Cultural Revolution on 350-351, 354, 368
    effect of overpopulation on 347
    grains in 357
    history of 347-351, 359-361
    in foreign countries 368-373

    in the Third World 370-373
    key to 354
    medicinal aspects of 347
    Northern 365
    regionality of 361-368
    sauces and dips for 356,
    seasonal aspects of 362
    Southern/Cantonese 365-367
    Soya derivatives in 354-356, variety in 347-349
    Western 367-368
    Western interest in 351-354
    wok cooking of 356-357
Food grain mania 111
Football 335
Forbidden City 227, 240, 246, 279, 301, 305, 318, 321, 322
    See also Beijing
Foreign currency 135, 279
    certificates 279
Foreigners, attitudes to 9, 10, 47, 273, 279, 284
    and religion 51, 273,
    fascination for 284
    influence of 10, 279-283
    purging of 52, 273
    suspicion of 273
    treatment of 284
Foreign experts, contemporary use of 130
Foreign films 282
Foreign influence, official disapproval of 47
Foreign lending 120
    by IMF 120
Foreign policy, China's 9, 273
Foreign religions in China 45, 49-54, 93
    adherents of 53
    downfall of 48
    edict against 47
    See also individual religions
Foreign tourism
    cities open to 240-269, 284-317
    cost of 283
    currency certificates for 279
    effet of 10, 237-240, 279-283
    foreign exchange from 135
    group tours for 283
    history of 273,279
    hotels for 273, 283-284, 285-289, 293, 294-295, 299, 306
    individual travel for 283
    regulations for 279
    transport for 284-285
    volume 283
Foreign trade, history of 273
    in Guangzhou 265, 269, 270
    promotion of 283
    See also Exports, Imports, and Trade
Forest felling 111
Foshan 290
    craft of 290
    history of 290
    Temple in 290
    tours of 290
Four Modernisations 9, 25, 99-139, 177
    agriculture 9, 108-116
    aims of 99, 130
    how to achieve 120, 128, 139
    industry 9, 116-126
    military power 9, 99-108
    science and technology 9, 126-128
Fourth National Games 336-339

Fourth National People's Congress 99
France 107
Friendship Stores 284, 295, 317
Fujian Province (Fukien), physical geography of 147
"Fung shui" 45

G

"Gang of Four" 16, 20-25, 54, 55, 65, 76, 99, 128
    arrest of 19, 22, 80
    as scapegoats 25
    demise 16, 22-23
    effect on education 128
    origins 20
    photographs of 29
    politics of 20-22
    victims of 65
Gansu (Kansu) Province 151
Genghis Khan 111
Geography of China, Topography 147-164
Gemoancy 44
Gold deposits 126
"Golden Age" 41, 43, 55
Grain crops, See Rice, and Wheat
"Grand Concept" of rule and society 55
Grazing lands 153, 173
Great Hall of the People 23, 351
Great Helmsman 22
    See also Mao Tse Tung
Great Leap Forward 17-19, 54, 73
    educational success in 54
    effect on development 99
    industrialisation in 54
Great Proletarian Cultural Revolution 9, 19, 25, 71, 99, 178, 345
    abolition of class privilege in 71, 76
    anti-foreign fury in 10
    as power struggle 20
    attitude to Overseas Chinese in 89
    educational success in 54
    effect on army 79
    effect on bureaucracy 12, 20
    effect on China International Travel Service 273-279
    effect on development 99, 126
    effect on education 126, 128
    effect on family life 54
    effect on research 126
    minorities during 27,
    monuments to 19
    persecution in 9, 76-77, 93,225
    return to purity in 54,99
    See also Red Guards
Great Wall 41, 245, 273, 307-310
    construction of 41, 183, 245
    pictures of 166, present day 245
    purpose of 183
    tours of 307-310
Great Yu 55
Group responsibility, doctrine of 51
Guangzhou
    architecture of 268, 289
    Cultural Park 233
    Food and restaurants of 268-269, 288-289
    Foreign Trade Fair 270
    foreign trade in 265
    geography of 289
    history of 265-268, 289
    hotels in 285-289
    Inhabitants of 268

    White Cloud Airport 293
Guan Yin 193
"Guest families", See Hakka people
Guilin 147
    food in 233
'Gwai lo' 273

H

Hainan Island, offshore oil blocks 121
Hakka people 187-193
Han Chinese 183, 193, 213, 273
Han Dynasty 41, 48, 183, 187
"Hanging lake" 161
Hangzhou 258-261, 293-294
    architecture of 258-259
    caves 60
    crafts of 293
    food and restaurants of 259-261
    history of 258
    hotels in 293
    scenery of 257, 258, 293-294
    tea of 258
    West Lake of 227, 233, 258, 293
Harrier aricraft 107
Heavy industry 116-120, 168
    investment in 116
    problems with 116-117
    purge of 120
    targets for 116
    versus light industry 120
    women working in 122
    zones and centres 177
Health care, See Acupuncture, Barefoot doctor, Chinese medicine, and Hospitals
Hebei Province, major cotton region 164
    soil of 156
Heilongjiang (Heilungkiang) 130, 151
"Helicopter cadres" 20
Henan (Honan) Province 154
Heroes, See Cult of Heroes
Himalayas 147, 156, 160
Hindu principles 51
Hong Kong 43-45, 89, 135
    Dollars 279
    entry to China from 284
    industrial zones around 177
Hospitals 126, 128
Hot anti-tank missile 107
Hotels, construction of 125, 273
    low standard of 273, 283
    meals in 288
    problems with 273
    See also individual cities
Housing 15, 139
    shortages in 125
Hovercraft 284
Huaihe River 151, 154
    early farming civilisations on 183
Hua Guofeng 15, 21, 22-23, 115, 122
    on agriculture 115-116
    on sport 336
    on textiles 122
    party selection of 21
    portraits of 10,15, 29, 30
Hubei Province, fish farming in 164
Hui people 204-210, 213, 218
"Hundred Flowers" campaign 17, 25, 54
Hu Yaobang 126
"Hutongs" 196
Hydro-electricity, coal burning stations 168
    on Yangtze River 111, 156

power supply 122
projects 111, 116, 173

I

Imperial Edict 57
Imperial Palace 243
  damage by pollutants 294
Imports 120-121
  cotton 120
  grain 120-121
  increase in 121
  mineral 120
  sugar !20
Incentives, worker 116
Inflation in '80s 135
Influence peddling 83-84
Inner Mongolia 151, 153, 189
Institutes of National Minorities 216
Intellectual élite 76
  Cultural Revolution assault on 76, 77
  present policy on 377-79
  travel for 76
  wages of 76
  See also Elites, and Classes in China
Intercontinental Ballistic Missile
  China's first 99, 127
  present strike force 107
Interest rates 135
International Monetary Fund 120
Iron deposits 126, 177
"Iron rice bowl" philosophy 132
Irrigation 111, 116, 154
Islands 147
  coral 164
  See also individual islands
Isolation in China 174

J

Japanese invasion 55
Jesuits 43, 273
Jiang Qing 20, 21, 22, 71, 77, 80, 84
Jiangsu, lakes in 161, 164
Jiangxi Province 161
Juvenile deliquency 119

K

Kang Shien 139
Koko Shili Mountains 156
Korea 147
Koreans in China 210, 215
Kublai Khan 170, 183, 187
"Kung fu" 233
Kuomintang 13, 17, 55

L

Labour heroes 127
Labour mobility 128
Lakes 161-164
  fish farming in 164
  "Hanging Lake" (Hungtse) 161
  highest (Namu) 161
  largest freshwater (Poyang) 161
  Taihu 161
  Tungping 151
"Land of silk" 164
Lao She, biographical sketch 26
Laser weaponry 107, 127
Law, Chinese 51, 83
Leadership 9
  criticism of 25, 108
  current 25

Legends, new 55
  old 53, 147
Leisure life 80, 203, 204, 210, 233-237
Lhasa 161
Liao Chengzhi, biographical sketch 140
Liaodong Peninsula 154
Libo, poetry of 149
Li Chi (Book of Rites) 361
Light industry 120, 122, 168, 177
  advances in 122
  overseas investments in 122
  zones and centres for 177
Lin Biao 15-16, 19, 20, 79-80
  Affair 15-16
  appointment of 19
  death of 79-80
  head of Red Guard 20
  history of, rewritten 16
Linxian Country, Communist Party
  Committee of 154
  water control system in 154-156
Lin Shaowen, biographical sketch 374
Li River 154
"Little Red Book" 19, 130
Liu Shaoqi 19-20, 84
Livestock raising 170-173
  encouragement of 111
  main grazing lands 173
  See also Crops and Livestock
Loess Plateau 151-154
Long March 13, 17, 41, 99
Lu Xun 26

M

Macau 89
  industrial zones around 177
Machine tool sector, modernisation
  of 122
Madame Liu 84
Madame Mao, See Jiang Qing
Magic, See Animism and ...
Mahayana 47
Manchu Dynasty 12, 183, 210, 273
Manchu people 210-215
Mandate of Heaven 43, 99
Manichaeism 47, 48
Maoism, as social doctrine 53
"Mao t'ai" 288
Mao Tse Tung 9, 10, 13, 15, 17, 23, 83,
  99, 116, 270
  and the Cultural Revolution 20
  attitude to foreigners 19
  bureaucratic opposition to 19
  death of 20-22
  early years 17
  experiments with revolution 17
  good grain mania 111
  Great Leap Forward 17
  "Hundred Flowers" campaign 17
  on agriculture 15, 111, on army 99
  on education 76, 128
  on peasant revolution 17, 116
  on sport 325, 329
  on tourism 273, 279
  poem by 147
  portraits of 10, 15, 29, 30,
  statue of 25
  swim by 334,
  tailoring of Marxism 53
  theory of criticism 83
  writings of 30, 50, 329
Markets 209, 370

free 367
  special 367
  state 367
Marksmen 332
Marxism 12, 31, 17
  in China 53
Mass campaign and Progaganda 12-17,
  23
"Mass line" 19
Material incentives 130-135
  See also Consumer Revolution
Ma Yinchu, biographical sketch 57
Mazdaism 45, 47
Mechanisation 227 See also Farm
  Machinery, Tractors Chinese
Metal industry 126
  backwardness of 126
Miao people 215
Middle Kingdom 273
Military Committee, gerontocracy
  of 108
Military establishment, See Peoples'
  Liberation Army
Military training 107
Minerals 122-126, 173-177 See also
  individual minerals
Ming dynasty 246, 273
Ming Tombs 245, 280, 283, 307, 310,
  313
Minister of Geology, See Sun Daqing
Minorities 183-224, 273
  areas/autonomous regions for 215
  constitutional standing of 218
  distribution 193-196
  official groups 196-201
  percentage of population 193, 220
  policies on and treatment of 218, 221
  preferential treatment of 189, 195
"Model peasants/workers" 55
Modern methods 9, 122
  economic 130
  problems faced 122
Monasteries, destruction of 48
Mongols 111, 183, 187, 215, 216, 218
Mongol Yuan Dynasty 183
Moslem-Arab settlements 48-50
Moslem faith, in China 47, 48, 50, 51,
  204-210, 213, 218
  mosques 48, 276
Mourning 201
Mythology, See Legends

N

Nachang 168
Nanjing 10, 299
  architecture of 10, 299
  crafts of 299
  gardens in 299
  history of 299
  hotels in 299
Nan Yue Kingdom 187
Napoleon, on China 99
National consciousness, development
  of 41, 47-48
  post-revolution development of 54
National Games, China 336-343
Nationalists 399, 116
Nationalities Committee 218
Navy, China's 103-107
Nestorianism 47, 48
New China Bookstores 237
Nightlife 237
  See also Cities and individual cities

North China Plain 151, 154
  cotton plantations on 164
Nuclear power, in China 107
  in Soviet Union 107
  See also Intercontinental Ballistic
    Missile

O

Oil
  fields 173, 177
  offshore 121, 173
  problems faced 121
  production 121
  See also Exports
Oil crops 170
  See also Crops and Livestock
Olympic Games 326, 337, 343
  Chinese entrants in 325
  Committee decision on China 334-335
  Moscow 336, 339
One child families 139
  benefits to 139
Opera 65, 317
  Beijing 65, 317
  masks 46, 284
Opium trade 10, 283
Opium Wars 25, 51, 249, 273
Optical fibres 127
Overseas Chinese 84-89
  attitudes to 89
  preferential treatment of 89
  relatives of 84-89
  returned 84-89

P

Pamirs 147
Panchen Lama, biographical sketch 93
P'an Ku 147
Party and Government hierarchy 80-84
  power of 80
  privileges of 80, 83
  public treatment of 83, 84
Pearl River 154
Peasant Movement Institute 270
Peng Dehuai 16
  purge of 19
Penglung people 218
Peoples Daily 84, 111, 237
Peoples Liberation Army 13, 22, 29, 34,
  99-108
  educational level of 108
  élitism of 103
  equipment 16, 29
  faults of 99-103, 108
  modernisation of 99, 108
  obsolescence of 99-103
  origins of 99
  strengths of 103
  See also Airforce, Armour, and Navy
Perkins, Dwight H. 108
Philosophy, See Chinese ....
Physical culture 36, 233, 325
Physical geography, China 147-164, 273
  area/size 147, 183
  coastline 147-151
  land frontier 147
  See also Canals, Deserts, Islands,
    Lakes, Rivers, and Underground
    Water
Physics, high energy 107
  investment in 127
Ping Pong 331

Plant species, China 147
Police, See Public Security Branch
Politburo 12, 15, 23, 80
Politics, Chinese 9-25
 Capriciousness of 15-16
 conflicts in 12, 17, 23
 factions and power struggles 19-22
 history of 9-10
 stability of 23
 See also Chinese politics, Western analysis of, Chinese socio-political system, Mass campaign, Gang of Four
Pollution 119, 227-232
 See also Cities
Pol Pot 116
Population, China 99
 age breakdown 99,
 as a resource 13, 17
 Control 139
 density 147, 170
 distribution 147, 170
 growth 139
 targets 139
Population control 139
 measures taken in 139
 minority exemption from. 189
 one child family policy for 139
Port facilities, containerisation of 112
 in Shanghai 112
Pottery 51, 53, 56, 66
Power cuts 122
Press 80, 83, 128-130
 See also individual newspapers
Price rises, 1979 132
Private enterprise in the '80s 132
Private lots 116
Profit distribution 135
Propaganda 84
 See also Mass campaigns
Protestant Christianity in China 45
Provinciality 232-233
 in cooking 233
Public Security Bureau 13

Q
Qing Dynasty, See Manchu Dynasty
Qin Dynasty 183, 185
Qinghai Province 156
Qinghai-Tibet Plateau 147, 151, 156, 161
Qinshihuangdi 41
 construction of canals 154
 construction of Great Wall 41
 tomb of 48
 See also Qin Dynasty

R
Radio Beijing 325
Railway 284-285
 See also Transportation
Rainfal 156
 See also Climate
Rare earth deposits 126
Red Guards 9, 10, 12, 19, 20
 anti-foreign fury of 10
 function of 20
 on food 350-351
 presecution by 26, 71, 77, 140, 225, 345
 raids by 20
Red Flag 13
Red Flag Canal, construction of 154

Refrigeration facilities 115
Relaxation, See Leisure life
Renminbi 121
"Resettled youth" 73, 195, 215
Resources, manpower 13, 115
Restaurants 286, 350, 351, 358, 370, 373
 See also Food, Cities, and individual cities
Ricci, Matteo 273
Rice 168, 170, 177
 area under paddy 170
 See also Crops and Livestock
"Rice-Christians" 53
Rickshaws 84
Rivers 151-161
 fish farming in 164
 flood control of 151
 inland 156
 northern 156
 southern 156
 world's highest 156
 See also individual rivers
Romanisation of language 41
Roof of the World, See Qinghai-Tibet Plateau
Rural drift, effect of 115, 125
Russia, religion in 51, 53
"Rusticated Youths", See "Resettled youth"
"Rustication" programme 73

S
Satellites, China's first 107
 developments in 107
Schools 76,222
 élitism in 76, 79
 high 130
 nursery 79, 130
 primary 10, 130
 See also Education
Science and Technology 9, 126, 128
 advances in 99
 during Cultural Revolution 126
 foreign 273
 in cities 227
 Institute 130
 inventions 127
 personnel in 127-128
 problems faced 127
 re-establishment after Cultural Revolution 126-127
 under Mao Tse Tung 128
Seismic Surveys, by Western firms 121
Self reliance 25
Senior citizens 198
Serica/Sera/Seres, See "Land of silk"
Shaanxi Province 83, 151, 154
Shakespeare 71
Shamanist cults 51, 221
Shandong (Shantung) Peninsula 147
Shanghai
 architecture of 233, 234, 250, 295
 European influence in 249, 250, 295
 food and restaurants in 251
 history of 250, 295
 hotels in 294-295
 industry in 168
 life in 250-251, 295
 parks in 299
 physical area of 249
 pollution in 119, 250
 population of 147, 249

shopping in 295
 sinking of 151
 Suzhou Creek in 237
Shang Yin Dynasty 183
Shanxi coalmine 121
 Province 151
Shengli 121
Shipbuilding industry 103
Shooting 325
Siberian railway 107
Sichuan (Szechuan) Province 147, 160
 food of 357
 tea gardens in 164
Silk 146-170, 257
 early trade in 164-170
 factory 114
 production areas for 170
 worms 170
 See also Crops and Livestock, and Textiles
Silk Route 10, 47, 122, 164-170
Silver deposits 126
Skiing 325
Smog 232
 See also Cities, and Pollution
Smuggling, from Hong Kong 135
 from Taiwan 135
Socialism in China, flexibility of 55
Social services, provision of 139
Soils, China 147, 153, 154, 156
Son of Heaven 227, 273
Song Dynasty 183, 187
Song Qingling, biographical sketch 375
Soviet Union 9, 84, 99
 aid in Chinese oil industry 121
 bureaucratic influence in China 17
 Navy 103
Space effort in China 107
Sport 325-343
 facilities for 325
 history of 325, 326
 interest in 325-33
 minority participation in 343
 participation in world events 331-336
 political role of 337
 training in 330-31
 treatment of injuries in 331
Sportsmen and women
 Ni Zhigin, high jumper 325-329
 Wu Lanyang, skeet shooter 329-330
 Yu Peisu, pentathlete 339
 Zou Zhenzian, triple jumper 339
Spring Festival 55
Stalin, Josef 20
Standardisation 41
Standard of living 71-76
 in rural areas 71-73
 in urban areas 73-76
State Planning Commission 121
State-run enterprises in the '80s 135
Steel 116
 plant 116
"Stinking ninth category" 76
"Street committees" 55
Strikes and Demonstrations 19, 22, 23
Strong, Anna Louise 93
Sugar 120
Sui Dynasty 183
 public examinations for administrators in 130
Summer Palace 245-246, 307, 317, 318
Sun Daqing 216
Sun Yat-sen 375
 founding of Kuomintang 270

Mausoleum 299
 Memorial Hall 286
 Statue 280
Superstition 55
 effect of Revolution on 53
Supremacy, Chinese
 historial 9-10
 to-day 9
Suzhou 71, 232, 251-258
 agriculture of 168
 architecture of 251
 canals of 255
 deep-sea fishing of 168
 fish farming of 168
 food and restaurants of 232, 251-258
 gardens of 251
 history of 251
 industry of 168
 inhabitants of 187, 251
Swimming and Diving 332, 334

T
Taching Oilfield, See Daqing
Taihang Mountains 154
Tai people 183, 187
"Tai Qi Chuan" 233, 289, 295, 325, 326, 329
Taiping Rebellion 45
Taklamakan 156-161
Tang Dynasty 47, 48, 54, 183, 187
Tanka people 193
Taoism 41, 45, 46, 47, 51, 53
Tarim Basin 161
Tarim River 161
Tea 164, 168, 294
 foreign exchange from 164
 picker 213
 plantations 164
 provinces where grown 164
 tree 164
Technology, See Science and ...
Television 142
Temple guards 46, 59
Temple of Heaven 68, 283, 317
Temples 43, 46, 48, 59, 60, 68
 See also Cities, and individual temples
Ten Great Oil Years 121
Tennis 343
Ten-year plan (1976-1985)
 key objectives 177
Textiles 115, 122
 cotton 115
 expansion of industry 122
 in pre-Communist China 122
 silk 155, 122
 synthetics 122
 women working in industry 122
 wool 155, 122
Thomas Cook, on China travel 283
"Three Hard years" 19
"Three Transcendant Powers" 55
Tibet 161
Tibetans 187, 215-216, 220
Tienanmien Gate 310
Tienanmien Square 23, 301, 310, 325
Tin deposits 126, 177
Tipping 283
Tobacco 170
 production areas 170
Tortoise 322
Tourism,
 courses on 279
 internal 279
 plans for 279

two-tier price system for 279
  See also Foreign Tourism
Tractors, Chinese 115
  See also Farm machinery
Trade deficit 121
Trading partners, for oil 121
Traditional values, See Values and Traditions
Transport 112
  by canal/water system 154
  by rail 112, 116, 284-285, 360
  in cities 227
  model cars 83
  traffic police 84
  underdevelopment of 173
  See also Bicycles, Port facilities
"Treasure basin" See Tsaidam Basin
Trishaws 84
Tsiadam Basin 161
Trikiang Dam Irrigation System 154
Tungping Lake 151
Tungsten deposits 126, 177
Turfan Depression 147

U
Uighurs 187, 216
Underground water 156, 161
U.N. Security Council 99
Universities and Institutes
  entrance examinations for 132
  "key" 130
  See also Education
Urban population growth 73

V
Values and Traditions 9, 61-63, 99
"Venice of the East", See Suzhou
Victory Oilfield, See Shengli
Vietnam, 1979 war with 103, 108
"Visa invitations" 283

W
Wages, China 283
  breaches in control 132
Wall posters 13, 16, 23, 29, 36, 83
Wang Dongxing 22, 83
Wang Hongwen 22
Wang Ming 17
Water conservation 154
  See also Irrigation, Water control
Water control, hydro-electric power supply 122
  hydro-electric projects 111, 116
  taming the Yangtse 111
Water polo 332
Water Splashing Festival 224
Weight-lifting 339
Weiqi 73
Wenhui Bao 282
West, See China and the West, Foreigners
Wheat 170
  Spring production areas 170
  winter production areas 170
  See also Crops and Livestock
Wok 356-357
Wool production, see Textiles

Worker morale 114, 116
World Cup, Chinese participation in 335
Writing, unification of Chinese manner of 41
Wuhan steel plant 116
Wu Hu Tartars 187

X
Xenophobia, Chinese 273
Xi'an 187, 261-262
  architecture of 261
  as Tang capital, Changan 47
  food and restaurants of 262
  history of 261
  inhabitants of 261
Xiang Jiang River 154
Xiao Liumang, biographical sketch 178
Xinjiang(Sinkiang) Uighur Autonomous Region
  climate of 151
  deserts in 156
  Kazakh people from 187
  lakes in 161
  population of 147
Xiongnu 183

Y
Yalu River 147
Yalutsangpo River 156
Yangtse River 116, 151, 161, 164
  course of 151, 156

dimensions of 156
flooding of 151
Middle-Lower Plain of 161
source of 156
taming of 111, 156
tea production along 164
Yao tribe 193
Yao Wenyuan 29
Yellow River, See Huang He
Yellow Sea 151, 164
Yenan 41
Yin-yang 50, 273
Yi people 191, 216
Young, Joanna, Biographical sketch 345
Youth 94, 142
Yunnan Province, ethnic diversity of 191
Yu Quili 121

Z
Zhang Chunqiao 21
Zhang Longguan 71, 126
Zhang Zushua 93
Zhao Ziyang, 99
  biographical sketch 271
Zhejiang (Chekiang) Province 164
  physical geography of 147
Zhejiang silk textile plant 122
Zhou Dynasty 183
Zhou Peiyuan, Biographical Sketch 323
Zhuang people 216
Zoos 36, 289
Zoroastrianism 45, 48